24.6.08

Designing and Supporting Computer Networks

CCNA Discovery Learning Guide

Part II: Labs

KT-373-479

Kenneth D. Stewart III

Aubrey Adams

Cisco Press

800 East 96th Street

Indianapolis, Indiana 46240 USA

Designing and Supporting Computer Networks
CCNA Discovery Learning Guide
Part II: Labs
Kenneth D. Stewart III and Aubrey Adams

Copyright ® 2008 Cisco Systems, Inc.

Published by:
Cisco Press
800 East 96th Street
Indianapolis, IN 46240 USA

Printed in the United States of America

First Printing April 2008

Library of Congress Cataloging-in-Publication Data
Stewart, Kenneth (Kenneth D.)
  Designing and supporting computer networks / Kenneth Stewart, E. Aubrey Adams.
      p. cm. -- (CCNA discovery learning guide)
  ISBN-13: 978-1-58713-212-4 (pbk. w/CD)
  ISBN-10: 1-58713-212-5 (pbk. w/CD)
 1. Computer networks. 2. Computer networks--Management. I. Adams, E. Aubrey. II. Title. III. Series.
  TK5105.5.S747 2008
  004.6--dc22
                          2008012080
ISBN-13: 978-1-58713-212-4
ISBN-10: 1-58713-212-5

This book is part of a two-book set. Not to be sold separately.

This book is part of the Cisco Networking Academy® series from Cisco Press. The products in this series support and complement the Cisco Networking Academy curriculum. If you are using this book outside the Networking Academy, then you are not preparing with a Cisco trained and authorized Networking Academy provider.

For more information on the Cisco Networking Academy or to locate a Networking Academy, please visit www.cisco.com/edu.

ı|ııı|ıı
CISCO.

Contents at a Glance

Part II: Labs

Contents

Introduction to Part II

The labs in the CCNA Discovery Designing and Supporting Computer Networks course have a number of features that are different from the first three courses in the CCNA Discovery curriculum.

Approximately half the labs are of a written type that, when completed, make up a network design portfolio. This portfolio provides you with a complete set of network design and testing documentation to be used in class presentation, and can form the basis of a job application.

This portfolio will contain network checklists and procedures including the following:

- ❑ Network Requirements
- ❑ Current Network Environment
- ❑ Proposed Physical Design
- ❑ Proposed Logical Design
- ❑ Prototype Test Results
- ❑ Implementation Plan
- ❑ Cost Proposal

Before starting each lab, read through the tasks that you are expected to perform. Record what you expect the result of performing those tasks will be. Every lab asks you to think about the content and tasks before you perform them.

Network design portfolio documents: To help you create a network design portfolio as you work through the labs in Part II, the CD bound into Part I of this book provides the following files:

- Example Test Plan (in Microsoft Word format)
- Prototype Network Installation Checklist (in PDF format)
- LAN Design Test Plan (in PDF and Microsoft Word format)
- Server Farm Design Test Plan (in PDF and Microsoft Word format)
- WAN Design Test Plan (in PDF and Microsoft Word format)
- VPN Design Test Plan (in PDF and Microsoft Word format)

A Word About the Discovery Server CD

The labs that use equipment often employ the Discovery Server CD to provide simulated network services. These labs also often make use of Cisco IOS features and other software tools to provide the network performance monitoring important in network benchmarking and design.

The CCNA Discovery series of courses is designed to provide a hands-on learning approach to networking. Many of the CCNA Discovery labs are based on Internet services. Because it is not always possible to allow students access to these services on a live network, the Discovery Server has been developed to provide them.

The Discovery Server CD is a bootable CD that transforms a regular PC into a Linux server running several preconfigured services for use with Discovery labs. Your instructor can download the CD files, burn a CD, and show you how to make use of the server. Hands-on labs that make use of the Discovery Server are identified within the labs themselves.

After the server has booted, it provides many services to clients including the following:

- Domain Name Services
- Web Services
- FTP
- TFTP
- Telnet
- SSH
- DHCP
- Streaming video

Introducing Network Design Concepts: Labs

The lab exercises included in this chapter cover all the Chapter 1 online curriculum labs to ensure that you have mastered the practical, hands-on skills needed to consider security and required services in network design. As you work through these labs, use Chapter 1 in Part I of this book or use the corresponding Chapter 1 in the Discovery Designing and Supporting Computer Networks online curriculum for assistance.

Lab 1-1: Creating an ACL (1.3.4)

Upon completion of this lab, you will be able to create access control lists (ACL) to filter traffic for security and traffic management.

This lab contains skills that relate to the following 640-802 CCNA exam objectives:

- Configure and apply ACLs based on network filtering requirements (including CLI/SDM).
- Configure and apply ACLs to limit Telnet and SSH access to the router (including SDM/CLI).
- Verify and monitor ACLs in a network environment.

Expected Results and Success Criteria

Before starting this lab, read through the tasks that you are expected to perform. What do you expect the result of performing these tasks will be?

_____

_____

_____

How is an understanding of ACLs useful in network administration?

_____

_____

_____

How will a network administrator know whether the ACL is working properly?

_____

_____

_____

_____

Background/Preparation

In this lab, you consider the need for data traffic control and filtering in a network and design the policies to achieve this.

The traffic security design is then applied to a sample network using ACLs.

ACLs are typically applied at the distribution layer. This lab uses a router connected to a server that provides sample network applications to demonstrate ACL placement and operation.

Figure 1-1 shows the network topology for this lab, and Table 1-1 documents the hostnames, addresses, and subnet masks for all the network devices in the topology.

Figure 1-1   Lab 1-1 Network Topology

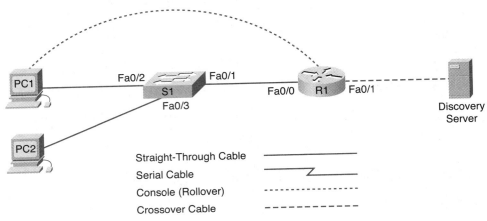

Table 1-1   Addressing Table for Lab 1-1

Device	Hostname	Address	Subnet Mask
Discovery Server	Server	172.17.1.1	255.255.0.0
R1	FC-CPE-1	Fa0/1 172.17.0.1	255.255.0.0
		Fa0/0 10.0.0.1	255.255.255.0
S1	FC-ASW-1	N/A	N/A
Host1	PC1	10.0.0.10	255.255.255.0
Host2	PC2	10.0.0.201	255.255.255.0

Task 1: Analyze the Traffic Filtering Requirements

Step 1.   Determine the access and filtering requirements.

For this lab, it has been determined that

- PC1 is a network administrator's workstation. This host must be permitted FTP and HTTP access to the network server and Telnet access to the router FC-CPE-1.

- PC2 is a general workstation that is to have HTTP access only. FTP services and Telnet access to the router is not permitted.

Step 2.   Having determined specific requirements, decide whether all other nonfiltered traffic is to be allowed or denied.

List the benefits and potential problems to the filtering scenario determined in Step 1:

- Benefits of allowing all other nonfiltered traffic:

  _____

- Potential problems with allowing all other nonfiltered traffic:

  _____

- Benefits of denying all other nonfiltered traffic:

  _____

  _____

- Potential problems with denying all other nonfiltered traffic:

  _____

Task 2: Design and Create the ACL

Step 1.   Review, and then apply, ACL recommended practice:

- Always plan thoroughly before implementation.

- The sequence of the statements is important. Put the more specific statements at the beginning and the more general statements at the end.

- Statements are added to the end of the ACL as they are written.

- Create and edit ACLs with a text editor and save the file.

- Use named ACLs wherever possible.

- Use comments (remark option) within the ACL to document the purpose of the statements.

- To take effect, ACLs must be applied to an interface.

- An interface can have one ACL per network layer protocol, per direction.

- Although there is an implicit deny any statement at the end of every ACL, it is good practice to configure this explicitly. This ensures that you remember that the effect is in place and allows logging of matches to this statement to be used.

- ACLs with many statements take longer to process, which may affect router performance.

- Placement of ACLs:

  - **Standard**: Closest to destination (if you have administrative authority on that router)

    - **Extended**: Closest to source (if you have administrative authority on that router)

Step 2.   Consider two approaches to writing ACLs:

- Permit specific traffic first, and then deny general traffic.

- Deny specific traffic first, and then permit general traffic.

When would it be best to permit specific traffic first and then deny general traffic?

_____

_____

_____

When is it best to deny specific traffic first and then permit general traffic?

_____

_____

_____

Step 3.   Select one approach and write the ACL statements that will meet the requirements of this lab.

_____

_____

_____

_____

_____

_____

_____

_____

_____

After an ACL is written and applied to an interface, it is useful to know whether the ACL statements are having the desired effect. The number of packets that meet the conditions of each ACL statement can be logged by adding the option **log** at the end of each statement.

Why is it important to know to how many times packets that match an ACL statement are denied?

_____

_____

Task 3: Cable and Configure the Given Network

Note: If the PCs used in this lab are also connected to your Academy LAN or to the Internet, ensure that you record the cable connections and TCP/IP settings so that these can be restored at the conclusion of the lab.

Step 1.   Referring to the topology diagram in Figure 1-1, connect the console (or rollover) cable to the console port on the router and the other cable end to the host computer with a DB-9 or DB-25 adapter to the COM 1 port. Ensure that power has been applied to both the host computer and the router.

Step 2.   Connect and configure the devices in accordance with the given topology and configuration. Your instructor may substitute Discovery Server with an equivalent server for this lab.

Step 3.   Establish a HyperTerminal, or other terminal emulation program, from PC1 to router R1. Confirm that the router is ready for lab configuration by ensuring that all existing configurations are removed. See the section "Erasing and Reloading the Router" in the "Lab Equipment Interfaces and Initial Configuration Restoration" appendix for these instructions.

Step 4.   From global configuration mode, issue the following commands:

```
Router(config)# hostname FC-CPE-1

FC-CPE-1(config)# interface FastEthernet0/0
FC-CPE-1(config-if)# ip address 10.0.0.1 255.255.255.0
FC-CPE-1(config-if)# no shutdown
FC-CPE-1(config-if)# exit

FC-CPE-1(config)# interface FastEthernet0/1
FC-CPE-1(config-if)# ip address 172.17.0.1 255.255.0.0
FC-CPE-1(config-if)# no shutdown
FC-CPE-1(config-if)# exit

FC-CPE-1(config)# line vty 0 4
FC-CPE-1(config-line)# password telnet
FC-CPE-1(config-line)# login
FC-CPE-1(config-line)# end
```

Step 5.   Ping between PC1 and Discovery Server to confirm network connectivity. Troubleshoot and establish connectivity if the pings fail.

Task 4: Test the Network Services Without ACLs

Perform the following tests on PC1:

Step 1.   Open a web browser on PC1 and enter the URL **http://172.17.1.1** at the address bar.

What page displayed?

_____

Step 2.   Open a web browser on PC1 and enter the URL **ftp://172.17.1.1** at the address bar.

What page displayed?

_____

Step 3.   On the Discovery FTP home directory, open the Discovery 1 folder. Click and drag a chapter file to the local desktop.

Did the file copy successfully?

_____

Step 4.   From the PC1 command-line prompt, issue the command **telnet 10.0.0.1**, or use a Telnet client (HyperTerminal or TeraTerm, for example) to establish a Telnet session to the router.

What response from the router displayed?

_____

Step 5.   Exit the Telnet session. What response displayed?

_____

Perform the following tests on PC2:

Step 1.   Open a web browser on PC2 and enter the URL **http://172.17.1.1** at the address bar.

What page displayed?

_____

Step 2.   Open a web browser on PC2 and enter the URL **ftp://172.17.1.1** at the address bar.

What page displayed?

_____

Step 3.   On the Discovery FTP home directory, open the Discovery 1 folder. Click and drag a chapter file to the local desktop.

Did the file copy successfully?

_____

Step 4.   From the PC2 command-line prompt, issue the command **telnet 10.0.0.1**, or use a Telnet client (HyperTerminal or TeraTerm, for example) to establish a Telnet session to the router.

What response from the router displayed?

_____

Step 5.   Exit the Telnet session. What response displayed?

_____

Why was each of the connections for PC1 and PC2 successful?

_____

_____

If any connection was not successful, troubleshoot the network and configurations and establish each type of connection from each host.

Task 5: Configure the Network Services ACL

Perform the steps that follow and issue the appropriate commands from global configuration mode:

Step 1.   Allow PC1 to access the web server:

```
FC-CPE-1(config)# ip access-list extended Server-Access
FC-CPE-1(config-ext-nacl)# remark Allow PC1 access to server
FC-CPE-1(config-ext-nacl)# permit tcp host 10.0.0.10 host 172.17.1.1 eq
   www log
```

Step 2.   Allow PC2 to access the web server:

```
FC-CPE-1(config-ext-nacl)# remark Allow PC2 to access web server

FC-CPE-1(config-ext-nacl)# permit tcp host 10.0.0.201 host 172.17.1.1 eq
    www log
```

Step 3.   Allow PC1 Telnet access to router:

```
FC-CPE-1(config-ext-nacl)# remark Allow PC1 to telnet router

FC-CPE-1(config-ext-nacl)# permit tcp host 10.0.0.10 host 10.0.0.1 eq
    telnet log
```

Step 4.   Deny all other traffic:

```
FC-CPE-1(config-ext-nacl)# remark Deny all other traffic
FC-CPE-1(config-ext-nacl)# deny ip any any log
FC-CPE-1(config-ext-nacl)# exit
```

What is the purpose of the **remark** statements in the commands in Steps 1 through 4?

_____

_____

Task 6: Apply the ACLs

Step 1.   Apply the extended ACL to the router interface closest to the source:

```
FC-CPE-1(config)# interface FastEthernet0/0
FC-CPE-1(config-if)# ip access-group Server-Access in
FC-CPE-1(config-if)# end
```

Step 2.   From the privileged EXEC mode, issue the **show running-configuration** command and confirm that the ACLs have been configured and applied as required.

Step 3.   Reconfigure if errors are noted.

Task 7: Test the Network Services with ACLs

Perform the following tests on PC1:

Step 1.   Open a web browser on PC1 and enter the URL **http://172.17.1.1** at the address bar.

What web page displayed?

_____

Step 2.   Open a web browser on PC1 and enter the URL **ftp://172.17.1.1** at the address bar.

What web page displayed?

_____

Step 3.   On the Discovery FTP home directory, open the Discovery 1 folder. Click and drag a chapter file to the local desktop.

Did the file copy successfully?

_____

Why is this the outcome?

_____

Step 4.   From the PC1 command-line prompt, issue the command **telnet 10.0.0.1**, or use a Telnet client (HyperTerminal or TeraTerm, for example) to establish a Telnet session to the router.

What response did the router display?

_____

Why is this the outcome?

_____

Step 5.   Exit the Telnet session.

Perform the following tests on PC2:

Step 1.   Open a web browser on PC2 and enter the URL **http://172.17.1.1** at the address bar.

What web page displayed?

_____

Why is this the outcome?

_____

Step 2.   Open a web browser on PC2 and enter the URL **ftp://172.17.1.1** at the address bar.

What web page displayed?

_____

Why is this the outcome?

_____

Step 3.   From the PC2 command-line prompt, issue the command **telnet 10.0.0.1**, or use a Telnet client (HyperTerminal or TeraTerm, for example) to establish a Telnet session to the router.

What response did the router display?

_____

Why is this the outcome?

_____

If any of these transactions did not result in the expected outcome, troubleshoot the network and configurations and retest the ACLs from each host.

Task 8: Observe the Number of Statement Matches

From privileged EXEC mode, issue the following command:

```
FC-CPE-1# show access-list Server-Access
```

List the number of matches logged against each ACL statement.

_____

Task 9: Clean Up

Erase the configurations and reload the routers and switches. Disconnect and store the cabling. For PC hosts that are normally connected to other networks (such as the school LAN or to the Internet), reconnect the appropriate cabling, and restore the TCP/IP settings.

Challenge

Rewrite the Server-Access ACL used in this lab to meet the following criteria:

- Administrator workstations are considered to be in the address range of 10.0.0.10 /24 to 10.0.0.15 /24 instead of in a single host.

- The general workstations have the address range of 10.0.0.16 /24 to 10.0.0.254 /24 instead of being in a single host.

_____

_____

_____

_____

_____

_____

_____

Lab 1-2: Monitoring VLAN Traffic (1.4.3)

Upon completion of this lab, you will be able to

- Observe broadcast traffic on a switch.

- Create and apply VLANs to separate local traffic.

- Observe broadcast traffic containment with VLANs.

This lab contains skills that relate to the following 640-802 CCNA exam objectives:

- Perform and verify initial switch configuration tasks, including remote-access management.

- Verify network status and switch operation using basic utilities (including: ping, traceroute, Telnet, SSH, ARP, ipconfig) and **show** and **debug** commands.

- Describe how VLANs create logically separate networks and the need for routing between them.

- Configure, verify, and troubleshoot VLANs.

Expected Results and Success Criteria

Before starting this lab, read through the tasks that you are expected to perform. What do you expect the result of performing these tasks will be?

_____

_____

_____

How is an understanding of VLANs useful in network administration?

_____

_____

_____

How will a network administrator know whether the VLAN is working correctly?

_____

_____

_____

Background/Preparation

This lab demonstrates the flow of network traffic from host PCs attached to a switch. Currently, the switch is not configured to segment network traffic into VLANs. In this lab, you initially observe the flow of traffic without VLANs. Then, you observe the data traffic after configuring the switch to contain local traffic within each respective VLAN. The effects of the VLANs on the network traffic are then observed and discussed.

The packet capture program Wireshark (formerly known as Ethereal) is required to be installed on each PC used in this lab. Wireshark is a free, open source program that you can download from http://www.wireshark.org/. See your instructor if this program is not available in the lab.

The Cisco IOS commands used in this lab apply to the Cisco 2960 switch. See your instructor about comparable commands if you are using other switch models in this lab.

Figure 1-2 shows the network topology for this lab, and Table 1-2 documents the names, addresses, and subnet masks for all the network devices in the topology.

Figure 1-2   Lab Topology

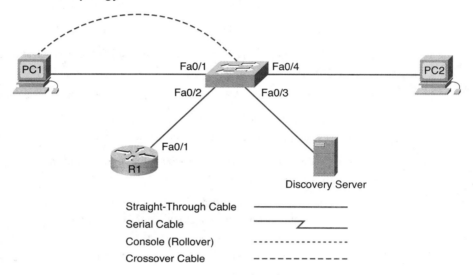

Table 1-2   Addressing Table for Lab 1-2

Device Designation	Device Name	Address	Subnet mask
S1	FC-ASW-1	N/A	N/A
PC1	Host1	172.17.1.10	255.255.0.0
PC2	Host2	172.17.1.11	255.255.0.0
Router	R1	172.17.0.1	255.255.0.0
Discovery Server	Server	172.17.1.1	255.255.0.0

Task 1: Demonstrate Broadcasts Across a Single LAN

Step 1.   Prepare the switch for configuration:

Note: If the PCs used in this lab are also connected to your Academy LAN or to the Internet, ensure that you record the cable connections and TCP/IP settings so that these can be restored at the conclusion of the lab.

a. Referring to the topology diagram in Figure 1-2, connect the console (or rollover) cable to the console port on the switch and the other cable end to the host computer with a DB-9 or DB-25 adapter to the COM 1 port. Ensure that power has been applied to both the host computer and switch.

b. Establish a HyperTerminal, or other terminal emulation program, connection from PC1 to the switch.

    c. Confirm that the switch is ready for lab configuration by ensuring that all existing VLAN and general configurations are removed. See the section "Erasing and Reloading the Switch" in the "Lab Equipment Interfaces and Initial Configuration Restoration" appendix for these instructions.

Step 2.   Configure the connected devices:

    a. Connect the two PCs to the switch as shown in the topology diagram in Figure 1-2.

    b. Configure the two PCs to have the IP addresses and subnet mask shown in Table 1-2.

    c. Clear the ARP cache on each PC by issuing the **arp -d** command at the PC command prompt.

    d. Confirm that the ARP cache is clear by issuing the **arp -a** command.

    e. Connect Discovery Server to the switch as shown in the topology diagram. Your instructor may substitute Discovery Server with a PC for this lab.

    f. Connect the 1841 router to the switch as shown in the topology diagram. Your instructor may substitute the router with a PC for this lab.

    g. Establish a console session to the router from one of the PCs and issue the following commands from the CLI global configuration mode:

```
Router(config)# interface fa0/1
Router(config-if)# ip address 172.17.0.1 255.255.0.0
Router(config-if)# no shutdown
Router(config-if)# exit
```

    h. If additional PCs have been used, or substituted for Discovery Server and the 1841 router, perform substeps a, b, c, and d for each PC.

Step 3.   Generate and examine ARP broadcasts:

    a. Launch Wireshark on each PC, and start the packet capture for the traffic seen by the NIC in each PC.

    b. From the command line of each PC, ping all connected devices.

    c. Monitor the operation of Wireshark. Note the ARP traffic registering on each PC.

    d. Stop the Wireshark capture on each PC.

    e. Examine the entries in the Wireshark Packet List (upper) pane.

How many ARP captures occurred for each device?

_____

List the source IP addresses of the ARP request and replies:

_____

_____

Did each device receive an ARP request from every PC connected to the switch?

_____

    f. Exit Wireshark. (You have the option to save the capture file for later examination.)

Task 2: Demonstrate Broadcasts Within Multiple VLANs

Step 1.   Configure the VLANs on the switch:

a.   Using the established console session from PC1 to the switch, set the hostname by issuing the following command from the global configuration mode:

```
Switch(config)# hostname FC-ASW-1
```

b.   Set interfaces Fa0/1 and Fa0/2 to VLAN 10 by issuing the following commands from the global configuration and interface configuration modes:

```
FC_ASW-1(config)# interface FastEthernet0/1

FC_ASW-1(config-if)# switchport access vlan 10
% Access VLAN does not exist. Creating vlan 10

FC_ASW-1(config-if)# interface FastEthernet0/2

FC_ASW-1(config-if)# switchport access vlan 10
```

c.   Set interfaces Fa0/3 and Fa0/4 to VLAN 20 by issuing the following commands from the interface configuration mode:

```
FC_ASW-1(config-if)# interface FastEthernet0/3

FC_ASW-1(config-if)# switchport access vlan 20
% Access VLAN does not exist. Creating vlan 20

FC_ASW-1(config-if)# interface FastEthernet0/4

FC_ASW-1(config-if)# switchport access vlan 20

FC_ASW-1(config-if)# end
```

d.   Confirm that the interfaces are assigned to the current VLANs by issuing the **show vlan** command from the privileged EXEC mode. If the VLANs are not assigned correctly, troubleshoot the command entries shown in Steps 1b and 1c and reconfigure the switch.

Step 2.   Prepare the PCs:

a.   Clear the ARP cache on each PC by issuing the **arp -d** command at the PC command prompt.

b.   Confirm the ARP cache is clear by issuing the **arp -a** command.

Step 3.   Generate ARP broadcasts:

a.   Launch Wireshark on each PC and start the packet capture for the traffic seen by the NIC in each PC.

b.   From the command line of each PC, ping each of the other three devices connected to the switch.

c.   Monitor the operation of Wireshark. Note the ARP traffic registering on the two PCs.

d.   Stop the Wireshark capture on each PC.

e. Examine the entries in the Wireshark Packet List (upper) pane.

How many ARP captures occurred for each PC?

_____

List the source IP addresses.

_____

What is the difference between the captured ARP packets for each PC this time and those captured in Task 1?

_____

How many Ethernet broadcast domains are present now?

_____

_____

f. Exit Wireshark. (You have the option to save the capture file for later examination.)

Task 3: Clean Up

Erase the configuration and reload the switch. Disconnect and store the cabling. For PC hosts that are normally connected to other networks (such as the school LAN or to the Internet), reconnect the appropriate cabling and restore the TCP/IP settings.

Reflection

Discuss the use of VLANs in keeping data traffic separated. What are the advantages of doing this?

_____

_____

_____

_____

List different criteria that could be used to divide a network into VLANs during the initial network design phase:

_____

_____

_____

_____

_____

_____

_____

_____

_____

Lab 1-3: Identifying Network Vulnerabilities (1.4.5)

Upon completion of this lab, you will be able to

- Use the SANS site to quickly identify Internet security threats.

- Explain how threats are organized.

- List several recent security vulnerabilities.

- Use the SANS links to access other security-related information.

This lab contains skills that relate to the following 640-802 CCNA exam objectives:

- Describe security recommended practices, including initial steps to secure network devices.

- Describe today's increasing network security threats and explain the need to implement a comprehensive security policy to mitigate the threats.

- Explain general methods to mitigate common security threats to network devices, hosts, and applications.

- Describe the functions of common security appliances and applications.

Expected Results and Success Criteria

Before starting this lab, read through the tasks that you are expected to perform. What do you expect the result of performing these tasks will be?

_____

_____

_____

How is an understanding of network vulnerabilities useful in network administration?

_____

_____

_____

How can a network administrator maintain network security?

_____

_____

_____

Background/Preparation

A popular and trusted website related to defending against computer and network security threats is SANS (SysAdmin, Audit, Network, Security). SANS contains several components, each a major contributor to information security.

In this lab, you are introduced to computer security issues and vulnerabilities. The SANS website is used as a tool for threat vulnerability identification, understanding, and defense.

To assist a corporate security administrator to quickly identify security threats, SANS and the U.S. Federal Bureau of Investigation (FBI) compile the SANS Top 20 Internet Security Attack Targets, which you can view at http://www.sans.org/top20/.

This list is regularly updated and is referred to in this lab. Your instructor will advise you if there are specific changes or issues you need to be aware of to complete this lab.

Task 1: Open the SANS Top 20 List

Step 1.   Using a web browser, go to http://www.sans.org/. On the Resources menu, choose Top 20 List.

The SANS Top 20 Internet Security Attack Targets list is organized by category.

Note the category headings.

_____

_____

_____

_____

_____

_____

Step 2.   Router and switch topics fall under the Network Devices category, N. Note the topics in this category.

_____

_____

_____

Task 2: Review Common Configuration Weaknesses

Step 1.   Click one of the hyperlinks (for example, N2. Network and Other Devices Common Configuration Weaknesses).

Step 2.   List the headings in this topic.

_____

_____

_____

_____

Task 3: Note CVE References

Under the N2. Network and Other Devices Common Configuration Weaknesses topic, or another selected from the Top 20 Security Risks page, locate references to CVE or Common Vulnerability Exposure. The CVE name is linked to the National Institute of Standards and Technology (NIST) National Vulnerability Database (NVD), sponsored by the U.S. Department of Homeland Security (DHS) National Cyber Security Division and US-CERT, which contains information about the vulnerability.

Task 4: Investigate a Topic and Associated CVE Hyperlink

Choose a topic to investigate, and click an associated CVE hyperlink. The link should open a new web browser connected to http://nvd.nist.gov/ and the vulnerability summary page for the CVE.

Note: Because the CVE list changes, the current list might not contain the same vulnerabilities as those listed in the following steps.

Task 5: Record Vulnerability Information

Complete the information about the vulnerability.

Original release date: _____

Last revised: _____

Source: _____

Overview:

_____

_____

_____

Task 6: Record the Vulnerability Impact

Under Impact, there are several values. The Common Vulnerability Scoring System (CVSS) severity is displayed and contains a value between 1 and 10.

Complete the information about the vulnerability impact.

CVSS Severity:

_____

Access complexity:

_____

Authentication:

_____

Impact type:

_____

Task 7: Record the Solution

The References to Advisories, Solutions, and Tools section contains links with information about the vulnerability and possible solutions.

Using the hyperlinks, write a brief description of the solution found on those pages:

_____

_____

_____

Task 8: Zero-Day Attack

If listed on the Top 20 Security Risks page, click the Zero-Day Attack link. Alternatively, if it is not listed, perform an Internet search for the definition of this term.

Review the information found. Briefly describe what a "zero-day attack" is and why such attacks can have an extreme impact on computer networks and systems:

_____

_____

_____

_____

Reflection

The number of vulnerabilities to computers, networks, and data continues to increase. Many national governments have dedicated significant resources to coordinating and disseminating information about security vulnerability and possible solutions. It remains the responsibility of the end user to implement the solution.

Retaining default configurations on networked devices can also create security vulnerabilities. For example, a Google search for "wireless router passwords" returns links to multiple sites that publish a list of wireless router default administrator account names and passwords. Failure to change the default password on these devices can lead to compromised security and vulnerability to attackers.

Think of ways that users can help strengthen security. Write down some user habits that create security risks:

_____

_____

_____

_____

_____

_____

_____

_____

_____

_____

_____

Challenge

Try to identify an organization that will meet with the class to explain how vulnerabilities are tracked and solutions applied. Finding an organization willing to do this might prove difficult, for security reasons, but will benefit students, who will learn how vulnerability mitigation is accomplished in the real world. It will also give representatives of the organization an opportunity to meet the class and conduct informal intern interviews.

Lab 1-4: Gaining Physical Access to the Network (1.4.6A)

Upon completion of this lab, you will be able to

- Gain access to a router or switch with unknown login and privileged mode passwords.

- Demonstrate the necessity and importance of physical security for network devices.

This lab contains skills that relate to the following 640-802 CCNA exam objectives:

- Implement basic router security.

- Describe today's increasing network security threats and explain the need to implement a comprehensive security policy to mitigate the threats.

- Explain general methods to mitigate common security threats to network devices, hosts, and applications.

- Describe the functions of common security appliances and applications.

- Describe recommended security practices, including initial steps to secure network devices.

Expected Results and Success Criteria

Before starting this lab, read through the tasks that you are expected to perform. What do you expect the result of performing these tasks will be?

_____

_____

_____

How is an understanding of network device access useful in network administration?

_____

_____

_____

How will a network administrator know if the device's physical access is secure?

_____

_____

_____

Background/Preparation

This lab demonstrates that physical access is required to access and change the password of Cisco routers and switches. At first, an attempt to telnet to the router or switch is made by trying to log in by guessing the password. When this proves unsuccessful, physical access to the console port on the router or switch is made so that the passwords can be changed and control of the device is established. This demonstrates why it is of critical importance that routers and switches have physical security to prevent unauthorized access, in addition to strong password protection.

Part 1: Access and Change Router Passwords

Figure 1-3 shows the network topology for this lab, and Table 1-3 documents the names, addresses, and subnet masks for all the network devices in the topology diagram.

Figure 1-3   Lab Topology: Part 1

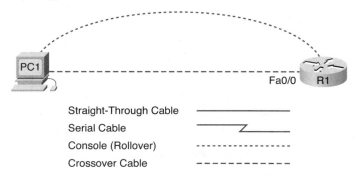

Table 1-3   Addressing Table for Part 1 of Lab 1-4

Device Designation	Device Name	Fast Ethernet Address	Subnet Mask
R1	FC-CPE-1	10.0.0.1	255.255.255.0
PC	PC1	10.0.0.254	255.255.255.0

The following principles apply to the process of accessing and changing the passwords of a router:

- Router passwords are in the startup configuration file stored in NVRAM. The router boot sequence is changed so that it starts without loading the configuration. When running without the startup configuration loaded, the router can be reconfigured with new, known passwords.

- A memory location in NVRAM, called the configuration register, holds a binary value that determines the router startup sequence. The configuration register value needs to be changed so that the router boots but does not load the startup configuration. When the passwords are changed, the configuration register is reset to a value that loads the changed startup configuration when the router next powers on.

To change existing but unknown router passwords, a physical console connection is required.

Task 1: Attempt Login to the Router

Note: If the PC used in this lab is also connected to your Academy LAN or to the Internet, ensure that you record the cable connections and TCP/IP settings so that these can be restored at the conclusion of the lab.

Step 1.   Referring to the topology in Figure 1-3, connect the host PC NIC Ethernet port to the router Fa0/0 Ethernet port using a crossover cable. Ensure that power has been applied to both the host computer and router.

Step 2.   Using the given preconfigured topology, attempt to telnet to the router from the PC command line.

Which IP address is used to telnet to the router?

What does the message-of-the-day display?

_____

_____

How many login attempts are allowed?

_____

What message is displayed to indicate failure of the login attempts?

_____

Step 3.   When this attempt at remote login fails, establish a direct physical connection to the router by making the necessary console connections between the PC and router. Then establish a terminal session using HyperTerminal or TeraTerm.

What does the message-of-the-day display?

_____

_____

Attempt to log in by guessing the password.

How many login attempts are allowed?

_____

What message is displayed to indicate failure of the login attempts?

_____

The configuration register needs to be changed so that the startup configuration is not loaded. Normally, this is this done from the global configuration mode; but because you cannot log in at all, the boot process must first be interrupted so that the change can be made in the ROM Monitor mode.

Task 2: Enter the ROM Monitor Mode

ROM Monitor (ROMMON) mode is a limited command-line environment used for special purposes, such as low-level troubleshooting and debugging. ROMMON mode is invoked when a Break key sequence sent to the console port interrupts the router boot process. This can only be done via the physical console connection.

The actual Break key sequence depends on the terminal program used:

- With HyperTerminal, the key combination is Ctrl+Break.

- For TeraTerm, it is Alt+B.

The list of standard break key sequences is available at http://www.cisco.com/warp/public/701/61.pdf.

Step 1.   To enter ROMMON mode, turn the router off, wait a few seconds, and turn it back on.

Step 2.   When the router starts displaying "System Bootstrap, Version" on the terminal screen, press the Ctrl key and the Break key together if using HyperTerminal, or the Alt key and the B key together if using TeraTerm.

The router will boot in ROMMON mode. Depending on the router hardware, one of several prompts might display, such as the following:

```
rommon 1 >
```

or simply

```
>
```

Example output may be similar to this:

```
Router>System Bootstrap, Version 12.3(8r)T8, RELEASE SOFTWARE (fc1)
Cisco 1841 (revision 5.0) with 114688K/16384K bytes of memory.

Self decompressing the image :
###################################
monitor: command "boot" aborted due to user interrupt
rommon 1 >
```

Task 3: Change the Configuration Register Setting to Bypass the Startup Configuration File

First examine the available ROMMON mode commands by using Help. Enter **?** at the prompt. The output should be similar to this:

```
rommon 1 > ?
alias       set and display aliases command
boot        boot up an external process
break       set/show/clear the breakpoint
confreg     configuration register utility
context     display the context of a loaded image
dev         list the device table
dir         list files in file system
dis         display instruction stream
help        monitor builtin command help
history     monitor command history
meminfo     main memory information
repeat      repeat a monitor command
reset       system reset
set         display the monitor variables
sysret      print out info from last system return
tftpdnld    tftp image download
xmodem      x/ymodem image download
```

Task 4: Change the Configuration Register Setting to Boot Without Loading the Configuration File

Change the configuration register setting to boot without loading the configuration file. From ROMMON mode, enter **confreg 0x2142** to change the configuration register:

```
rommon 2 > confreg 0x2142
```

Note: The ROMMON prompt increments when a command is issued; this is normal behavior. The increment does not mean a change of mode. The same ROMMON commands are still available.

0x (zero x) denotes that 2142 is a hexadecimal value. What is this value in binary?

Task 5: Restart the Router

From ROMMON mode, enter **reset**, to restart the router or power cycle the router:

```
rommon 3 > reset
```

Because of the new configuration register setting, the router will not load the configuration file. After restarting, the system prompts as follows:

```
"Would you like to enter the initial configuration dialog? [yes/no]:"
```

Enter **no** at the prompt.

Task 6: View and Change Passwords

The router is now running without a loaded configuration file.

Step 1.   At the user mode prompt Router>, issue the **enable** command to go to the privileged mode without a password.

Step 2.   Use the command **copy startup-config running-config** to restore the existing configuration. Because the user is already in privileged EXEC, no password is needed.

Step 3.   Issue **show running-config** to display the configuration details. Note that all the passwords are shown. Record all the passwords.

_____

_____

_____

What two measures could be taken to prevent the passwords from being readable?

_____

_____

_____

Step 4.   If the passwords were not readable, they can be changed. To change the passwords, issue the **configure terminal** command to enter the global configuration mode.

Step 5.   In global configuration mode, use these commands to change the passwords:

```
FC-CPE-1(config)# enable password cisco
FC-CPE-1(config)# line console 0
FC-CPE-1(config-line)# password console
FC-CPE-1(config-line)# login
FC-CPE-1(config-line)# line vty 0 4
FC-CPE-1(config-line)# password telnet
FC-CPE-1(config-line)# login
```

Task 7: Change the Configuration Register Setting to Boot and Load the Configuration File

Step 1.   The instructor will provide you with the original configuration register value, most likely 0x2101. While still in the global configuration mode, enter **config-register 0x2101** (or the value provided by your instructor):

```
FC-CPE-1(config)# config-register 0x2101
```

Step 2.   Use the Ctrl+Z combination to return to the privileged EXEC mode.

Step 3.   Use the **copy running-config startup-config** command to save the new configuration.

Step 4.   Before restarting the router, verify the new configuration setting. From the privileged EXEC prompt, enter the **show version** command.

Verify that the last line of the output reads as follows, or the equivalent:

```
Configuration register is 0x2142 (will be 0x2101 at next reload).
```

Step 5.   Use the **reload** command to restart the router.

Task 8: Verify the New Password and Configuration

Step 1.   When the router reloads, log in and change mode using the new passwords.

Step 2.   Issue the **no shutdown** command on the fa0/0 interface to bring it up to working status:

```
FC-CPE-1(config-if)# no shutdown
```

Step 3.   Save the running configuration to the startup configuration:

```
FC-CPE-1# copy run start
```

Step 4.   Disconnect the console cable. Access the router using Telnet from the PC command line.

The newly configured passwords will allow a successful remote login.

Task 9: Clean Up

Erase the configurations and reload the router. Disconnect and store the cabling. For PC hosts that are normally connected to other networks (such as the school LAN or to the Internet), reconnect the appropriate cabling and restore the TCP/IP settings.

Part 2: Access and Change Switch Passwords

Figure 1-4 shows the network topology for this lab, and Table 1-4 documents the names, addresses, and subnet masks for all the network devices in the topology diagram.

Figure 1-4   Lab Topology: Part 2

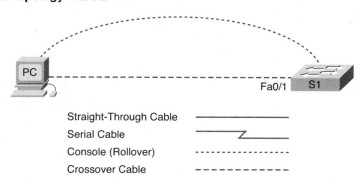

Straight-Through Cable	———————
Serial Cable	——⌐———
Console (Rollover)	- - - - - - - - - -
Crossover Cable	— — — — — —

Table 1-4   Addressing Table for Part 2 of Lab 1-4

Device Designation	Device Name	IP Address	Subnet Mask
S1	FC-ASW-1	10.0.0.2	255.255.255.0
PC	PC1	10.0.0.254	255.255.255.0

This part of the lab demonstrates that physical access is required to access and change the password of Cisco switches, and again why it is of critical importance that routers and switches also have physical security to prevent unauthorized access.

After unsuccessful attempts to remotely log in, a console connection is made, and the following principles are applied to the process of accessing and changing the passwords of a switch:

■ Switch passwords are in the configuration file called config.text, which is stored in flash memory. The switch boot sequence is changed so that it starts without loading the configuration.

■ When running without the configuration loaded, the switch can be reconfigured with new, known passwords.

Task 1: Attempt Login to the Switch

Note: If the PC used in this lab is also connected to your Academy LAN or to the Internet, ensure that you record the cable connections and TCP/IP settings so that these can be restored at the conclusion of the lab.

Step 1. Referring to the topology in Figure 1-4, connect the host PC NIC Ethernet port to the switch Fa0/1 Ethernet port using a straight-through cable. Ensure that power has been applied to both the host computer and switch.

Step 2. Using the given preconfigured topology, attempt to telnet to the switch from the PC command line.

Which IP address is used to telnet to the switch?

_____

What does the message-of-the-day display?

_____

_____

How many login attempts are allowed?

_____

What message is displayed to indicate failure of the login attempts?

_____

_____

Step 3. When this attempt at remote login fails, establish a direct physical connection to the switch by making the necessary console connections between the PC and switch. Then establish a terminal session using HyperTerminal or TeraTerm.

What does the message-of-the-day display?

_____

_____

Attempt to log in by guessing the password.

How many login attempts are allowed?

_____

What message is displayed to indicate failure of the login attempts?

_____

To prevent the configuration from loading, the config.text file is renamed so that the switch IOS cannot locate and load a valid configuration file. To rename the file, the boot process must be interrupted so that the change can be made in the "switch" mode.

Task 2: Enter "Switch" Mode

Step 1.   Power off the switch.

Step 2.   Locate the MODE button on the front of the switch.

Step 3.   Hold down the MODE button on the front of the switch while powering on the switch. Release the MODE button after 10 seconds.

Output similar to the following should display:

```
Base ethernet MAC Address: 00:0a:b7:72:2b:40
Xmodem file system is available.
The password-recovery mechanism is enabled.

The system has been interrupted prior to initializing the
flash files system. The following commands will initialize
the flash files system, and finish loading the operating
system software:

flash_init
load_helper
boot

switch:
```

Step 4.   To initialize the file system and finish loading the operating system, enter the following commands at the switch: prompt:

```
switch: flash_init
switch: load_helper
```

Step 5.   To view the contents of flash memory, enter **dir flash:** at the switch: prompt:

```
switch: dir flash:
```

Note: Do not forget to type the colon (**:**) after the word _flash_ in the **dir flash:** command.

The file config.text should be seen listed.

Step 6. Enter **rename flash:config.text flash:config.old** to rename the configuration file. This file contains the current password definitions.

```
switch:_rename_flash:config.text_flash:config.old
```

Step 7. Enter **dir flash:** at the switch: prompt to view the name change:

```
switch: dir flash:
```

Task 3: Restart the Switch

Step 1. Enter **boot** to restart the switch:

```
switch: boot
```

Step 2. The configuration file config.text cannot be located; therefore, the switch boots into setup mode:

```
Would you like to terminate autoinstall? [Yes]: Y
Would you like to enter the initial configuration dialog? [yes/no] N
Switch>
```

Task 4: View and Change Passwords

The switch is now running without a loaded configuration file.

Step 1. Issue the **enable** command at the user mode prompt to go to privileged mode without a password:

```
Switch>enable
```

Step 2. Enter **rename flash:config.old flash:config.text** to rename the configuration file with its original name:

```
Switch# rename flash:config.old flash:config.text
Destination filename [config.text]?
Press Enter to confirm file name change.
```

Step 3. Copy the configuration file into RAM:

```
Switch# copy flash:config.text system:running-config
Destination filename [running-config]?
Press Enter to confirm file name.
```

Step 4. Press Enter to accept the default filenames:

```
Source filename [config.text]?
Destination filename [running-config]
```

The configuration file is now loaded.

Step 5. Issue **show running-config** to display the configuration details. Note that all the passwords are shown. Record all the passwords. If the passwords were not readable, they can be changed.

_____

_____

_____

What two measures could be taken to prevent the passwords from being readable?

_____

_____

_____

Step 6.   To change the passwords, issue the **configure terminal** command to enter global configuration mode.

Step 7.   In global configuration mode, use these commands to change the passwords:

```
FC-ASW-1# configure terminal
FC-ASW-1(config)# enable password cisco
FC-ASW-1(config)# line console 0
FC-ASW-1(config-line)# password console
FC-ASW-1(config-line)# line vty 0 15
FC-ASW-1(config-line)# password telnet
FC-ASW-1(config-line)# exit
FC-ASW-1(config)# exit
```

Task 5: Save the Configuration File

Issue the **copy running-config startup-config** command to save the new configuration:

```
FC-ASW-1# copy running-config startup-config
Destination filename [startup-config]?
Building configuration...
[OK]
FC-ASW-1#
```

Task 6: Verify the New Password and Configuration

Step 1.   Power cycle the switch.

Step 2.   When the switch reloads, log in and change mode using the new passwords.

Step 3.   Disconnect the console cable. Access the switch using Telnet from the PC command line.

The newly configured passwords will allow a successful remote login.

Task 7: Clean Up

Erase the configurations and reload the switch. Disconnect and store the cabling. For PC hosts that are normally connected to other networks (such as the school LAN or to the Internet), reconnect the appropriate cabling and restore the TCP/IP settings.

Reflection

Consider the different methods of securing physical access to networking devices such as routers and switches. List how only those people who require access can be identified and how this security can be implemented:

Note: It is important to remember that the passwords (console, cisco, class, telnet) used in these labs are for convenience only. These are *not* secure passwords that would be used in production networks.

Lab 1-5: Implementing Port Security (1.4.6B)

Upon completion of this lab, you will be able to

- Configure port security on individual Fast Ethernet ports on a switch.

- Test and confirm the configured switch port security.

This lab contains skills that relate to the following 640-802 CCNA exam objectives:

- Perform and verify initial switch configuration tasks, including remote-access management.

- Verify network status and switch operation using basic utilities (including ping, traceroute, Telnet, SSH, ARP, ipconfig) and **show** and **debug** commands.

- Implement basic switch security (including port security, trunk access, management VLAN other than VLAN 1, and so on).

Expected Results and Success Criteria

Before starting this lab, read through the tasks that you are expected to perform. What do you expect the result of performing these tasks will be?

_____

_____

_____

Why do you think that network administrators implement port security in their network?

_____

_____

_____

How will a network administrator know whether port security is working properly?

_____

_____

_____

Background/Preparation

Network security is an important responsibility for network administrators and network designers. Access layer switch ports are accessible through the structured cabling at wall outlets. Anyone can plug in a PC, laptop, or wireless access point at one of these outlets. These outlets are potential entry points to the network by unauthorized users.

Switches provide a feature called port security. With port security, it is possible to limit the number of MAC addresses that can be learned on an interface. The switch can be configured to take an action (for example, shut down, if this number is exceeded). The number of MAC addresses per port can be limited, commonly to one. The first address dynamically learned by that switch for that port becomes the secure address.

Figure 1-5 shows the network topology for this lab, and Table 1-5 documents the hostnames, addresses, and subnet masks for all the network devices in the topology.

Figure 1-5   Lab 1-5 Network Topology

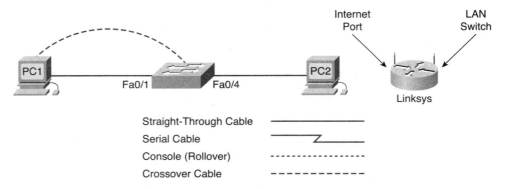

Table 1-5   Addressing Table for Lab 1-5

Device Designation	Device Name	VLAN 1 Address	Subnet Mask
S1	FC-ASW-1	10.0.0.2	255.255.255.0
PC1	Host 1	10.0.0.254	255.255.255.0
PC2	Host 2	10.0.0.253	255.255.255.0
Linksys Internet Port	Intruder	10.0.0.252	255.255.255.0

Using the given topology, this lab configures a switch to provide network access to only two PCs, and tests this security by attempting to connect an "intruder" device, the Linksys wireless router, to the secure port.

Task 1: Configure and Test the Switch Connectivity

If the PCs used in this lab are also connected to your Academy LAN or to the Internet, ensure that you record the cable connections and TCP/IP settings so that these can be restored at the conclusion of the lab.

Step 1: Prepare the Switch for Configuration

1. Referring to the topology diagram in Figure 1-5, connect the console (or rollover) cable to the console port on the switch and the other cable end to the host computer with a DB-9 or DB-25 adapter to the COM 1 port. Ensure that power has been applied to both the host computer and switch.

2. Establish a HyperTerminal, or other terminal emulation program, connection from PC1 to the switch.

3. Confirm that the switch is ready for lab configuration by ensuring that all existing VLAN and general configurations are removed. see the section "Erasing and Reloading the Switch" in the "Lab Equipment Interfaces and Initial Configuration Restoration" appendix for these instructions.

Step 2: Configure the Switch

Configure the hostname and VLAN 1 interface IP address as shown in the addressing table.

Step 3: Configure the Hosts Attached to the Switch

1. Configure the two PCs to use the same IP subnet for the address and mask as shown in the table.

2. Connect PC1 to switch port Fa0/1 and PC2 to switch port Fa0/4. The Linksys device is not connected at this stage of the lab.

Step 4: Verify Host Connectivity

Ping between all PCs and the switch to verify correct configuration. If any ping was not successful, troubleshoot the hosts and switch configurations.

Step 5: Record the Host MAC Addresses

Determine and record the Layer 2 addresses of the PC network interface cards.

(For Windows 2000, XP, or Vista, check by using Start > Run > **cmd** > **ipconfig /all**.)

PC1 MAC address: _____

PC2 MAC address: _____

Step 6: Determine What MAC Addresses the Switch Has Learned

1. At the privileged EXEC mode prompt, issue the **show mac-address-table** command to display the PC MAC addresses that the switch has learned:

   FC-ASW-1# **show mac-address-table**

   Record the details displayed in the table:

   _____

   _____

   _____

   _____

   _____

   _____

   _____

   _____

2. Record the MAC addresses shown and the associated switch ports. Confirm that these addresses and ports match the connected PCs.

   How were these MAC addresses and port associations learned?

   _____

   _____

Task 2: Configure and Test the Switch for Dynamic Port Security

This task consists of the following steps, all of which are described in the sections that follow:

Step 1.   Set port security options.

Step 2.   Verify the configuration.

Step 3.   Verify the port security.

Step 4.   Test the port security.

Step 5.   Reactivate the port.

Step 1: Set Port Security Options

1. Disconnect all the PC's Ethernet cables from the switch ports.

2. Ensure that the MAC address table is clear of entries. To confirm this, issue the **clear mac-address-table dynamic** and **show mac-address-table** commands.

   a. Clear the MAC address table entries:

      ```
      FC-ASW-1# clear mac-address-table dynamic
      ```

   b. Issue the **show mac-address-table** command and record the table entries:

      _____

      _____

      _____

      _____

3. Determine the options for setting port security on interface FastEthernet 0/4. From the global configuration mode, enter **interface fastethernet 0/4**:

   ```
   FC-ASW-1(config)# interface fa 0/4
   ```

   Enabling switch port security provides options, such as specifying what happens when a security setting is violated.

4. To configure the switch port FastEthernet 0/4 to accept only the first device connected to the port, issue the following commands from configuration mode:

   ```
   FC-ASW-1(config-if)# switchport mode access
   FC-ASW-1(config-if)# switchport port-security
   ```

5. In the event of a security violation, the interface should be shut down. Set the port security action to **shutdown**:

   ```
   FC-ASW-1(config-if)# switchport port-security violation shutdown
   FC-ASW-1(config-if)# switchport port-security mac-address sticky
   ```

   What other action options are available with port security?

   _____

6. Exit configuration mode.

Step 2: Verify the Configuration

1. Display the running configuration.

   What statements in the configuration directly reflect the security implementation?

   _____

   _____

   _____

   _____

2. Show the port security settings:

   FC-ASW-1# **show port-security interface fastethernet 0/4**

   Record the details displayed in the table:

Step 3: Verify the Port Security

1. Connect PC1 to switch port Fa0/1 and PC2 to switch port Fa0/4.

2. From the command prompt, ping from PC1 to PC2.

   Was this successful?

3. From the command prompt, ping from PC2 to PC1.

   Was this successful?

4. From the console terminal session, issue the **show mac-address-table** command.

   Record the details displayed in the table.

   _____

   _____

   _____

   _____

   _____

   _____

   _____

5. Show the port security settings:

   FC-ASW-1# `show port-security interface fastethernet 0/4`

   Record the details displayed in the table.

   _____

   _____

   _____

   _____

   _____

   _____

   _____

   _____

   _____

   _____

   _____

   _____

   Note the difference between these entries and those recorded for **show port-security interface fastethernet 0/4** in Step 2.

   _____

   _____

   _____

6. Confirm the status of the switch port:

   ALSwitch# `show interface fastethernet 0/4`

   What is the state of this interface?

   FastEthernet 0/4 is ____ and line protocol is ____.

Step 4: Test the Port Security

1. Disconnect PC2 from Fa0/4

2. Connect PC2 to the Linksys using one of the ports on the Linksys LAN switch.

3. Use the Basic Setup tab to configure the Internet IP address on the Linksys device to the address and mask, as shown in the address table.

4. Configure PC2 to get an IP address using DHCP. Verify that PC2 receives an IP address from the Linksys device.

5. Connect the Internet port on the Linksys to Fa0/4.

6. Ping from PC1 to PC2.

   Was this successful?

   _____

7. Ping from PC2 to PC1.

   Was this successful?

   _____

   Record the output displayed on the console screen at the switch command line.

   _____

   _____

   _____

   _____

   _____

8. Issue the **show mac-address-table** command.

   Record the details displayed in the table.

   _____

   _____

   _____

   _____

   _____

9. Show the port security settings:

   FC-ASW-1# `show port-security interface fastethernet 0/4`

   Record the details displayed in the table.

   _____

   _____

   _____

   _____

   _____

   _____

   _____

   _____

   _____

   _____

   _____

   _____

   Note the difference in entries recorded from the **show port-security interface fastethernet 0/4** command in Step 3.

   _____

   _____

   _____

10. Confirm the status of the switch port:

    FC-ASW-1# `show interface fastethernet 0/4`

    What is the state of this interface?

    FastEthernet 0/4 is _____ and line protocol is _____.

Step 5: Reactivate the Port

1. If a security violation occurs and the port is shut down, enter interface Fa0/4 configuration mode, disconnect the offending device, and use the **shutdown** command to temporarily disable the port.

2. Disconnect the Linksys and reconnect PC2 to port Fa0/4. Issue the **no shutdown** command on the interface.

3. Ping from PC1 to PC2. You might have to repeat this multiple times before success.

   List reasons why multiple ping attempts might be necessary before success is achieved.

   _____

   _____

   _____

Discuss Switch Port Security Using Dynamic MAC Address Assignment

Advantages:

_____

_____

_____

Disadvantages:

_____

_____

_____

_____

_____

Task 3: Clean Up

Erase the configurations and reload the switches. Disconnect and store the cabling. For PC hosts that are normally connected to other networks (such as the school LAN or to the Internet), reconnect the appropriate cabling and restore the TCP/IP settings.

Reflection

When considering designing a typical enterprise network, it is necessary to think about points of security vulnerability at the access layer. Discuss which access layer switches should have port security and those for which it might not be appropriate. Include possible future issues with regard to wireless and guest access to the network.

_____

_____

_____

_____

_____

_____

_____

_____

_____

Gathering Network Requirements: Labs

The lab exercises included in this chapter cover all the Chapter 2 online curriculum labs to ensure that you have mastered the practical, hands-on skills needed to gather network requirements. As you work through these labs, use Chapter 2 in Part I of this book, or use the corresponding Chapter 2 in the Discovery Designing and Supporting Computer Networks online curriculum for assistance.

Lab 2-1: Creating a Project Plan (2.1.3)

Upon completion of this lab, you will be able to

- Describe the Plan phase of the network lifecycle.
- Create a checklist with outcomes for the Plan phase of the network lifecycle.

Expected Results and Success Criteria

Before starting this lab, read through the tasks that you are expected to perform. What do you expect the result of performing these tasks will be?

_____

_____

_____

What benefits are gained from designing a network upgrade using a network lifecycle approach?

_____

_____

_____

How will a network administrator know if the project plan has succeeded?

_____

_____

_____

Background/Preparation

FilmCompany is an expanding small advertising company moving into interactive advertising media, including video presentations. This company has just been awarded a large video support contract by the StadiumCompany. With this new contract, FilmCompany expects to see their business grow approximately 70 percent.

To facilitate this growth, the FilmCompany has decided to significantly upgrade its data network. In this lab, you have the role of network design consultant. Your job is to develop network design and project documents for the FilmCompany that will meet the requirements of this upgrade.

This lab is the first of a series of labs that explore the FilmCompany existing network and its upgrade requirements.

In this lab, you will use the information in the separate document, Appendix C, "FilmCompany Story," and on the accompanying CD-ROM to examine the second phase of the six phases of the Cisco Lifecycle Services:

- The Prepare phase
- **The Plan phase**
- The Design phase
- The Implement phase
- The Operate phase
- The Optimize phase

For the Plan phase, you will perform a site and operations assessment. The details of the project and its implementation will be developed in forthcoming labs.

Task 1: Evaluate the Current Network, Operations, and Network Management Infrastructure

Step 1.   Use word processing software to create a Project Plan Checklist document based on this lab.

Step 2.   From the case study, document, identify, and assess the current state of the following factors:

- Physical facilities

  _____

- Environmental facilities

  _____

- Electrical facilities

  _____

For each factor, indicate whether it is at capacity or has scope for growth. Include these factors on the checklist with your assessment.

Step 3.   Assess the ability of the current operations and network management infrastructure to support a new technology solution. On the checklist, list the following categories and include what changes must be completed before the implementation of any new technology solution.

- Infrastructure

- Personnel

- Processes

- Tools

Step 4.   Identify and add to the checklist any custom applications that may be required for the new network.

Task 2: Outline the Project Plan

Step 1.   To manage the project, the project plan includes five components. List these five components and an example of each, and then add them to the checklist.

1. _____

2. _____

3. _____

4. _____

5. _____

Step 2.   The plan needs to be within the scope, cost, and resource limits established by the business goals. List any potential issues that the FilmCompany may need to consider to meet these goals, and then add them to the checklist.

_____

_____

_____

Step 3.   The FilmCompany and the stadium management need to assign staff to manage the project from each of their perspectives. List the desirable skills and knowledge that these individuals should possess, and then add them to the checklist.

_____

_____

_____

_____

Step 4.   Save your Project Plan Checklist document. You will use it during the next stages of this network design case study.

Reflection

Sometimes apparent urgency, pressure to present results, and enthusiasm for a project can create a work environment that causes projects to be started before proper planning has been completed.

Consider and discuss the potential problems that result from starting a network upgrade before completely assessing the existing network.

_____

_____

_____

_____

_____

_____

Lab 2-2: Observing Traffic Using Cisco Network Assistant (2.1.6)

Upon completion of this lab, you will be able to

- Explain what occurs during the Operate phase of the network lifecycle.

- Use Cisco Network Assistant to monitor the outcomes of the Operate phase of the network lifecycle.

- Establish network baseline performance.

This lab contains skills that relate to the following 640-802 CCNA exam objectives:

- Describe the purpose and functions of various network devices.

- Verify device configuration and network connectivity using ping, traceroute, Telnet, SSH, or other utilities.

- Determine the path between two hosts across a network.

Expected Results and Success Criteria

Before starting this lab, read through the tasks that you are expected to perform. What do you expect the result of performing these tasks will be?

_____

_____

_____

What benefits are gained from determining the network baseline performance of a network?

_____

_____

_____

What are the probable outcomes if the network baseline performance is exceeded?

_____

_____

_____

Background/Preparation

FilmCompany is an expanding small advertising company moving into interactive advertising media, including video presentations. This company has just been awarded a large video support contract by the StadiumCompany. With this new contract, FilmCompany expects to see their business grow approximately 70 percent.

To facilitate this growth, the FilmCompany has decided to significantly upgrade its data network. In this lab, you have the role of network design consultant. Your job is to develop network design and project documents for the FilmCompany that will meet the requirements of this upgrade.

After the network is upgraded, the FilmCompany personnel will manage the network to ensure that it is performing to the design specifications outlined in the Prepare and Plan phases.

The Operate and Optimize phases of the network lifecycle are ongoing. They represent the day-to-day operations of a network. The purpose of this lab is to introduce the Cisco Network Assistant as a tool to monitor the current FilmCompany network and establish a network baseline. A network baseline will help the company achieve maximum availability, scalability, security, and manageability.

The lab examines the principle of determining a network baseline. Cisco Network Assistant is required to be installed on one PC used in this lab. Cisco Network Assistant is a network management and monitoring program that is provided for free and can be downloaded from http://www.cisco.com. See your instructor if this program is not available in the lab.

Figure 2-1 shows the network topology for this lab and Table 2-1 documents the names, addresses, and subnet masks for all of the network devices in that topology.

Figure 2-1   Lab 2-2 Topology

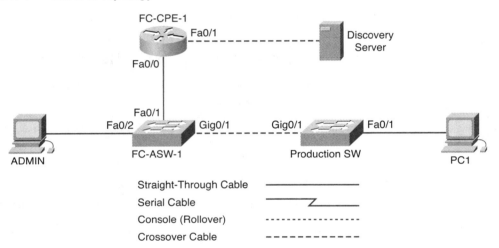

Table 2-1   Addressing Table for Lab 2-2

Device Designation	Device Name	IP Address	Subnet Mask
Switch 1	FC-ASW-1	VLAN1 10.0.0.2	255.255.255.0
Switch 2	Production SW	VLAN1 10.0.0.3	255.255.255.0
Admin PC	ADMIN	10.0.0.4	255.255.255.0
PC1	PC1	10.0.0.5	255.255.255.0
Router	FC-CPE-1	Fa0/0 interface: 10.0.0.1	255.255.255.0
		Fa0/1 interface: 172.17.0.1	255.255.0.0
Discovery Server	Discovery Server	172.17.1.1	255.255.0.0

Task 1: Establish the Network Baseline Criteria

Network baselining is the measuring and rating of the performance of a network as it transports data in real time.

A baseline is a type of "network snapshot" of the devices and their performance. Creating a baseline enables you to see the current network load and, by maintaining that baseline, identify network issues before they become critical. For example, with all the network routers baselined, including the CPU capability and usage, if gradual increases in CPU usage are noted, the issue can be addressed before network performance deteriorates.

List the devices in the lab network and the characteristics that should be monitored:

_____

_____

_____

_____

_____

_____

Task 2: Configure Network Connectivity

Note: If the PCs used in this lab are also connected to your Academy LAN or to the Internet, ensure that you record the cable connections and TCP/IP settings so that these can be restored at the conclusion of the lab.

Step 1.   Connect the devices in accordance with the topology given in Figure 2-1 and configured in accordance with Table 2-1. Your instructor may substitute Discovery Server with an equivalent server for this lab.

Step 2.   See your instructor regarding device configuration. If the devices are not configured, then from the Admin PC, establish a terminal session in turn to each switch and the router using HyperTerminal or TeraTerm. Configure these devices in accordance with the configuration details provided.

Step 3.   Ping between all devices to confirm network connectivity. Troubleshoot and establish connectivity if the pings fail.

Task 3: Set Up Cisco Network Assistant

Step 1.   From the Admin PC, launch the Cisco Network Assistant program.

Step 2.   Set Cisco Network Assistant to discover the network. One method is to establish a "community" of devices. From the Application menu, click **Communities**. A dialog box as shown in Figure 2-2 will display.

Figure 2-2   Cisco Network Assistant Communities

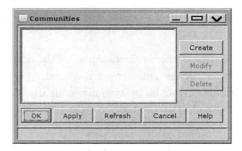

Step 3.   If there are communities listed, highlight each name and click **Delete**. When all existing communities have been deleted, or if there were none listed, click **Create**. The Create Community dialog as shown in Figure 2-3 displays.

Figure 2-3   Cisco Network Assistant Create Community

Step 4.   In the Name field, enter **FilmCompany**.

Step 5.   List the four options available in the **Discover** field:

_____

_____

_____

_____

Step 6.   From the Discover drop-down list, select **Devices in an IP address range**.

Step 7.   At the Start IP address, enter **10.0.0.1**

Step 8.   At the End IP address, enter **10.0.0.3**

Step 9.   Click **Start**. The devices found will be listed similar to that shown in Figure 2-4.

Figure 2-4   Cisco Network Assistant FilmCompany Community

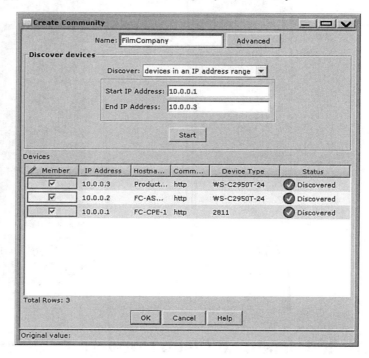

Step 10.   Click **OK** in the **Create Community** and **Communities** dialog boxes.

Step 11.   On the **Application** menu, highlight **Connect** and click **Connect To**. Select **FilmCompany** from the drop-down menu and click **Connect**. A range of icons is now available on the top toolbar and a network topology similar to Figure 2-5 should be displayed. If a topology is not displayed, click the **Topology** icon on the top toolbar and view the topology that Cisco Network Assistant has created.

Figure 2-5   Cisco Network Assistant Topology View

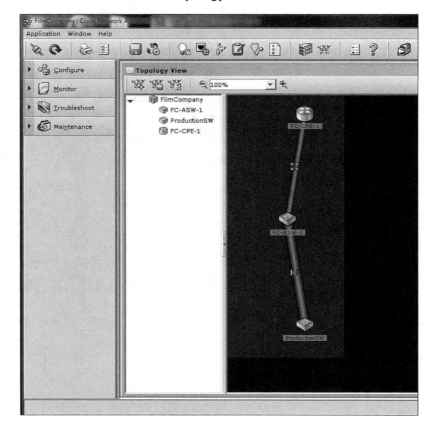

Task 4: Examine Cisco Network Assistant Features

Cisco Network Assistant provides a range of features to display text and graphical information about the network devices. From the topology view window, right-click each device's ID and select **Properties**.

What protocol is used to discover and obtain the device information displayed?

Task 5: Examine Sample Cisco Network Assistant Output

After devices are added to the community, the device links and operation can be monitored using the Monitor tab of Cisco Network Assistant.

Step 1.   Under **Monitor > Reports**, click **Port Statistics** to display information similar to Figure 2-6.

Figure 2-6   Cisco Network Assistant Port Statistics

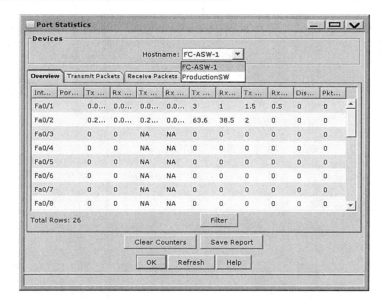

Step 2.   On the **Monitor > Reports** menu, click **Bandwidth Graphs**. Select Hostname **ProductionSW** and **Bar** type. This will display a graph similar to Figure 2-7.

Figure 2-7   Cisco Network Assistant Bar Type Bandwidth Graph

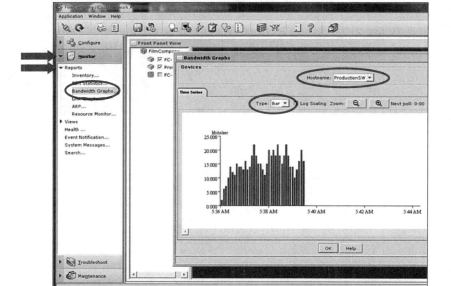

Step 3.   Ping between the Admin and PC1 hosts and Discovery Server to generate sample network traffic. Launch a web browser on each PC and access the URL **http://172.17.1.1**. Observe the changing graphical report.

Step 4.   From the Bandwidth Graphs window, change the Type from **Bar** to **Line.** Output similar to Figure 2-8 will be displayed.

Figure 2-8   Cisco Network Assistant Line Type Bandwidth Graph

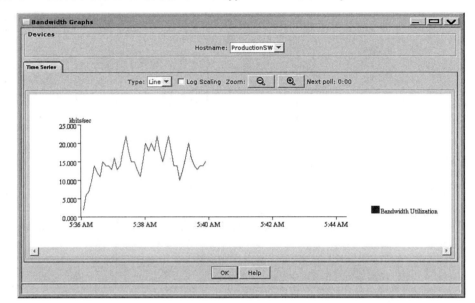

Step 5.   From the Bandwidth Graphs window, select Hostname **FC-ASW-1** and repeat Steps 2, 3 and 4 for this device. Observe the changing graphical reports.

Step 6.   Click **Link Graphs** on the **Monitor > Reports** menu. Select Hostname **ProductionSW** Interface **Fa0/1** and **Bar** type. This will display a graph similar to Figure 2-9.

Figure 2-9   Cisco Network Assistant Bar Type Link Graph

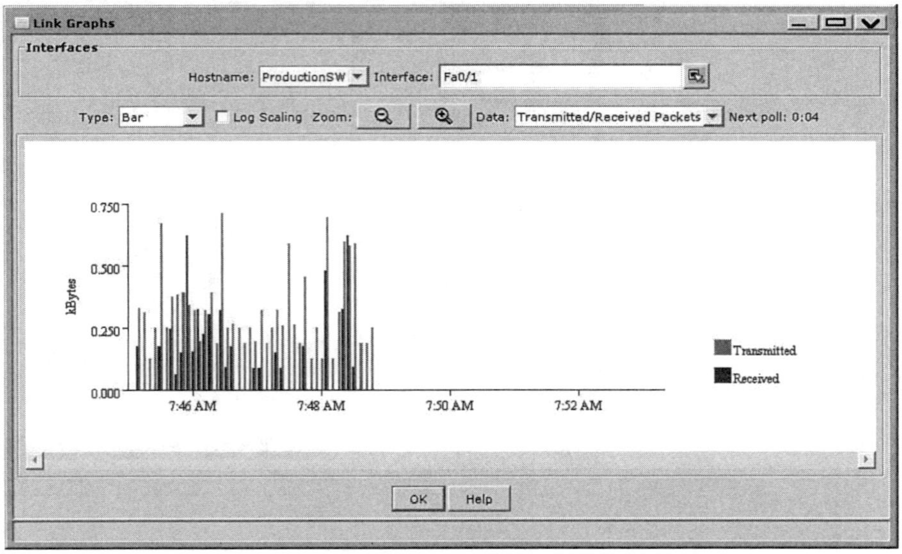

Step 7.   Ping between the Admin and PC1 hosts and Discovery Server to generate sample network traffic. Launch a web browser on each PC and access the URL **http://172.17.1.1**. Observe the changing graphical report.

Step 8.   From the Link Graphs window, change the Type from **Bar** to **Line.** Output similar to Figure 2-10 will be displayed.

Figure 2-10   Cisco Network Assistant Line Type Link Graph

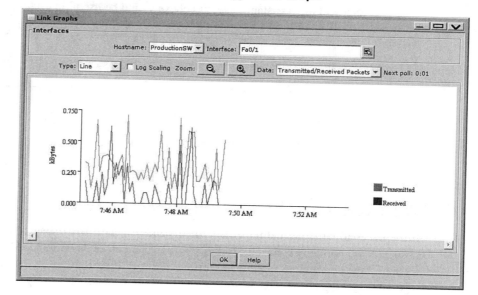

Step 9.   From the Link Graphs window, select Hostname **FC-ASW-1** and repeat Steps 6, 7, and 8 above for this device. Observe the changing graphical reports.

Step 10.   Click **Health** from the **Monitor > View** menu. This will display a graph similar to Figure 2-11.

Figure 2-11   Cisco Network Assistant Health Graphs

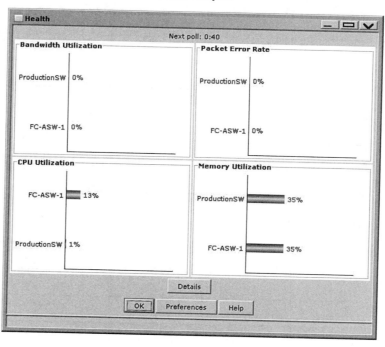

Step 11.   Ping between the Admin and PC1 hosts and Discovery Server to generate sample network traffic. Launch a web browser on each PC and access the URL **http://172.17.1.1**. Observe the changing graphical report. Observe changes in the displayed CPU and Memory Utilization for each device.

Step 12.   Examine the different toolbar functions and note any particular features and tools of Cisco Networking Assistant that you believe would be useful in establishing a network baseline:

_____

_____

_____

_____

_____

_____

Task 6: Clean Up

Erase the configurations and reload the routers and switches. Disconnect and store the cabling. For PC hosts that are normally connected to other networks (such as the school LAN or to the Internet), reconnect the appropriate cabling and restore the TCP/IP settings.

Reflection

This lab focused on monitoring individual devices in a network. Consider, research, and discuss the network factors that should be included in network baseline measurements.

_____

_____

_____

_____

_____

_____

_____

_____

_____

_____

_____

_____

_____

_____

Lab 2-3: Creating a Network Organization Structure (2.3.2)

Upon completion of this lab, you will be able to explain and diagram the structure of the customer organization.

Expected Results and Success Criteria

Before starting this lab, read through the tasks that you are expected to perform. What do you expect the result of performing these tasks will be?

_____

_____

_____

When designing a network upgrade, what benefits are gained from determining the range and type of users?

_____

_____

_____

Background/Preparation

FilmCompany is an expanding small advertising company moving into interactive advertising media, including video presentations. This company has just been awarded a large video support contract by the StadiumCompany. With this new contract, FilmCompany expects to see their business grow approximately 70 percent.

To facilitate this growth, the FilmCompany has decided to significantly upgrade its data network. You have the role of network design consultant. Your job is to develop network design and project documents for the FilmCompany that will meet the requirements of this upgrade.

This lab is one of a series of labs that explore the FilmCompany existing network and its upgrade requirements.

A comprehensive network project plan has to include details of how the network users interact with the network resources and services. To ensure that all user requirements are met, the network designer gathers information about all internal and external access to the existing network infrastructure.

In this lab, you will create a network organization structure of the FilmCompany. All stakeholders in the structure—internal network users, IT organizations, external customers, suppliers, and partners— are to be included.

Task 1: Determine the Network Users

Step 1.   Use word processing software to create a network organization structure document.

Step 2.   Examine the FilmCompany case study document and the sample interview.

Step 3.   Identify and list the potential end users.

_____

_____

_____

Step 4.   Diagram the relationship between these users.

Task 2: Assess Impact of User Network Access

Step 1.   Identify and include the different types of existing and potential new network services the listed users may require. Group the users under the type of network services they use.

_____

Step 2.   The impact of adding new user groups to the network also needs to be assessed. Identify and include the following in the network organization structure document:

- New user groups
- The type of access required
- Where access is allowed
- The overall impact on security

Step 3.   Save your network user structure document and network organization diagram and retain it for the next stages of this network design case study.

Reflection

The total number of users has a direct impact on the scale of the network at the access layer. The type of users and the services they require also have implications for the network structure.

Discuss and consider the impact that the range of network services required by even a relatively small number of users can have on the network structure:

_____

_____

_____

_____

_____

_____

_____

_____

Lab 2-4: Prioritizing Business Goals (2.3.3)

Upon completion of this lab, you will be able to determine and prioritize the project business goals.

Expected Results and Success Criteria

Before starting this lab, read through the tasks that you are expected to perform. What do you expect the result of performing these tasks will be?

_____

_____

_____

What benefits does the network designer gain from determining the business goals and assigning priorities to them?

_____

_____

_____

What problems could arise in a network project if goals and priorities were not set?

_____

_____

_____

Background/Preparation

FilmCompany is an expanding small advertising company moving into interactive advertising media, including video presentations. This company has just been awarded a large video support contract by the StadiumCompany. With this new contract, FilmCompany expects to see their business grow approximately 70 percent.

To facilitate this growth, the FilmCompany has decided to significantly upgrade its data network. You have the role of network design consultant. Your job is to develop network design and project documents for the FilmCompany that will meet the requirements of this upgrade.

This lab is one of a series of labs that explore the FilmCompany existing network and its upgrade requirements.

A comprehensive network project plan has to include details of the project business goals and priorities. In this lab, to ensure that the information gathered is accurate, you will create a checklist that lists the business goals and priorities of the FilmCompany network upgrade project.

Task 1: Determine the Business Goals

Step 1.   Use word processing software to create a business goals document.

Step 2.   From the sample interview in the FilmCompany case study document, identify and list the business goals that the network upgrade is expected to provide:

_____

_____

_____

_____

These goals can be financial, for example:

- **Profitability**: Can the project reduce costs or help the business avoid costs in the future?

- **Business growth and market share**: Can the project help the business grow more efficiently or create competitive advantages?

Or the goals may be strategic:

- **Customer satisfaction**: Can the project improve the customer experience and increase customer loyalty?

- **Reputation and industry standing**: Will the project develop specific core technology competencies in the organization?

Step 3.   Identify and list at least four business goals from the case study interview.

_____

Discuss these goals with another student, or in a group, to clarify understanding of the goals.

Task 2: Prioritize the Business Goals

Step 1.   Rank the following list of business goals in order of priority. Base this ranking on the information in the case study document and discussion with other students.

Step 2.   List the ranked business goals in a table and assign a priority value as a percentage. The total of the percentage values must equal 100.

Prioritizing Business Goals	Priority
Total	100%

Step 3.   Discuss your priority values with other students. If there are differences in priorities, discuss why this has occurred and attempt to resolve them.

Step 4.   Save your Project Prioritized Business Goals Checklist document and retain it for the next stages of this network design case study.

Reflection

Having prioritized the business goals as the stated objectives of a network upgrade project does not necessarily ensure that the project will be a success. These objectives need to be measured against success criteria to determine whether the business goals were achieved.

Before a project can be declared a success, the objectives must be shown to have met the success criteria statements.

Consider and discuss possible success criteria based on the business goals for the FilmCompany network upgrade:

_____

_____

_____

_____

_____

_____

_____

_____

Lab 2-5: Establishing Technical Requirements (2.4.1)

Upon completion of this lab, you will be able to identify and document the project technical requirements.

This lab contains skills that relate to the following 640-802 CCNA exam objectives:

- Describe the purpose and functions of various network devices.
- Select the components required to meet a network specification.

Expected Results and Success Criteria

Before starting this lab, read through the tasks that you are expected to perform. What do you expect the result of performing these tasks will be?

_____

_____

_____

What benefits are gained from identifying the technical requirements of a project before it is started?

_____

_____

_____

Why is it important to consider both the technical requirements and the business requirements of a project?

_____

_____

_____

Background/Preparation

FilmCompany is an expanding small advertising company moving into interactive advertising media, including video presentations. This company has just been awarded a large video support contract by the StadiumCompany. With this new contract, FilmCompany expects to see their business grow approximately 70 percent.

To facilitate this growth, the FilmCompany has decided to significantly upgrade its data network. You have the role of network design consultant. Your job is to develop network design and project documents for the FilmCompany that will meet the requirements of this upgrade.

This lab is one of a series of labs that explore the FilmCompany existing network and its upgrade requirements.

A comprehensive network project plan has to include details of technical requirements of the project. In this lab, you will create and prioritize the technical requirements for the network so that it meets the FilmCompany business goals and priorities.

Task 1: Determine the Technical Requirements

Step 1.   Use word processing software to create a technical requirements document.

Step 2.   From the case study document and checklists developed in previous labs, identify and list the technical requirements that will enable the network upgrade to meet the FilmCompany business goals. The technical requirements document provides direction for the network designer in the following decisions:

- Selecting network equipment

- Designing the topology

- Choosing protocols

- Selecting network services

Step 3.   Discuss these technical requirements with another student, or in a group. Consider the range of possible technical solutions to meet the business goals of the FilmCompany.

_____

_____

_____

_____

Task 2: Prioritize the Technical Requirements

The network designer works with the customer to create a prioritized list of technical requirements. This list will be used to define the project scope.

Step 1.   Rank the list of technical requirements in order of priority. Base this ranking on the information in the case study document and discussion with other students.

It is useful to categorize the technical requirements into the following areas:

- Availability and Performance

- Security

- Scalability

- Manageability

Step 2.   List the ranked technical requirements in a table and assign a priority value as a percentage. The total of the percentage values must equal 100.

Category	Prioritized Technical Requirements	Priority
Availability and Performance		
Security		
Scalability		
Manageability		
	TOTAL	100

Step 3.   Discuss your priority values with other students. If there are differences in priorities, discuss why this has occurred and attempt to resolve them:

_____

_____

_____

_____

Step 4.   Save your Project Prioritized Technical Requirements Checklist document and retain it for the next stages of this network design case study.

Reflection

When discussing technical requirements with the customer, the network designer must consider the technical level of the audience. Technical terms and jargon may not be clearly understood by the customer. Such terms should either be avoided or tailored to the level of detail and complexity that the customer can understand.

Compile a list of networking technical terms and jargon that may need to be expressed or explained to a nontechnical business customer. Develop an explanation or definition for each term that a nontechnical business customer can understand for the purpose of discussing a network upgrade with them:

_____

_____

_____

_____

_____

_____

_____

_____

_____

_____

Lab 2-6: Identifying Organizational Constraints (2.4.2)

Upon completion of this lab, you will be able to identify the constraints that affect the network design, including cost, schedule, and resource constraints.

Expected Results and Success Criteria

Before starting this lab, read through the tasks that you are expected to perform. What do you expect the result of performing these tasks will be?

_____

_____

_____

Why is identifying the constraints that apply to a project an important part of the network design?

_____

_____

_____

Background/Preparation

FilmCompany is an expanding small advertising company moving into interactive advertising media, including video presentations. This company has just been awarded a large video support contract by the StadiumCompany. With this new contract, FilmCompany expects to see their business grow approximately 70 percent.

To facilitate this growth, the FilmCompany has decided to significantly upgrade its data network. You have the role of network design consultant. Your job is to develop network design and project documents for the FilmCompany that will meet the requirements of this upgrade.

This lab is one of a series of labs that explore the FilmCompany existing network and its upgrade requirements.

A comprehensive network project plan has to include details of constraints that apply to the project. In this lab, you will identify the organizational constraints that apply to the FilmCompany case study network upgrade project design.

Task 1: Identify Possible Project Constraints

Step 1.   Use word processing software to create a project constraints document.

Step 2.   Develop a list of possible constraints that set limits or boundaries on the network upgrade project by brainstorming ideas with other students:

_____

_____

_____

Step 3.   Classify each constraint as one of the four following types:

- Budget

- Policy

- Schedule

- Personnel

Task 2: Tabulate the Relevant Constraints

Step 1.   Relate the list of constraints to the prioritized business goals of the FilmCompany.

Step 2.   Develop a definitive list of items that apply specifically to the FilmCompany case study.

Step 3.   Enter the constraints into a table.

FilmCompany Constraints

Constraint	Gathered Data	Comments
Budget		
Policy		
Schedule		
Personnel		

Step 4.   Save your Project Constraints Checklist document and retain it for the next stages of this network design case study.

Reflection

The constraints imposed on this network design project are determined by the internal requirements of the FilmCompany. Consider and discuss external constraints. Include constraints that may be beyond the control of the business but which, in some circumstances, affect a network design project:

_____

_____

_____

_____

_____

Lab 2-7: Monitoring Network Performance (2.5.2)

Upon completion of this lab, you will be able to describe methods of monitoring network performance to ensure that the network design is working appropriately.

This lab contains skills that relate to the following 640-802 CCNA exam objectives:

- Describe the purpose and functions of various network devices.
- Select the components required to meet a network specification.
- Determine the path between two hosts across a network.

Expected Results and Success Criteria

Before starting this lab, read through the tasks that you are expected to perform. What do you expect the result of performing these tasks will be?

_____

_____

_____

What benefits are gained from monitoring network performance?

_____

_____

_____

What are possible actions a network administrator could take if network performance was noted to be deteriorating?

_____

_____

_____

Background/Preparation

FilmCompany is an expanding small advertising company moving into interactive advertising media, including video presentations. This company has just been awarded a large video support contract by the StadiumCompany. With this new contract, FilmCompany expects to see their business grow approximately 70 percent.

To facilitate this growth, the FilmCompany has decided to significantly upgrade its data network. You have the role of network design consultant. Your job is to develop network design and project documents for the FilmCompany that will meet the requirements of this upgrade.

After the network is upgraded, the FilmCompany personnel will manage the network to ensure that it is performing to the design specifications outlined in the Prepare and Plan phases.

This lab simulates the monitoring of the current FilmCompany network during its operations. It is used to note whether baseline performance is exceeded. This information will help determine how the network needs to be upgraded to meet the requirements of the new stadium contract.

The network management and monitoring program Cisco Network Assistant is required to be installed on each PC used in this lab. Cisco Network Assistant is a program provided free and can be downloaded from http://www.cisco.com. See your instructor if this program is not available in the lab.

Figure 2-12 shows the network topology for this lab and Table 2-2 documents the names, addresses, and subnet masks for all of the network devices in that topology.

Figure 2-12   Lab 2-7 Topology

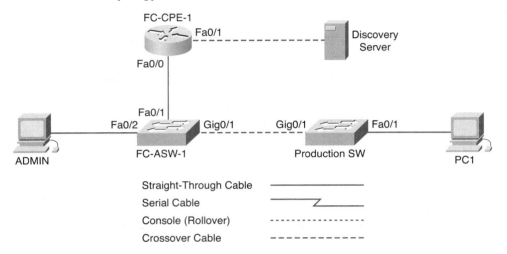

Table 2-2   Addressing Table for Lab 2-7

Device Designation	Device Name	IP Address	Subnet mask
Switch 1	FC-ASW-1	VLAN 10.0.0.2	255.255.255.0
Switch 2	ProductionSW	VLAN 10.0.0.3	255.255.255.0
Admin PC	ADMIN	10.0.0.4	255.255.255.0
PC1	PC1	10.0.0.5	255.255.255.0
Router	FC-CPE-1	Fa0/0 10.0.0.1	255.255.255.0
		Fa0/1 172.17.0.1	255.255.0.0
Discovery Server	Discovery Server	172.17.1.1	255.255.0.0

Task 1: Configure Network Connectivity

Note: If the PCs used in this lab are also connected to your Academy LAN or to the Internet, ensure that you record the cable connections and TCP/IP settings so that these can be restored at the conclusion of the lab.

Step 1. Connect the devices in accordance with the given topology and configuration. Your instructor may substitute Discovery Server with an equivalent server for this lab.

Step 2. See your instructor regarding device configuration. If the devices are not configured from the Admin PC, establish a terminal session in turn to each switch and the router using HyperTerminal or TeraTerm. Configure these devices in accordance with the configuration details provided.

Step 3. Ping between all devices to confirm network connectivity. Troubleshoot and establish connectivity if the pings fail.

Task 2: Set Up Cisco Network Assistant

Step 1. From the Admin PC, launch the Cisco Network Assistant program.

Step 2. Set Cisco Network Assistant to discover the network by establishing a "community" of devices.

    a. From the Application menu, select **Communities**.

    b. In the Name field, enter **FilmCompany**.

    c. From the Discover drop-down list, select **Devices in an IP address range**.

    d. Enter the start and end addresses of the router and two switches.

    _____

    _____

    e. Click **Start**. List the devices found:

    _____

    _____

    _____

    _____

    f. Click **OK** in the **Create Community** and **Communities** dialog boxes.

Step 3. On the **Application** menu, highlight **Connect** and click **Connect To**. Select **FilmCompany** from the drop-down menu and click **Connect**. A range of icons is now available on the top toolbar and a network topology similar to Figure 2-13 should be displayed. If a topology is not displayed, click the **Topology** icon on the top toolbar and view the topology that Cisco Network Assistant has created.

Figure 2-13   Cisco Network Assistant Topology View

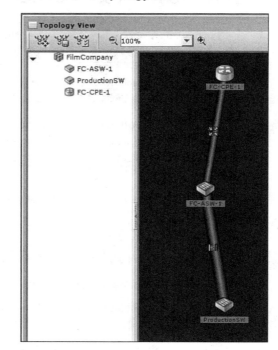

Task 3: Monitor Network Traffic

For each switch, FC-ASW-1 and ProductionSW, examine the different bandwidth and link utilization graphs for a range of traffic.

Determine which graphs are the most useful for monitoring network traffic at this stage.

Use PC1 to generate network traffic to be monitored. This can include the following:

- Ping and telnet to Discovery Server.

- Opening the Discovery Server home web page in a browser on PC1.

- Using FTP to download files from Discovery Server.

Figures 2-14 through Figure 2-18 provide samples of the device bandwidth monitoring information that can be observed.

Figure 2-14   Device ProductionSW Bandwidth Graph 1 (Bar Type)

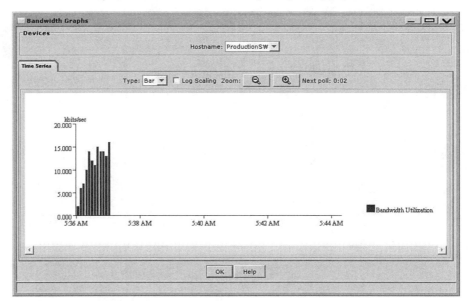

Figure 2-15   Device ProductionSW Bandwidth Graph 2 (Bar Type)

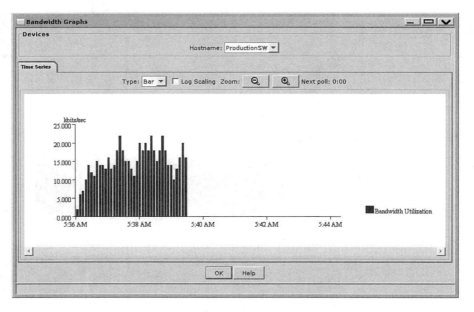

Figure 2-16   Device ProductionSW Bandwidth Graph 2 (Line Type)

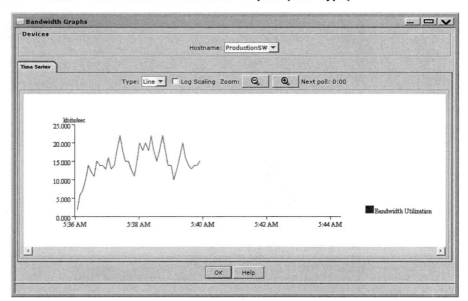

Figure 2-17   Device ProductionSW Bandwidth Graph 3 (Bar Type)

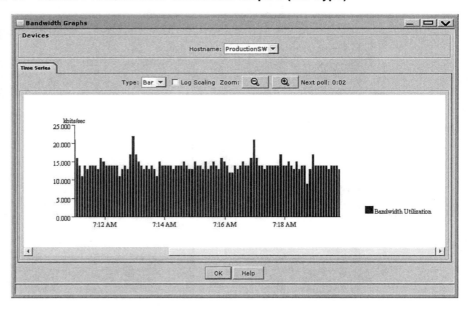

Figure 2-18   Device ProductionSW Bandwidth Graph 3 (Line Type)

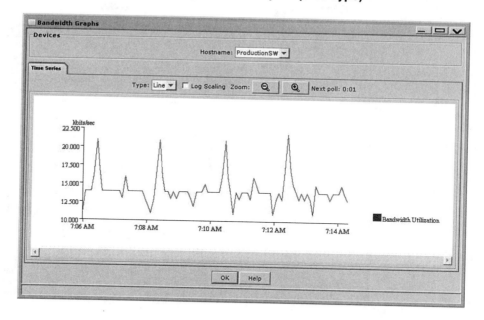

Figures 2-19 through Figure 2-23 provide samples of the device link monitoring information that can be observed.

Figure 2-19   Device ProductionSW Link Interface Fa0/1 Packets Transmitted and Received (Bar Type)

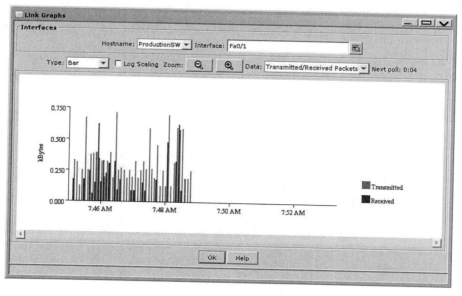

Figure 2-20   Device ProductionSW Link Interface Fa0/1 Packets Transmitted and Received (Line Type)

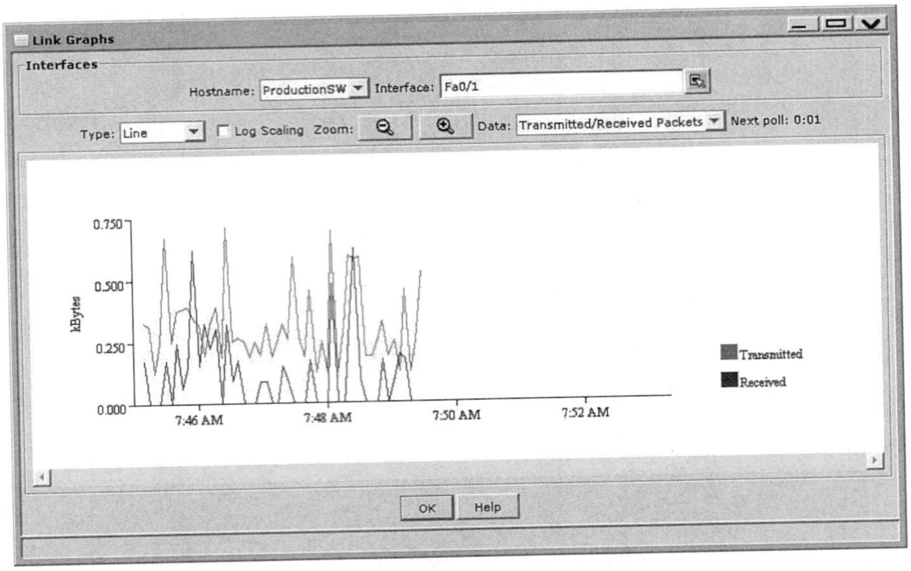

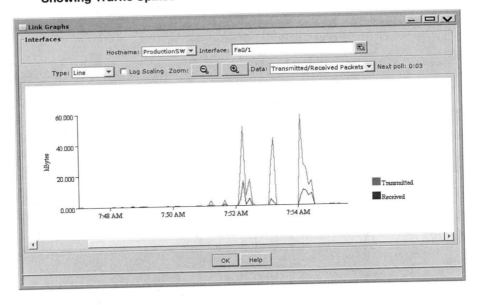

Figure 2-21   Device ProductionSW Link Interface Fa0/1 Packets Transmitted and Received Showing Traffic Spikes

Figure 2-22   Device ProductionSW Link Interface Gigabit Interface 0/1 Packets Transmitted and Received (Line Type)

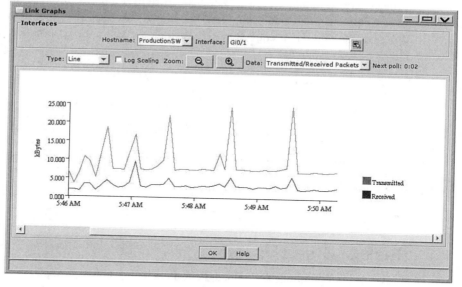

Figure 2-23   Device ProductionSW Link Interface Gigabit Interface 0/1 Utilization Spike

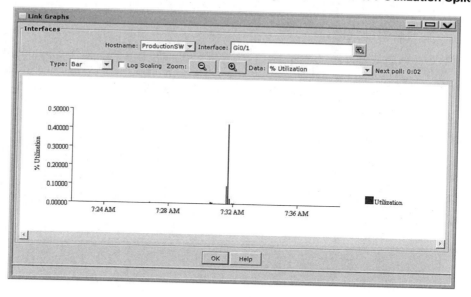

List the four types of data that can be monitored for a device link.

_____

_____

_____

_____

Task 4: Review the Data

Typical network monitoring would be performed over a period of time. Discuss with other students and record here what conclusions could be drawn from the limited information monitored in this lab. What area do you think requires more investigation before the information would be useful in planning a network upgrade?

_____

_____

_____

_____

_____

_____

Task 5: Clean Up

Erase the configurations and reload the routers and switches. Disconnect and store the cabling. For PC hosts that are normally connected to other networks (such as the school LAN or to the Internet), reconnect the appropriate cabling and restore the TCP/IP settings.

Reflection

The usefulness of monitoring network traffic and performance is maximized when the full range of network usage and service situations has been recorded. Consider and discuss when recorded network performance data should be considered for network design purposes and occasions when it should not be included:

_____

_____

_____

_____

_____

Lab 2-8: Investigating Network Monitoring Software (2.5.3)

Upon completion of this lab, you will be able to describe how network monitoring tools can be used to page or send e-mail to on-call technicians.

Expected Results and Success Criteria

Before starting this lab, read through the tasks that you are expected to perform. What do you expect the result of performing these tasks will be?

_____

_____

_____

What benefits are gained from network support technicians understanding what network monitoring tools are available?

_____

_____

_____

What problems could arise if network problems are not immediately detected and acted on by technical or network support staff?

_____

_____

_____

Background/Preparation

FilmCompany is an expanding small advertising company moving into interactive advertising media, including video presentations. This company has just been awarded a large video support contract by the StadiumCompany. With this new contract, FilmCompany expects to see their business grow approximately 70 percent.

To facilitate this growth, the FilmCompany has decided to significantly upgrade its data network. In this lab, you have the role of network design consultant. Your job is to develop network design and project documents for the FilmCompany that will meet the requirements of this upgrade.

After the network is upgraded, the FilmCompany personnel will manage the network to ensure that it is performing to the design specifications outlined in the Prepare and Plan phases.

In this lab, research the possible range of networking utility programs that use SNMP to monitor network performance and notify support staff when an out-of-limits condition is detected.

Task 1: SNMP Overview

Simple Network Management Protocol is a common network management protocol. The protocol enables network administrators to gather data about the network and corresponding devices. SNMP management system software is available in tools such as CiscoWorks. SNMP management agent software is often embedded in operating systems on servers, routers, and switches.

SNMP has four main components:

- Management station
- Management agents
- Management Information Base (MIB)
- Network management protocol

Descriptions of SNMP are available at the following URLs:

http://www.cisco.com/univercd/cc/td/doc/cisintwk/ito_doc/snmp.htm

http://www.protocols.com/pbook/tcpip9.htm#SNMP

As part of a network management system, SNMP tools can respond to network errors or failures in several ways. Generally, when a network fault occurs, or when predefined thresholds are met, the SNMP tools can react by sending the following:

- An alert on the network
- A message to a pager
- An email to an administrator

The FilmCompany is required to maintain a specified level of network service to meet its StadiumCompany contract obligations. They need to purchase network management software that enables them to monitor and manage the new upgraded network.

Task 2: Search for SNMP Monitoring Programs

Step 1.   Using a computer with Internet access, use a web browser to search for examples of SNMP monitoring programs. Use search terms such as the following:

- SNMP reporting
- SNMP notification
- SNMP monitoring

Step 2.   List other appropriate search terms.

_____

_____

_____

_____

_____

_____

Step 3.   Note and compare the features of a number of the monitoring programs found.

Name: _____

Website: _____

Key features:

_____

_____

_____

Name: _____

Website: _____

Key features:

_____

_____

_____

Name: _____

Website: _____

Key features:

_____

_____

_____

Name: _____

Website: _____

Key features:

_____

_____

_____

Step 4.   Select a program that would be suitable for the FilmCompany network and give reasons for your selection. Discuss your choice of program with other students.

Program: _____

Website: _____

Reasons:

_____

_____

_____

Task 3: Example SNMP Program

An example of an SNMP monitoring program is Plixer Denika v7.

Step 1.   Go to the website for this program at http://www.plixer.com/products/denika.php.

Step 2.   List the type of reports that this program can generate:

_____

_____

_____

_____

_____

_____

_____

Step 3.   Read the details for each type of report. Select the report type that would be most applicable to ensure that a problem with the performance of the link carrying real-time video data from the StadiumCompany to FilmCompany was addressed as soon as possible. Summarize the features of this reporting provided by this program.

Type of report:

_____

Features:

_____

_____

_____

_____

_____

_____

Reflection

Consider and discuss the organizational or business support necessary to make best use of network monitoring programs with event-triggered notification features:

_____

_____

_____

_____

Characterizing the Existing Network: Labs

The lab exercises included in this chapter cover all the Chapter 3 online curriculum labs to ensure that you have mastered the practical, hands-on skills needed to investigate and characterize the existing network to enable development of a network Design Requirements document. As you work through these labs, use Chapter 3 in Part I of this book, or use the corresponding Chapter 3 in the Discovery Designing and Supporting Computer Networks online curriculum for assistance.

Lab 3-1: Creating a Logical Network Diagram (3.1.2)

Upon completion of this lab, you will be able to

- Use router and switch commands to obtain information about an existing network.
- Use Cisco Network Assistant to obtain information about an existing network.
- Develop a logical network diagram.

This lab contains skills that relate to the following 640-802 CCNA exam objectives:

- Describe the purpose and functions of various network devices.
- Interpret network diagrams.
- Determine the path between two hosts across a network.
- Verify network status and switch operation using basic utilities (including ping, traceroute, Telnet, SSH, ARP, ipconfig), and **show** and **debug** commands.
- Interpret the output of various **show** and **debug** commands to verify the operational status of a Cisco switched network.
- Verify device configuration and network connectivity using ping, traceroute, Telnet, SSH, or other utilities.
- Verify router hardware and software operation using **show** and **debug** commands.

Expected Results and Success Criteria

Before starting this lab, read through the tasks that you are expected to perform. What do you expect the result of performing these tasks will be?

_____

_____

_____

What are the benefits of a logical network diagram to a network administrator?

_____

_____

_____

What possible actions could a network administrator take if monitoring the highlighted issues?

_____

_____

_____

Background/Preparation

In this lab, you have the task of documenting an existing precabled and configured enterprise network. However, you do not have physical access to the devices, cabling information, or other documentation.

You will first discover as much information as possible by telnetting from an administrator PC into the network devices and using router and switch commands. The Telnet access password for all devices is cisco, and the password to enter privileged EXEC mode is class. You will record this information and use it to draw a logical topology diagram of the network.

You will then use the network management and monitoring program Cisco Network Assistant to display the topology graphically. This program is required to be installed on each PC used in this lab. Cisco Network Assistant is a program provided free and can be downloaded from http://www.cisco.com. See your instructor if this program is not available in the lab.

Figure 3-1 represents the network topology for this lab.

Figure 3-1   Student Lab 3-1 Network Topology

ADMIN

Part 1: Use Cisco IOS Commands to Obtain Information About the Network

First, you use some Cisco IOS commands to obtain information about the network.

Task 1: Discover and Document the First Device

Note: If the PCs used in this lab are also connected to your Academy LAN or to the Internet, ensure that you record the cable connections and TCP/IP settings so that these can be restored at the conclusion of the lab.

Step 1.   Your instructor will advise you as to which PC is configured for Administrator access to the network. Access this Admin PC and issue the **ipconfig** command from the command prompt to discover the default gateway.

Step 2.   Telnet from the command prompt (or use a terminal program such as HyperTerminal or TeraTerm) to the IP address of the gateway device and enter privileged EXEC mode using the passwords given previously.

Step 3.   Issue Cisco IOS commands, such as those shown here, and others you choose to use, to learn about the device:

```
show running-config

show ip route

show interfaces

show ip interface brief

show version
```

Record this information in Table 3-1 at the end of this lab.

Step 4.   Issue Cisco IOS commands such as those shown here to discover information about connected devices:

```
show cdp neighbors

show cdp neighbors detail
```

It might take a few minutes for the network to converge. If you do not see any neighboring devices initially, repeat the command until you do.

Document the information you gather in the appropriate device tables.

Step 5.   Close the Telnet session by issuing the **exit** command.

Task 2: Discover the Remaining Devices

Step 1.   Telnet to the IP address of a device connected to the first device interrogated, and repeat the processes in Task 1. Document this new device in an appropriate device table at the end of this lab.

Step 2.   Repeat this process until you have discovered and documented all devices in the network.

As you work through the network devices, record the details of each and sketch a diagram of the network devices and their interconnections.

When IP address information has been recorded, what other commands could you use to confirm connectivity and trace interconnections between devices?

_____

_____

Can a connectivity trace be relied upon to return details of all the pathways between devices? Give reasons for your response:

_____

_____

Part 2: Use Cisco Network Assistant to Obtain Information About the Network

In this part of the lab, you use Cisco Network Assistant to obtain information about the network.

Task 1: Launch Cisco Network Assistant

Step 1.   Launch the Cisco Network Assistant program on the Admin PC connected to the network.

Step 2.   Network devices can be accessed for monitoring and information gathering. From the Applications menu, click **Connect**.

Step 3.   In the Connect dialog box, select the **Connect To** option and enter the default gateway of the Admin PC in the field.

Task 2: Record the Network Topology

Step 1.   Record the displayed topology. Click each device to display its properties.

Step 2.   Continue to use Cisco Network Assistant to connect to each known device. Record the topology displayed with each connection and compare it with the diagram that you created from the results of Part 1.

Task 3: Collate the Network Information

Assemble your completed network device tables and topology diagrams into your FilmCompany case study portfolio for use in later labs.

Task 4: Clean Up

Erase the configurations and reload the routers and switches. Disconnect and store the cabling. For PC hosts that are normally connected to other networks (such as the school LAN or to the Internet), reconnect the appropriate cabling and restore the TCP/IP settings.

Reflection

1. These techniques were used to discover and document an enterprise LAN. Would the same techniques work for an enterprise network that includes WAN links?

_____

_____

2. Could these techniques be used in a network that includes routers and switches from a manufacturer other than Cisco? Why or why not?

_____

_____

Device Tables

Router

Hostname _____

Model _____

IOS version _____

Table 3-1

Interface	IP Address	Subnet Mask	Connects to Device	Connects to Interface

Router

Hostname _____

Model _____

IOS version _____

Table 3-2

Interface	IP Address	Subnet Mask	Connects to Device	Connects to Interface

Router

Hostname _____

Model _____

IOS version _____

Table 3-3

Interface	IP Address	Subnet Mask	Connects to Device	Connects to Interface

Router

Hostname _____

Model _____

IOS version _____

Table 3-4

Interface	IP Address	Subnet Mask	Connects to Device	Connects to Interface

Switch

Hostname _____

Model _____

IOS version _____

IP address _____

Subnet mask _____

Default gateway _____

Table 3-5

Trunk Ports	Connects to Device	Connects to Interface

Active Access Ports	VLAN Number	VLAN Name

Switch

Hostname _____

Model _____

IOS version _____

IP address _____

Subnet mask _____

Default gateway _____

Table 3-6

Trunk Ports	Connects to Device	Connects to Interface

Active Access Ports	VLAN Number	VLAN Name

Switch

Hostname _____

Model _____

IOS version _____

IP address _____

Subnet mask _____

Default gateway _____

Table 3-7

Trunk Ports	Connects to Device	Connects to Interface

Active Access Ports	VLAN Number	VLAN Name

Switch

Hostname _____

Model _____

IOS version _____

IP address _____

Subnet mask _____

Default gateway _____

Table 3-8

Trunk Ports	Connects to Device	Connects to Interface

Active Access Ports	VLAN Number	VLAN Name

Switch

Hostname _____

Model _____

IOS version _____

IP address _____

Subnet mask _____

Default gateway _____

Table 3-9

Trunk Ports	Connects to Device	Connects to Interface

Active Access Ports	VLAN Number	VLAN Name

Network Diagram

Use this page to sketch a logical network topology diagram based on the information that you tabulated and noted in Parts 1 and 2.

Lab 3-2: Using show version to Create an Inventory List (3.2.2)

Upon completion of this lab, you will be able to

- Use IOS **show** commands to determine the version and capabilities of an installed Cisco IOS.

- Use Cisco.com website tools to determine the features and capabilities of a Cisco IOS.

This lab contains skills that relate to the following 640-802 CCNA exam objectives:

- Perform and verify initial switch configuration tasks, including remote-access management.

- Verify router hardware and software operation using **show** and **debug** commands.

Expected Results and Success Criteria

Before starting this lab, read through the tasks that you are expected to perform. What do you expect the result of performing these tasks will be?

_____

_____

_____

_____

How is an understanding of the Cisco networking device IOS useful in network administration?

_____

_____

_____

Why would a network administrator change the Cisco networking device IOS to a different version or feature set?

_____

_____

_____

Background/Preparation

The features and capabilities of the Cisco IOS image installed on a router and switch determine which network features it can provide. When considering a network upgrade, it is important to determine precisely what the current devices can do. If shortcomings are found in Cisco device IOS capabilities, the planned upgraded services cannot be provided, and the device IOS will have to be upgraded.

In this lab, you examine the installed Cisco IOS image on a router and on a switch, and then use Cisco.com to more precisely list the features of that Cisco IOS.

This lab is based on the Cisco 1841 Integrated Services Router (ISR) and Cisco Catalyst 2960 switch. The results of this lab will vary accordingly if other devices are used.

Part 1: Determine the Capabilities of the IOS of a Cisco 1841 ISR

In this part of the lab, you determine the capabilities of the IOS image running on a Cisco router.

Task 1: Inspect the Installed Cisco IOS

Note: If the PCs used in this lab are also connected to your Academy LAN or to the Internet, ensure that you record the cable connections and TCP/IP settings so that these can be restored at the conclusion of the lab.

Step 1. Referring to the lab network topology given in Figure 3-2, connect the console (or rollover) cable to the console port on the router and the other cable end to the host computer with a DB-9 or DB-25 adapter to the COM 1 port. Ensure that power has been applied to both the host computer and router.

Figure 3-2   Lab Network 3-2 Topology: Part 1

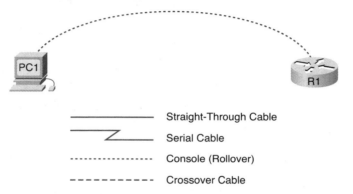

Step 2. Establish a HyperTerminal or other terminal emulation program connection to the router.

Step 3. From the privileged EXEC mode prompt of the terminal, issue the **show version** command. Record the following details:

Cisco IOS version: _____

Name of the system image (IOS) file: _____

Cisco IOS feature set: _____

Date of code build: _____

Where the router IOS image booted from:_____

Type of processor board:_____

Amount of DRAM:_____

Number of Ethernet interfaces:_____

Number of serial interfaces: _____

Amount of NVRAM: _____

Amount of flash memory:_____

Configuration register: _____

Step 4.   Issue the **show flash** command. Record the following details:

The amount of flash memory available and used: _____

The size of the IOS file: _____

Step 5.   Issue the **show running-configuration** command. Record features that indicate what the router is capable of:

_____

_____

_____

Task 2: Examine a Cisco IOS Feature Set on Cisco.com

Step 1.   Launch a web browser on a PC connected to the Internet and access the website http://www.cisco.com.

Step 2.   The Cisco main website changes frequently, so the steps listed here are only representative of the procedure for accessing the resources. If the options do not appear as listed, check with your instructor or use the Cisco.com search functions to find the Cisco IOS Software Selector.

Step 3.   Roll over the **Support** tab and select **Support**.

Step 4.   On the Support page, under Frequently Used Resources, click **Tools & Resources**.

Step 5.   At the bottom of the Tools & Resources page, click the **Show All Tools** button to display tools by category.

Step 6.   Scroll down and click **Cisco IOS Software Selector**.

Step 7.   Click **Search by Release/Product Code/Platform**.

■ At Platform, select **1841**. Click **Continue**.

■ At Release, select **12.4(3c)**.

■ At Feature Set, select **IP BASE**.

Print or select and save the search results.

Note: The list of features may be more than 10 printed pages.

Step 8.   Examine the listed features. From your understanding of Cisco IOS features, group three or four features under headings such as these:

Routing: _____

Security: _____

IP services: _____

Converged services: _____

Network management: _____

Other: _____

Task 3: Examine Your Cisco IOS Feature Set on Cisco.com

Step 1. If your router Cisco IOS version differs from the IOS version in Task 2, repeat this search using your IOS version. Record your results.

Step 2. Compare this list of features with the list from Task 2.

Task 4: Clean Up

Erase any configurations and reload the router. Disconnect and store the cabling. For PC hosts that are normally connected to other networks (such as the school LAN or to the Internet), reconnect the appropriate cabling and restore the TCP/IP settings.

Part 2: Determine the Capabilities of the IOS of a Cisco 2960 Switch

In this part of the lab, you determine the capabilities of the IOS image running on a Cisco switch.

Task 1: Inspect the Installed Cisco IOS

Note: If the PCs used in this lab are also connected to your Academy LAN or to the Internet, ensure that you record the cable connections and TCP/IP settings so that these can be restored at the conclusion of the lab.

Step 1. Referring to the network topology in Figure 3-3, connect the console cable to the console port on the switch and the other cable end to the host computer with a DB-9 or DB-25 adapter to the COM 1 port. Ensure that power has been applied to both the host computer and switch.

Figure 3-3   Lab 3-2 Network Topology: Part 2

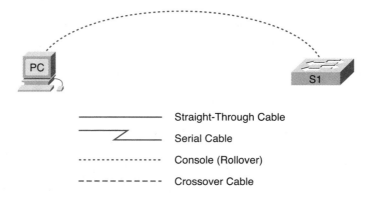

Straight-Through Cable

Serial Cable

Console (Rollover)

Crossover Cable

Step 2. Establish a HyperTerminal or other terminal emulation program to the switch.

Step 3. From the privileged EXEC mode prompt of the terminal, issue the **show version** command. Record the following details:

IOS version: _____

Name of the system image (IOS) file: _____

IOS feature set: _____

Date of code build: _____

Type of processor board and processor: _____

_____

Amount of DRAM: _____

Number of Fast Ethernet interfaces: _____

Number of Gigabit Ethernet interfaces: _____

Amount of NVRAM: _____

Amount of flash memory: _____

Configuration register: _____

Step 4.   Issue the **show flash** command. Record the following details:

The amount of flash memory available and used: _____

_____

The size of the IOS file: _____

Task 2: Examine a Cisco IOS Feature Set on Cisco.com

Step 1.   Launch a web browser on a PC connected to the Internet and access the website http://www.cisco.com.

Step 2.   Roll over the tab and select **Support**.

Step 3.   On the Support page, under Frequently Used Resources, click **Tools & Resources**.

Step 4.   At the bottom of the Tools & Resources page, click the **Show All Tools** button to display tools by category.

Step 5.   Click **Cisco IOS Software Selector**.

Step 6.   Click **Cisco Feature Navigator** from the Tool Index on the left side of the page.

Step 7.   Click **Search by Platform**.

- At Platform, scroll down and select **CAT2960**. Click **Continue**.
- At Major Release, select **12.2SEE** (the screen will refresh after each selection).
- At Release, select **12.2(25)SEE3**.
- At Feature Set, select **LAN BASE**.

Print or select and save the search results.

Note: The list of features may be more than ten printed pages.

Step 8.   Examine the listed features. From your understanding of IOS features, group one or two features under headings such as these:

Routing: _____

Security: _____

IP services: _____

Converged services: _____

Network management: _____

Other: _____

Task 3: Examine your Cisco IOS Feature Set on Cisco.com

Step 1.   If your switch Cisco IOS version differs from the IOS version in Task 2, repeat this search using your IOS version. Record your results.

Step 2.   Compare this list of features with the list from Task 2.

Task 4: Clean Up

Erase any configurations and reload the switch. Disconnect and store the cabling. For PC hosts that are normally connected to other networks (such as the school LAN or to the Internet), reconnect the appropriate cabling and restore the TCP/IP settings.

Challenge

To develop familiarity with using the Cisco.com website, conduct an equivalent Cisco IOS for each different Cisco networking device in your lab. Compare the devices for Cisco IOS functionality and features.

Lab 3-3: Using Feature Navigator (3.2.3)

Upon completion of this lab, you will be able to

- Set up a Cisco.com Guest registration.

- Select Cisco IOS images using the Cisco.com Feature Navigator.

Expected Results and Success Criteria

Before starting this lab, read through the tasks that you are expected to perform. What do you expect the result of performing these tasks will be?

_____

_____

_____

How is an understanding of the Cisco.com Feature Navigator useful in network administration?

_____

_____

_____

What are the benefits of using the Cisco.com Feature Navigator in network design?

_____

_____

_____

Background / Preparation

This lab introduces the features of the Cisco Systems, Inc. website, http://www.cisco.com, as a resource for supporting Cisco networking devices.

You use the website tools to examine the features available in versions of Cisco IOS Software for the Cisco 1841 ISR and Catalyst 2960 switch.

The ability to navigate and access the services and information on Cisco.com is critical to maintaining current knowledge of router and switch features that applies to network configuration and troubleshooting.

Part 1: Create a Cisco.com Guest Registration

Part 1 covers setting up a Cisco.com Guest registration (formerly known as CCO, Cisco Connection Online). If you already have a current working Cisco.com Registration, omit this task.

Note: Cisco.com Guest registration is completely separate from your Cisco Networking Academy student account. During the registration process, you may find it convenient to register the same username as your student username, if it is available.

Task 1: Access the Cisco.com Registration Service

Step 1.   Launch a web browser on a PC connected to the Internet and access the website http://www.cisco.com.

Step 2.   On the upper right of the page, click **Register** as shown in Figure 3-4. The page that opens is Step 1 of 4 in the registration process.

Figure 3-4   Online Cisco.com Registration

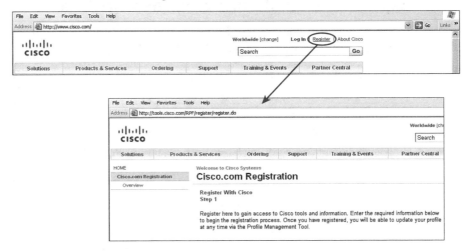

Task 2: Complete the Registration Process

Step 1.   Complete the registration information required for Step 1 of the online process:

- A valid e-mail address must be used.

- The user ID can be the same as your Networking Academy name (if it is available).

- Do not select any check boxes under Register for Additional Access.

- You may choose to receive information from Cisco by selecting Yes or No as you prefer.

- Read the Cisco Privacy Statement and click **Yes**.

- Click **Submit**.

Step 2.   On the next page, Step 2 of 4 of the process, select **Home Address**, and enter either your academy address details or your personal address, and a telephone number. Click **Submit**.

Step 3.   At the Your Interest and Preferences screen under Step 3 of 4, click **Skip This Step** if you are not employed. Completing this information is optional.

Step 4.   At Step 4 of 4, the Complete Registration screen appears. You will be directed to your e-mail account to activate your registration with Cisco.com.

Step 5.   Check the e-mail account you registered with for a message with the subject "Cisco.com Registration: Action required." In the body of the e-mail, click the Cisco.com account activation link, or copy and paste it into a browser address window.

- You will see the Successful Registration screen.

- You will receive a Cisco.com Registration Confirmation e-mail with your user ID.

You can now access Cisco.com by clicking Log In at the top of the Cisco.com web page and entering your user ID and password.

Task 3: Test Your Cisco.com Guest Registration

Step 1.   Launch a web browser on a PC connected to the Internet and access the website http://www.cisco.com.

Step 2.   At the upper right of the page, click **Log In** and log in using your Cisco.com username and password.

Note: As a security precaution, you will be prompted to change your password when you log in if you have not changed it within the past 3 months.

Once logged in, you might not notice any change in appearance of the website (other than Logged In and Profile links at the top of each page). However, when services on the Support menu are accessed, the range and detail of features may increase.

Note: Guest registration does not provide access to IOS Software downloads. Additional access registration is required to access IOS Software. These registrations can be of the following types:

- Service Contract (SMARTnet) Owner.
- Cisco Channel Partner or Authorized Company.
- Purchase Direct from Cisco.
- Customer of a Cisco Certified Partner Initiated Customer Access (PICA) Partner.
- You are a Cisco Certified Internetwork Expert (CCIE User).

Part 2: Access Cisco.com Feature Navigator

In Part 2 of this lab, you access and examine the various Cisco.com Feature Navigator search tools.

Task 1: Access and Log In to Cisco.com

Step 1.   Launch a web browser on a PC connected to the Internet and access the website http://www.cisco.com.

Step 2.   At the upper right of the page, click **Log In** and log in using your Cisco.com username and password.

Step 3.   Click **Products and Services**.

Step 4.   Under Product Research Tools, click the **Cisco Feature Navigator** link.

Note: If you do not have a Cisco.com Registration or the preceding steps do not lead you to the Cisco Feature Navigator, you can access it directly by using the URL http://www.cisco.com/go/cfn.

Task 2: Examine the Feature Navigator Tools

List the six tools offered by the Feature Navigator.

_____

_____

_____

_____

_____

_____

It might be necessary to use more than one tool. For example, you might not know the exact description of a feature set, but you may know the platform and image name. In this lab, you use a combination of tools to provide all the necessary information.

Part 3: Examine 1841 Router IOS Features

In this part of the lab, you perform a detailed search of the features of a particular Cisco router.

Note: It is important to distinguish between a *Cisco IOS feature* and an IOS *feature set*.

A Cisco IOS feature is a specific facility that an IOS supports. Examples include support for a particular routing protocol (EIGRP or BGP), a WAN service (Frame Relay), or a security facility (IPsec).

A feature set is a group of features that differentiates one Cisco IOS image from another. Feature sets have generalized names such as the following:

- IP Base
- Advanced IP Services
- Advanced Enterprise Services

Task 1: Search by Feature

This Feature Navigator tool requires that you know which features you want your upgraded network to have. For this lab task, sample features are used.

Step 1.   From the Cisco Feature Navigator page, click the **Search by Feature** link.

Step 2.   From the Available Features list, select the following features (click **Add** after selecting each feature):

- CallManager Express (CME) 3.0
- IPv6 (Internet Protocol Version 6)
- Mobile IP
- Videoconferencing for the Cisco Multiservice IP-to-IP Gateway
- Voice over IP (VoIP)

These features are a sample of services that the FilmCompany may consider adding to their network; you may add others for this exercise.

Tip: Filtering by using the first letter links across the top of the page or using the Search field makes finding each feature easier.

Step 3.   Click **Continue**.

Step 4.   On the next screen, from the Platform drop-down menu, select **1841**. From the Feature Set drop-down menu, select **Advanced IP Services**.

Output similar to what Table 3-10 shows will display.

Table 3-10   Cisco IOS Releases Matching Selected Feature Sets for 1841 Router

Release	Image Name	DRAM	Flash
12.3(14)YT1	c1841-advipservicesk9-mz.123-14.YT1.bin	192	48
12.3(14)YT	c1841-advipservicesk9-mz.123-14.YT.bin	192	48
12.3(8)YG4	c1841-advipservicesk9-mz.123-8.YG4.bin	192	64
12.3(8)YG3	c1841-advipservicesk9-mz.123-8.YG3.bin	192	64
12.3(8)YG2	c1841-advipservicesk9-mz.123-8.YG2.bin	192	64
12.3(8)YG	c1841-advipservicesk9-mz.123-8.YG.bin	192	64

Step 5.   Note the DRAM and flash requirements for each image.

Does your router have the DRAM and flash resources to support these advanced services?

How can the DRAM and flash available on your router be determined?

The required and suitable Cisco IOS image can be selected and the appropriate arrangements made to download it. Downloading a Cisco IOS is covered in Lab 3-4.

Task 2: Search by Platform

Step 1.   From the Cisco Feature Navigator page, click the **Search by Platform** link.

Step 2.   List the four search objectives available.

Step 3.   From the Platform drop-down menu, select **1841**. Click **Continue**.

Task 3: Search by Feature Set

Step 1.   From the Feature Set drop-down menu, select **IP Base**.

Step 2.   Examine the list of features.

List the interior routing protocols supported.

List the exterior routing protocols supported.

Step 3. From the Feature Set drop-down menu, select **Advanced IP Services**.

Observe that the extra features listed include such features as the following:

- Analog Centralized Automatic Message Accounting E911 Trunk
- Analog DID (Direct Inward Dial)
- Call Admission Control for H.323 VoIP Gateways
- Caller ID
- Caller ID on Analog Voice Interfaces
- CallManager Express (CME) 3.1
- Cisco IOS Telephony Service (ITS) Version 2.1

And various features for the following:

- H323
- MGCP (Media Gateway Control Protocol)
- Mobile IP
- SIP (Session Initiation Protocol)
- Videoconferencing for the Cisco Multiservice IP-to-IP Gateway
- VoIP

This presentation provides feature details but makes direct comparison between different feature sets difficult.

Task 4: Compare Images

This task demonstrates the case where you know some release and version details about the IOS images but not the exact features of each.

Step 1. Click the **Compare Images** tab on the current page or the **Compare Images** link on the Cisco Feature Navigator page.

Step 2. Under Select First Image Parameters, make a selection from each drop-down list, for example:

- Software: IOS
- Major Release: 12.4
- Release Number: 12.4(1a)
- Platform: 1841
- Feature Set: IP Base

Step 3. Under Select Second Image Parameters, make a selection from each drop-down list, for example:

- Software: IOS
- Major Release: 12.4
- Release Number: 12.4(10b)

- Platform: 1841

- Feature Set: Advanced IP Services

Step 4.   Note the information displayed:

- Image information for each IOS

- Features unique to each image

- Common features in both images (scroll halfway down the page)

Does your router have the DRAM and flash resources to support these advanced services?

_____

How can the DRAM and flash available on your router be determined?

_____

What extra Layer 3 protocol support is with the Advanced IP Services feature set?

_____

Step 5.   Examine some of the unique features listed by clicking the links.

Describe the enhanced network services and features users could expect if an IOS upgrade to the Advanced IP Services feature set were performed.

_____

_____

_____

_____

Part 4: Examine 2960 Switch IOS Features

In this part of the lab, you perform a detail search of the features of a particular Cisco switch.

Task 1: Search by Platform

Step 1.   Return to the Cisco Feature Navigator page and click the **Search by Platform** link.

Step 2.   From the Platform drop-down menu, select **CAT2960** and click **Continue**.

Task 2: Search by Feature Set

Step 1.   From the Feature Set drop-down menu, select **LAN Base**.

Step 2.   Read through the list of features.

Step 3.   Examine some of the features listed by clicking the links.

Step 4.   Select various Major Release and Release values from those respective menus. Note the IOS image filenames and memory requirements.

Step 5.   Return to the Cisco Feature Navigator. From the Platform drop-down menu, select **CAT3560** and click **Continue**.

Step 6.   Examine the list of features.

Which significant Layer 3 protocol family is included in the feature set?

_____

What is the significance of this difference between 2960 and 3560 switches?

_____

_____

Reflection

The recording and documentation of network features and services, and the devices that provide them, are important features of network management.

Consider and explore the Cisco.com resources and information that can facilitate this task.

_____

_____

Lab 3-4: Installing a Cisco IOS Software Image (3.2.4)

Upon completion of this lab, you will be able to

- Download the correct Cisco IOS and transfer the file to the Cisco router.

- Use TFTP to save and restore a Cisco IOS image.

This lab contains skills that relate to the following 803-640 CCNA exam objectives:

- Manage IOS configuration files, including save, edit, upgrade, restore.

- Verify router hardware and software operation using **show** and **debug** commands.

Expected Results and Success Criteria

Before starting this lab, read through the tasks that you are expected to perform. What do you expect the result of performing these tasks will be?

_____

_____

_____

How is an understanding of the Cisco networking device IOS transfer to and from a TFTP server useful in network administration?

_____

_____

_____

How will a network administrator know whether the Cisco IOS was transferred and saved correctly?

_____

_____

_____

Background / Preparation

This lab demonstrates backing up a Cisco router IOS image file to a TFTP server and uploading an IOS image to a Cisco router.

For recovery purposes, it is important to keep backup copies of router IOS images. These can be stored in a central location, such as a TFTP server, and retrieved if necessary.

Cisco IOS files have a specific name structure that reflects the platform, IOS version, feature set, and file type. It is strongly recommended that Cisco IOS image files not be renamed for any reason.

The configuration output used in this lab matches that of an 1841 series router. The same commands can be used with other Cisco routers but may produce slightly different output.

Part 1: Back Up the Cisco Router IOS File

In this part of the lab, you back up the current Cisco IOS image from the router flash memory to the TFTP server.

Task 1: Configure Network Connectivity

Figure 3-5 shows the network topology for this lab, and Table 3-11 documents the hostnames, addresses, and subnet masks for all the network devices in the topology diagram in Figure 3-5.

Note: If the PCs used in this lab are also connected to your Academy LAN or to the Internet, ensure that you record the cable connections and TCP/IP settings so that these can be restored at the conclusion of the lab.

Figure 3-5   Lab 3-4 Network Topology

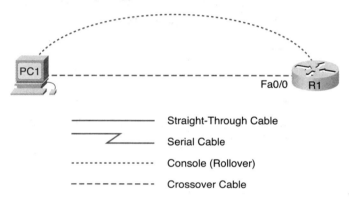

Table 3-11   Addressing Table for Lab 3-4

Device Designation	Device Name	Fast Ethernet Address	Subnet mask
R1	ACC-CPE-1	10.0.0.1	255.255.255.0
PC	PC1	10.0.0.254	255.255.255.0

Step 1.   Refer to the lab topology diagram in Figure 3-5, and connect the console (or rollover) cable to the console port on the router and the other cable end to the host computer with a DB-9 or DB-25 adapter to the COM 1 port. Use a crossover cable to connect PC1 NIC interface to router interface Fa0/1. Ensure that power has been applied to both the host computer and router.

Step 2.   Using the IP address information from Table 3-11, configure computer PC1.

Step 3.   On PC1, establish a console session to the router using HyperTerminal or TeraTerm.

Step 4.   Configure the router hostname and interface as given in the table.

Step 5.   Ping PC1 from the CLI prompt to verify connectivity between the router and the PC. Troubleshoot the configuration of the router and PC if connectivity is not verified.

Task 2: Run the TFTP Server

Step 1.   Check that a TFTP server such as SolarWinds is installed on PC1. If not, see your instructor to arrange the installation. This software must be installed and running before the any file transfer can be initiated from the router.

Note: For convenience, PC1 is both used both for the terminal session and as a TFTP server in this lab. In a production environment, the server can be any appropriately configured and accessible secure computer on the network.

Step 2.   Start the TFTP program (SolarWinds). Depending on the version, an active TFTP server window similar to that shown in Figure 3-6 will appear.

Figure 3-6   SolarWinds TFTP Server Window

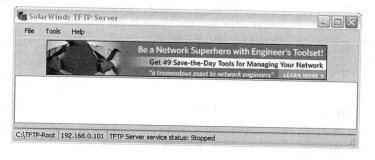

Task 3: Configure the TFTP Server

Step 1.   On the TFTP server File menu, select **Configure**. A configuration window similar to Figure 3-7 will display.

Figure 3-7   SolarWinds TFTP Server Configuration

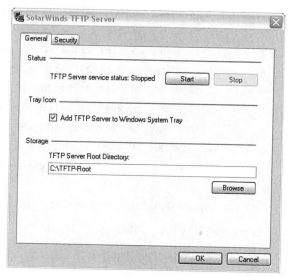

Step 2.   Verify the settings listed in Table 3-12 in the TFTP Server Configuration window by clicking the appropriate tab.

Table 3-12   TFTP Server Settings

Setting	Value
TFTP Root Directory	TFTP-Root
Security	Transmit and Receive Files
Advanced Security	<all IP addresses>
Auto-Close	Never
Log	Enable Log Requests to the Following File. Leave the default file.

Note: The layout of the configuration window and the number of tabs displayed will vary in accordance with the SolarWinds TFTP server version. However, these settings, or equivalent, are available in all versions of this, or any other, TFTP server program.

Step 3.   When finished, click **OK**.

Task 4: Collect Information to Document the Router

It is important to document the features and information about the router before backing up the Cisco IOS file, in case any recovery action has to be taken.

Step 1.   Issue the **show flash** command.

Sample output:

```
ACC-CPE-1# show flash:
-#- --length-- -----date/time------ path
1     13937472 May 05 2007 21:13:20 +00:00 c1841-ipbase-mz.124-1c.bin
2         1821 May 05 2007 21:29:36 +00:00 sdmconfig-18xx.cfg
3      4734464 May 05 2007 21:30:14 +00:00 sdm.tar
4       833024 May 05 2007 21:30:42 +00:00 es.tar
5      1052160 May 05 2007 21:31:10 +00:00 common.tar
6         1038 May 05 2007 21:31:36 +00:00 home.shtml
7       102400 May 05 2007 21:32:02 +00:00 home.tar
8       491213 May 05 2007 21:32:30 +00:00 128MB.sdf
9      1684577 May 05 2007 21:33:16 +00:00 securedesktop-ios-3.1.1.27-k9.pkg
10      398305 May 05 2007 21:33:50 +00:00 sslclient-win-1.1.0.154.pkg

8679424 bytes available (23252992 bytes used)
```

Is there an IOS image file stored in flash? _____

Note the exact name of that file: _____

What is the size of that file? _____

What is the amount of flash that is available or unused? _____

What attributes can be identified from codes in the Cisco IOS filename? _____

_____

Step 2. Issue the **show version** command and record the following information.

Sample output:

```
ACC-CPE-1# show version
Cisco IOS Software, 1841 Software (C1841-IPBASE-M), Version 12.4(1c),
  RELEASE SO
FTWARE (fc1)
Technical Support: http://www.cisco.com/techsupport
Copyright (c) 1986-2005 by Cisco Systems, Inc.
Compiled Tue 25-Oct-05 17:10 by evmiller


ROM: System Bootstrap, Version 12.4(13r)T, RELEASE SOFTWARE (fc1)


R1 uptime is 2 days, 12 hours, 29 minutes
System returned to ROM by reload at 21:21:02 UTC Fri Aug 24 2007
System image file is "flash:c1841-ipbase-mz.124-1c.bin"


Cisco 1841 (revision 7.0) with 114688K/16384K bytes of memory.
Processor board ID FTX1118X0AB
2 FastEthernet interfaces
2 Serial(sync/async) interfaces
2 Low-speed serial(sync/async) interfaces
DRAM configuration is 64 bits wide with parity disabled.
191K bytes of NVRAM.
31360K bytes of ATA CompactFlash (Read/Write)


Configuration register is 0x2102
```

Configuration-register value: _____

Size of flash memory: _____

Is there at least 16 MB of flash? _____

Version number of boot ROM: _____

Is the boot ROM version 5.2 or later? _____

Task 5: Copy Cisco IOS Image to the TFTP Server

Step 1. Before copying the files, verify that the TFTP server is running. In the version of the server described in this lab, the TFTP service is activated by clicking Start in the General tab of the Configuration window.

Step 2. Record the IP address of the TFTP server.

Step 3.   From privileged EXEC mode, issue the **copy flash tftp** command. At the prompt, enter the filename for your system as recorded in Task 4 Step 1. To ensure accuracy, select the filename as shown in the **show flash:** output and copy and paste it at the source filename prompt. Then, enter the IP address of the TFTP server. At the destination filename, press **Enter** to accept the name displayed.

Sample output:

```
ACC-CPE-1# copy flash tftp
Source filename []? c1841-ipbase-mz.124-1c.bin
Address or name of remote host []? 10.0.0.254
Destination filename [c1841-ipbase-mz.124-1c.bin]?
!!!!!!!!!!!!!!!!!!!!!!!!!!!!!!!!!!!!!!!!!!!!!!!!!!!!!!!!!!!!!!!!!!!!!!!!!!!!!!!!!
!!!!!!!!!!!!!!!!!!!!!!!!!!!!!!!!!!!!!!!!!!!!!!!!!!!!!!!!
13937472 bytes copied in 37.627 secs (370412 bytes/sec)
```

Task 6: Verify the Transfer to the TFTP Server

Step 1.   To verify a successful upload transfer, open the TFTP server log file. For a default installation of Version 9 of SolarWinds TFTP server, this file is located at

C:\Program Files\SolarWinds\TFTPServer\Logging\TFTPService.log

Earlier versions may have the log at

C:\Program Files\SolarWinds\Free Tools\TFTP-Server.txt

The log content should include information similar to the following example:

```
3/25/2007 12:29 :Receiving c1841-ipbase-mz.124-1c.bin from  (10.0.0.1)
3/25/2007 12:29 :Received c1841-ipbase-mz.124-1c.bin from  (10.0.0.1),
   13937472 bytes
```

Step 2.   Verify the flash image size in the TFTP server directory. Using Windows Explorer or My Computer, locate the TFTP root directory. Display file details and record the file size.

The file size shown in the **show flash:** command output should be the same as the file size of the file stored on the TFTP server. If the file sizes are not identical, check with your instructor.

Part 2: Restore or Upgrade the Current IOS

In this part of the lab, you upload an IOS image from the TFTP server to the router flash memory as you would to restore a corrupt or missing IOS or to upgrade the router IOS.

Task 1: Prepare to Restore or Update the IOS Image

Step 1.   Before copying the file, verify that the TFTP server is running and that the required Cisco IOS image file is in the TFTP root directory. Note the exact filename.

Step 2.   Ping PC1 to confirm that connectivity between the router and the PC has been maintained.

Step 3.   Confirm that the flash memory capacity is of sufficient size to hold the Cisco IOS image.

Which command is issued to confirm flash memory size?

Task 2: Copy the IOS Image from the TFTP Server

Step 1.   From privileged EXEC mode, issue the **copy tftp flash** command.

Step 2.   At the prompt, enter the IP address of the TFTP server.

Step 3.   Enter the filename for your system, as noted in Part 1, Task 4, Step 1 of this lab.

Step 4.   At the destination filename, press **Enter** to accept the name displayed.

Note: If prompted to overwrite an existing file with the same name, press **Enter** to confirm. Do not interrupt the process.

Sample output:

```
ACC-CPE-1# copy tftp flash
Address or name of remote host []? 10.0.0.254
Source filename []? c1841-ipbase-mz.124-1c.bin
Destination filename [c1841-ipbase-mz.124-1c.bin]?
%Warning:There is a file already existing with this name
Do you want to over write? [confirm]
Accessing tftp://10.0.0.254/ c1841-ipbase-mz.124-1c.bin...

Loading c1700-y-mz.122-11.T.bin from 10.0.0.254 (via FastEthernet0/0):
!!!!!!!!!!!!!!!!!!!!!!!!!!!!!!!!!!!!!!!!!!!!!!!!!!!!!!!!!!!!!!!!!!!!!!!!!
!!!!!!!!!!!!!!!!!!!!!!!!!!!!!!!!!!!!!!!!!!!!!!!!!!!!!!!!!!!!!!!!!!!!!!!!!
!!!!!!!!!!!!!!!!!!!!!!!!!!!!!!!!!!!!!!!!!!!!!!!!!!!!!!!!!!!!!!!!!!!!!
[OK - 13937472 bytes]
Verifying checksum... OK (0x9C8A)
13937472 bytes copied in 37.627 secs (370412 bytes/sec)
```

If successful, the checksum OK output is displayed. If the checksum fails, the IOS upload steps will need to be repeated.

Some older systems may require that flash be erased. If the **Erase flash: before copying?** prompt is confirmed, all files in flash will be removed. In contrast, other systems have sufficient capacity to store multiple files. If the router prompts to erase flash, output similar to the following will occur before the new image is uploaded to flash.

Sample output:

```
Erase flash: before copying? [confirm][Enter]
Erasing the flash filesystem will remove all files! Continue? [confirm]
Erasing device...
```

```
eeeeeeeeeeeeeeeeeeeeeeeeeeeeeeeeeeeeeeeeeeeeeeeeeeeeeeeeeeeeeeeeeeee
eeeeeeeeeeeeeeeeeeeeeeeeeeeeeeeeeeeeeeeeeeeeeeeeeeeeeeeeeeeeeeeeeeeee
...erased
Erase of flash: complete
```

Task 3: Test the Restored IOS Image

Step 1.   Verify that the router IOS image is correct. Power cycle the router power and observe the startup process to confirm that no flash errors occurred. If there are none, the router IOS should have started correctly.

Step 2.   Further verify the IOS image in flash by issuing the **show version** command, which will show an output similar to this:

```
System image file is "flash: c1841-ipbase-mz.124-1c.bin"
```

Task 4: Clean Up

Erase the configurations and reload the router. Disconnect and store the cabling. For PC hosts that are normally connected to other networks (such as the school LAN or to the Internet), delete the IOS image file from the TFTP directory, reconnect the appropriate cabling, and restore the TCP/IP settings.

Challenge

Challenge 1: Switch IOS Upgrade—As a challenge lab, research and list the steps required to back up the Cisco IOS image file from a switch to a TFTP server. In addition, list the steps and commands to restore or upgrade the Cisco IOS image from the TFTP server to the switch.

Challenge 2: Nonoperational Device—The performance of Cisco IOS image backup and upgrade for routers and switches as described in this lab presumes that the device has a current, fully operational IOS to allow the configuration of IP connectivity before copying the image file. However, in some cases, the current IOS is corrupt or for some other reason the device will not boot with an operational IOS.

1.   Research and record the ROMMON process that enables a router to be configured and its IOS uploaded if the device has this problem.

2.   Research and record the Xmodem or similar process that enables the IOS of a switch to be uploaded using the serial (console) connection if the device has this problem.

Lab 3-5: Observing the Router Startup Process (3.2.5)

Upon completion of this lab, you will be able to identify and explain the stages of the router startup process.

This lab contains skills that relate to the following 640-802 CCNA exam objective:

- Describe the operation of Cisco routers, including the router boot process, POST, and router components.

Expected Results and Success Criteria

Before starting this lab, read through the tasks that you are expected to perform. What do you expect the result of performing these tasks will be?

_____

_____

_____

How is an understanding of the router startup process useful in network administration?

_____

_____

_____

How will a network administrator know whether the router started correctly?

_____

_____

_____

Background/Preparation

During this lab, you observe the startup process of a Cisco router while logged in to a console terminal session.

Information about the state of the router startup process, platform, and IOS details is displayed on the terminal screen as the router starts up.

You can record this information for future use to help troubleshoot startup problems.

The sample output used in this lab matches that of a particular Cisco 1841 series router and IOS platform. Other Cisco routers and IOS versions may produce slightly different output.

Task 1: Connect and Set Up the Router

This lab will uses the network topology shown in Figure 3-8.

Note: If the PCs used in this lab are also connected to your Academy LAN or to the Internet, ensure that you record the cable connections and TCP/IP settings so that these can be restored at the conclusion of the lab.

Figure 3-8   Lab 3-5 Network Topology

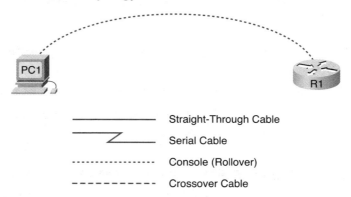

Straight-Through Cable

Serial Cable

Console (Rollover)

Crossover Cable

Step 1.   Referring to the lab topology diagram (Figure 3-8), connect the console (or rollover) cable to the console port on the router and the other cable end to the host computer with a DB-9 or DB-25 adapter to the COM 1 port. Ensure that power has been applied to both the host computer and router.

Step 2.   Establish a HyperTerminal or other terminal emulation program connection to the router.

Task 2: Restart the Router and Observe the Output

Step 1.   From the privileged EXEC prompt, issue the **reload** command. Confirm the reload when prompted.

Step 2.   Observe the output as the router restarts.

Output similar to this will display:

```
POST information:
System Bootstrap, Version 12.4(13r)T, RELEASE SOFTWARE (fc1)
Technical Support: http://www.cisco.com/techsupport
Copyright (c) 2006 by cisco Systems, Inc.
PLD version 0x10
GIO ASIC version 0x127
c1841 platform with 131072 Kbytes of main memory
Main memory is configured to 64 bit mode with parity disabled

Locating and Loading information:
Readonly ROMMON initialized
program load complete, entry point: 0x8000f000, size: 0xcb80
program load complete, entry point: 0x8000f000, size: 0xcb80

program load complete, entry point: 0x8000f000, size: 0xd4a9a0
Self decompressing the image : ##############################################
##############################################################################
  ########### [OK]

Smart Init is enabled
smart init is sizing iomem
```

```
     ID              MEMORY_REQ          TYPE
                     0X003AA110 public buffer pools
                     0X00211000 public particle pools
     0X0013          0X00035000 Card in slot 0
                     0X000021B8 Onboard USB
```

If any of the above Memory Requirements are
"UNKNOWN", you may be using an unsupported
configuration or there is a software problem and
system operation may be compromised.

Allocating additional 7692243 bytes to IO Memory.
PMem allocated: 117440512 bytes; IOMem allocated: 16777216 bytes

Restricted Rights Legend

Use, duplication, or disclosure by the Government is
subject to restrictions as set forth in subparagraph
(c) of the Commercial Computer Software - Restricted
Rights clause at FAR sec. 52.227-19 and subparagraph
(c) (1) (ii) of the Rights in Technical Data and Computer
Software clause at DFARS sec. 252.227-7013.

          cisco Systems, Inc.
          170 West Tasman Drive
          San Jose, California 95134-1706

Cisco IOS Software, 1841 Software (C1841-IPBASE-M), Version 12.4(1c),
RELEASE SO
FTWARE (fc1)
Technical Support: http://www.cisco.com/techsupport
Copyright (c) 1986-2005 by Cisco Systems, Inc.
Compiled Tue 25-Oct-05 17:10 by evmiller
Image text-base: 0x6007ECA0, data-base: 0x61480000

Port Statistics for unclassified packets is not turned on.
Cisco 1841 (revision 7.0) with 114688K/16384K bytes of memory.
Processor board ID FTX1118X0BN
2 FastEthernet interfaces
2 Low-speed serial(sync/async) interfaces
DRAM configuration is 64 bits wide with parity disabled.
191K bytes of NVRAM.
31360K bytes of ATA CompactFlash (Read/Write)

Task 3: Examine the Router Startup Output

The startup process has three stages, as described in the following steps.

Step 1.   Performing the POST and loading the bootstrap program

Examine the output displayed. Look at the highlighted section in the sample output in this lab that relates to the POST. Mark any differences between your observed output and this sample.

What are possible reasons for these differences?

_____

What does the POST test in the router?

_____

If the POST is successful, what is loaded into RAM?

_____

What is the purpose of the program loaded into RAM?

_____

What would happen if the POST is unsuccessful, and what could this mean?

_____

_____

Step 2.   Locating and loading the IOS software

Examine the displayed output. Look at the sample output in this lab that relates to the IOS loading. Mark any differences between your observed output and this sample.

What are possible reasons for these differences?

_____

What are the three possible locations of the IOS image?

_____

_____

How is the IOS image location to be used specified?

_____

What will be the result if an IOS image cannot be located and loaded?

_____

Step 3.   Locating and executing the startup configuration file or entering setup mode

Examine the displayed output. Look at the sample output in this lab that relates to the startup configuration loading. Mark any differences between your observed output and this sample.

What are possible reasons for these differences?

_____

What is the output if the router does not have a configuration to load?

_____

_____

_____

What displays if a startup configuration is loaded?

_____

Task 4: Clean Up

Erase the configurations and reload the router. Disconnect and store the cabling. For PC hosts that are normally connected to other networks (such as the school LAN or to the Internet), delete the IOS image file from the TFTP directory, reconnect the appropriate cabling, and restore the TCP/IP settings.

Reflection/Challenge

Prepare a troubleshooting checklist based on the router startup stages and the hardware and software features associated with each stage. Format the checklist so that if it is noted that a stage was unsuccessful, the possible problems can be readily identified. For example, for "IOS not loaded," note "ROMMON prompt displayed."

Prepare a second checklist listing possible router faults or problems (for example, "No cooling fan sound," "LEDs not illuminated or showing unusual behavior," or "Unexpected ROMMON prompt displayed." For each problem listed, enter the stage of the router startup process that failed.

Lab 3-6: Determining the Router Hardware Options (3.3.2)

Upon completion of this lab, you will be able to

- Determine the correct hardware options available on a specific Cisco device.
- Determine which hardware options on a specific Cisco device are scalable.

Expected Results and Success Criteria

Before starting this lab, read through the tasks that you are expected to perform. What do you expect the result of performing these tasks will be?

_____

_____

_____

How is an understanding of networking device hardware capabilities useful in network administration?

_____

_____

_____

How does a network administrator know what hardware capabilities a networking device possesses?

_____

_____

_____

Background/Preparation

When considering expanding or upgrading a network, it is not always necessary to completely replace existing network devices. Some devices may be capable of being individually upgraded or expanded.

In this lab, you examine the hardware features of a Cisco 1841 Integrated Services Router (ISR) and determine whether it is suitable for upgrading to meet the potential requirements of a planned network expansion.

In the FilmCompany case study in Appendix B, "FilmCompany Story," there is a need to consider how the existing 1841 routers can be upgraded to reduce the cost of the network upgrade.

A physical examination of the router will be performed, as will an examination of its technical documentation. The examination details will be recorded for use in the Planning and Design phases of the network upgrade.

This lab is based on the 1841 ISR. Any router platform that supports adding hardware modules can be substituted for the 1841. The search criteria and results will vary accordingly.

Part 1: Inspect a Cisco 1841 ISR

Part 1 requires you to perform a physical inspection of an 1841 ISR in the lab and then use a console terminal session to determine the interfaces available.

Task 1: Physically Inspect the External Features of the Router

Step 1. Examine the router. In Table 3-13, identify and match each item number in Figure 3-9 with the description. In addition, record on the table, with its description, the number of each interface and port on the router.

Figure 3-9   Cisco 1841 Integrated Services Router

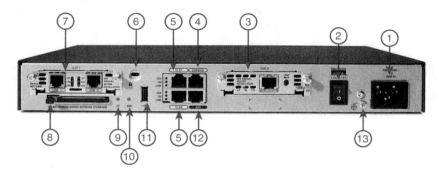

Table 3-13   Cisco 1841 Router Items

Item	Description	Item	Description
	CompactFlash (CF) LED		Chassis ground connection
	Kensington security slot		Input power connection
	Slot 0 (WIC, VWIC—data only, or HWIC)		Console port (No.)
	AIM LED		USB port (No.)
	Fast Ethernet interfaces and LEDs (No.)		Aux port (No.)
	On/Off switch		CompactFlash memory card slot
	Slot 1 (WIC, VWIC—data only, or HWIC)		

Is a module installed in Slot 0?: _____

If yes, record the module and interface(s) type:_____

How many Fast Ethernet interfaces does the router have?_____

How many and what type of other interfaces does the router have? _____

_____

Is a module installed in Slot 1? _____

If yes, record the module and interface(s) type:_____

Which of the modules and ports have the potential to be upgraded to improve the router's capabilities?_____

Task 2: Use IOS **show commands** to Inspect the Router

Note: If the PCs used in this lab are also connected to your Academy LAN or to the Internet, ensure that you record the cable connections and TCP/IP settings so that these can be restored at the conclusion of the lab.

Step 1. Referring to the topology diagram in Figure 3-10, connect the console (or rollover) cable to the console port on the router and the other cable end to the host computer with a DB-9 or DB-25 adapter to the COM 1 port. Ensure that power has been applied to both the host computer and router.

Figure 3-10 Lab 3-6 Network Topology

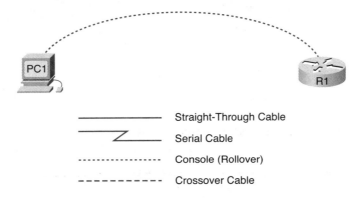

Step 2. Establish a HyperTerminal or other terminal emulation program connection to the router.

Step 3. From the privileged EXEC mode prompt of the terminal, issue **show run** and **show flash:** commands.

Record the number and type of interfaces.

_____

_____

_____

_____

Record the details of the memory (DRAM, flash) modules.

_____

Task 3: Compare the Physical and IOS Inspections

Are there any differences between the physical and IOS inspections?_____

If yes, explain the reason for any differences and solutions.

_____

_____

_____

_____

_____

Part 2: Examine 1841 Router Hardware Options

After establishing the current hardware status of the router, in this part you examine the technical documentation to determine the potential for upgrading and growth.

Task 1: Access the Cisco.com Documentation

Step 1.   Launch a web browser on a PC connected to the Internet and access the website http://www.cisco.com. Be aware that the Cisco website structure changes frequently. You might need to use the website search tool if the following steps do not much the current website.

Step 2.   In the Quick Links pane on the right, select **Documentation**.

Step 3.   Under Select a Category, click **Routers**. Under Select a Product, click the **Cisco 1800 Series Integrated Services Routers** link.

Step 4.   Review the documentation links that display.

Step 5.   Under Product Literature on the right side of the page, click the **Data Sheets** link. Note the range of datasheet documentation available.

Step 6.   Click **Cisco 1800 Series Integrated Services Routers: Cisco 1841 Router (Modular)**.

Task 2: Record the Router Hardware Information

Step 1.   Read through the *Cisco 1800 Series Integrated Services Routers: Cisco 1841 Router (Modular)* document, noting the structure and format of the information.

Step 2.   From Table 1 in this document, Architecture Features and Benefits of Cisco 1841 Router, record the following information:

The number of different modules and interface cards that are supported:_____

Default memory capacity:_____

_____

Cisco IOS versions supported: _____

Step 3.   From Table 5, Product Specifications of Cisco 1841 Router, in the document, locate and record the following specifications from the Architecture section.

DRAM type

_____

DRAM capacity

_____

Flash memory

_____

Flash memory capacity

_____

Modular slots-total

_____

Modular slots for
WAN access

_____

Modular slots for HWICs

_____

Modular slots for voice
support

_____

Analog and digital voice
support

_____

VoIP support

_____

Onboard Ethernet ports

_____

Onboard USB ports

_____

Console port

_____

Auxiliary port

_____

Onboard Advanced
Integration Module (AIM) slots

_____

Step 4.   From Table 6, Modules and Interface Cards the Cisco 1841 Router Supports, in the document, list the ten different categories of interface card (WIC) supported by the 1841 platform.

_____

_____

_____

_____

_____

_____

_____

_____

_____

_____

Step 5.   From Table 6 in the document, what feature does the Advanced Integration Module (AIM) enable to be installed in an 1841 router?

Task 3: Consider Possible Hardware Options

The 1841 ISR has removable and interchangeable modules. Various optional modules can be installed in the router to provide specific capabilities. These modules are installed either by inserting them into slots on the chassis or by opening the chassis and plugging them into connectors inside.

Flash memory and interface cards fit into slots on the chassis and are installed and removed without opening the chassis.

There are three types of interface cards for the 1800 series modular routers:

- WAN interface cards (WICs)

- Voice WAN interface cards (VWICs, in data mode only on the Cisco 1841)

- High-speed WAN interface cards (HWICs)

The following components plug into connectors inside the chassis and are installed and removed only by opening the chassis:

- Advanced Integration Module (AIM)

- Synchronous dynamic RAM (SDRAM) small-outline dual in-line memory module (SODIMM)

The 1841 router memory specifications are as follows.

Description	Specification
SDRAM	128 MB, expandable to 384 MB; default 128 MB
Flash memory	32, 64, or 128 MB; default 32 MB
Boot/NVRAM	2/4 MB flash memory

Summarize the changes that are possible for this router. This information is important to have and consider when planning and designing the network upgrade.

_____

_____

_____

_____

_____

_____

Task 4: Clean Up

Erase any configurations and reload the router. Disconnect and store the cabling. For PC hosts that are normally connected to other networks (such as the school LAN or to the Internet), reconnect the appropriate cabling and restore the TCP/IP settings.

Reflection

Network device capabilities are continuously developing. Consider the advantages of a modular platform over that of a device with a fixed hardware platform.

_____

_____

_____

_____

Lab 3-7: Preparing for a Site Survey (3.4.1)

Upon completion of this lab, you will be able to

- Explain the process of setting up a customer site visit.
- Prepare to conduct a professional site visit.

Expected Results and Success Criteria

Before starting this lab, read through the tasks that you are expected to perform. What do you expect the result of performing these tasks will be?

_____

_____

_____

In what ways can conducting a site visit benefit a network designer?

_____

_____

_____

What do you think are the most important aspects of a site visit, from a customer perspective and a network designer perspective?

_____

_____

_____

Background/Preparation

FilmCompany is an expanding, small advertising company moving into interactive advertising media, including video presentations. This company has just been awarded a large video support contract by the StadiumCompany. With this new contract, FilmCompany expects to see their business grow approximately 70 percent.

As the network designer with the task of designing and planning the upgrade for the FilmCompany data network expansion, you need to document their current network and services.

This is done by visiting FilmCompany premises, talking to their management, and inspecting their network.

The visit should be well planned and professionally conducted. This will ensure that the necessary information is collected and recorded and that you establish a professional working relationship with your customer, FilmCompany.

This lab covers the planning and preparation for this site visit.

Task 1: Clarify and Document the Purpose of the Site Visit

Step 1.   List and discuss reasons for conducting a site visit.

_____

_____

_____

_____

_____

_____

_____

_____

_____

_____

_____

_____

_____

_____

Step 2.   List the FilmCompany personnel who are most likely to be able to answer your questions and whom you would need to talk to on site.

_____

_____

_____

_____

_____

_____

Step 3.   Examine the FilmCompany case study document in Appendix B, the existing network topology diagram (see Figure 3-11), and the floor plan (see Figure 3-12).

Figure 3-11   FilmCompany Existing Network Topology

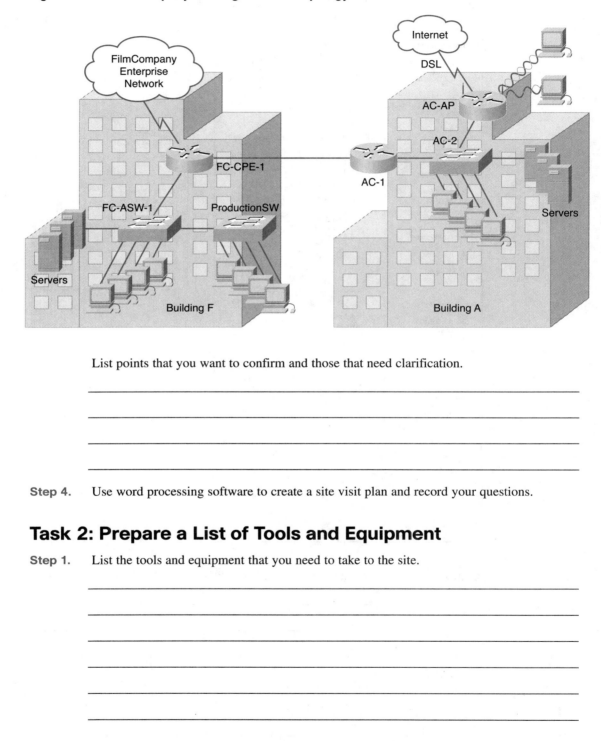

List points that you want to confirm and those that need clarification.

_____

_____

_____

_____

Step 4.   Use word processing software to create a site visit plan and record your questions.

Task 2: Prepare a List of Tools and Equipment

Step 1.   List the tools and equipment that you need to take to the site.

_____

_____

_____

_____

_____

_____

_____

_____

Figure 3-12   FilmCompany Floor Plan

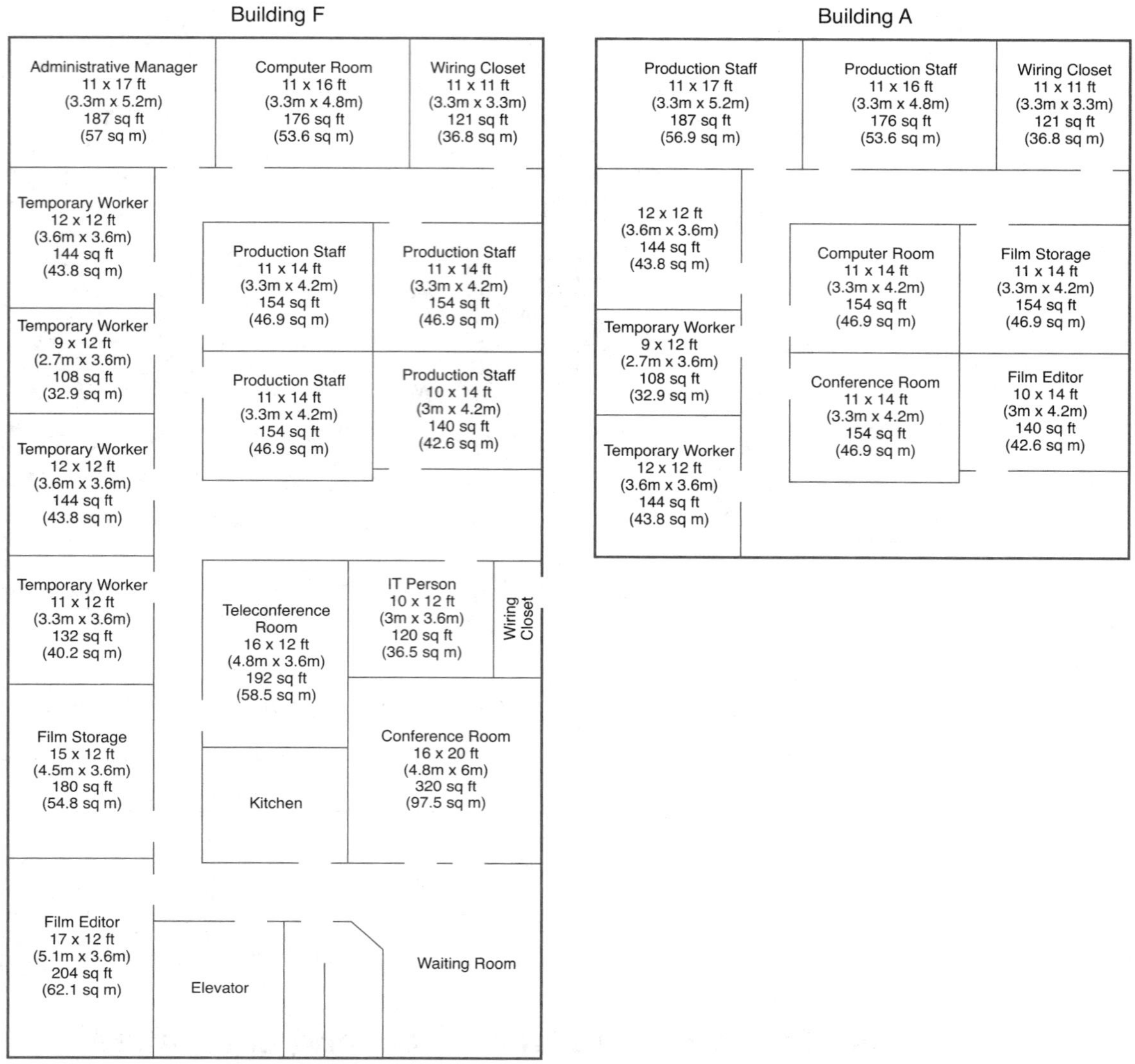

Building F

Administrative Manager	Computer Room	Wiring Closet
11 x 17 ft	11 x 16 ft	11 x 11 ft
(3.3m x 5.2m)	(3.3m x 4.8m)	(3.3m x 3.3m)
187 sq ft	176 sq ft	121 sq ft
(57 sq m)	(53.6 sq m)	(36.8 sq m)

Temporary Worker
12 x 12 ft
(3.6m x 3.6m)
144 sq ft
(43.8 sq m)

Production Staff
11 x 14 ft
(3.3m x 4.2m)
154 sq ft
(46.9 sq m)

Production Staff
11 x 14 ft
(3.3m x 4.2m)
154 sq ft
(46.9 sq m)

Temporary Worker
9 x 12 ft
(2.7m x 3.6m)
108 sq ft
(32.9 sq m)

Production Staff
11 x 14 ft
(3.3m x 4.2m)
154 sq ft
(46.9 sq m)

Production Staff
10 x 14 ft
(3m x 4.2m)
140 sq ft
(42.6 sq m)

Temporary Worker
12 x 12 ft
(3.6m x 3.6m)
144 sq ft
(43.8 sq m)

Temporary Worker
11 x 12 ft
(3.3m x 3.6m)
132 sq ft
(40.2 sq m)

Teleconference
Room
16 x 12 ft
(4.8m x 3.6m)
192 sq ft
(58.5 sq m)

IT Person
10 x 12 ft
(3m x 3.6m)
120 sq ft
(36.5 sq m)

Wiring Closet

Film Storage
15 x 12 ft
(4.5m x 3.6m)
180 sq ft
(54.8 sq m)

Kitchen

Conference Room
16 x 20 ft
(4.8m x 6m)
320 sq ft
(97.5 sq m)

Film Editor
17 x 12 ft
(5.1m x 3.6m)
204 sq ft
(62.1 sq m)

Elevator

Waiting Room

Building A

Production Staff	Production Staff	Wiring Closet
11 x 17 ft	11 x 16 ft	11 x 11 ft
(3.3m x 5.2m)	(3.3m x 4.8m)	(3.3m x 3.3m)
187 sq ft	176 sq ft	121 sq ft
(56.9 sq m)	(53.6 sq m)	(36.8 sq m)

12 x 12 ft
(3.6m x 3.6m)
144 sq ft
(43.8 sq m)

Computer Room
11 x 14 ft
(3.3m x 4.2m)
154 sq ft
(46.9 sq m)

Film Storage
11 x 14 ft
(3.3m x 4.2m)
154 sq ft
(46.9 sq m)

Temporary Worker
9 x 12 ft
(2.7m x 3.6m)
108 sq ft
(32.9 sq m)

Conference Room
11 x 14 ft
(3.3m x 4.2m)
154 sq ft
(46.9 sq m)

Film Editor
10 x 14 ft
(3m x 4.2m)
140 sq ft
(42.6 sq m)

Temporary Worker
12 x 12 ft
(3.6m x 3.6m)
144 sq ft
(43.8 sq m)

Step 2.   List the documentation, instrumentation, and software you need to take to the site.

_____

_____

_____

_____

_____

_____

Step 3.   Add these lists to the site visit plan.

Task 3: Arrange an Appointment to Visit the Site

Role-Play and Discussion

A site visit to FilmCompany must not disrupt the operation of the business and its network. Arrangements must be made to set a convenient visit time and duration. Access to the premises and to the required appropriate people must be organized.

Step 1.   Network designer role: Develop a list of questions and requests to ask when telephoning FilmCompany to arrange the site visit.

_____

_____

_____

_____

_____

_____

_____

_____

_____

Step 2.   Customer role: Develop a list of requirements relating to a proposed site visit by the network designer that the onsite technician can follow to ensure seamless interaction.

_____

_____

_____

_____

_____

_____

_____

_____

_____

Step 3.   Using the information recorded in Steps 1 and 2, the student performing the network designer role simulates a telephone conversation with the student performing the customer role, to arrange a site visit that meets the requirements of both roles.

Step 4.   Record the agreed-upon terms and details of the visit.

_____

_____

Step 5.   Add the agreed-upon details to the site visit plan.

Task 4: Approach to Site Visit

Step 1.   List points and issues that the network designer should follow while actually conducting the site visit.

Step 2.   Discuss the most commonly chosen answers and the least commonly chosen answers.

_____

_____

_____

_____

_____

_____

_____

_____

_____

_____

_____

_____

_____

_____

_____

_____

_____

_____

_____

_____

Reflection

Arranging a visit to a customer site to inspect their network and associated facilities can have many aspects. The data network of an organization is a vital part of their operations. Gaining access to inspect and record details of that network may require more detailed arrangements than this lab presents. Consider and discuss the arrangements required to visit a high-security area such as a government, aviation, or military location.

_____

_____

_____

_____

_____

_____

_____

_____

_____

Lab 3-8: Performing a Wireless Site Survey (3.4.3)

Upon completion of this lab, you will be able to use available tools to perform a wireless site survey.

This lab contains skills that relate to the following 640-802 CCNA exam objective:

- Identify common issues with implementing wireless networks, including interface and misconfiguration.

Expected Results and Success Criteria

Before starting this lab, read through the tasks that you are expected to perform. What do you expect the result of performing these tasks will be?

_____

_____

_____

What problems could arise if a wireless survey is not carried out before implementing a wireless LAN?

_____

_____

_____

Background/Preparation

An important consideration when building a wireless network is to understand how a wireless access point's radio signals travel. Many factors can reduce signal quality in a building. Signal strength and quality must be checked throughout the location to determine the best placement of the wireless access point (AP) device. Some locations may provide superior signal quality but are not secure. A survey of the building topology must be performed to determine the best possible location for both signal strength and security.

This lab focuses on signal strength by changing the location of a wireless router. Signal strength will be viewed by using the program NetStumbler. The AP does not need to be physically connected to the network via an Ethernet cable to perform this task. We are simply going to plug in the AP and its power source to an electrical outlet, at increasing distances from the wireless NIC in PC1, and view the signal strength on the PC1 device.

Task 1: Configure the Wireless Client PC1

Figure 3-13 shows the network topology for this lab, and Table 3-14 documents the hostnames, addresses, and subnet masks for all the network devices in the topology diagram.

Note: If the PCs used in this lab are also connected to your Academy LAN or to the Internet, ensure that you record the cable connections and TCP/IP settings so that these can be restored at the conclusion of the lab.

Figure 3-13   Lab 3-8 Network Topology

PC-PT
PC1

Linksys-WRT300N
Wireless Router

Table 3-14   Addressing Table for Lab 3-8

Device Designation	Device Name	Address	Subnet Mask
PC1	PC1	192.168.2.2	255.255.255.0
Wireless router	WR1	LAN 192.168.2.1	255.255.255.0

Step 1. Referring to the topology diagram in Figure 3-13, configure the PC1 wireless NIC address to match the address shown in Table 3-14.

Step 2. Ensure that power has been applied to the wireless router.

Step 3. From the command prompt of PC1, ping the wireless router to confirm network connectivity.

If the pings fail, troubleshoot and establish connectivity.

Task 2: Monitor Signal Strength Using NetStumbler

Step 1. The program NetStumbler will be used to evaluate the wireless signal quality in the building.

On PC1, launch NetStumbler. If NetStumbler, or an equivalent program is not installed on PC1, see your instructor.

Step 2. In the Network Stumbler window, expand the SSIDs section and locate the service set identifier (SSID) of the wireless router being used in this demonstration. Your instructor will provide you with the SSID number if it is not apparent.

Note: It might be possible that more than one SSID is detected and listed. Other wireless devices in the area may be configured to broadcast their SSIDs.

Step 3. Expand the SSID number to find the wireless router MAC address. Click that address to open the Signal/Noise monitoring window to the right.

The green vertical bars in the moving graph indicate signal strength. Red bars indicate signal noise. The higher the green bars, the stronger the signal.

Additional information may be found in the Help menu of the NetStumbler program (**Help > User Interface > Configuration Dialog > Graph View**).

Step 4. Record the signal strength of the wireless router at its current location and include its distance from PC1.

What unit does NetStumbler use to measure the radio signal strength?

_____

_____

_____

_____

Task 3: Relocate the Wireless AP

Step 1. Disconnect the power cord on the wireless router and move the device to a location outside the room, preferably at least 30 feet (10 meters) away. Power up the wireless router at that location.

Step 2. Wait for the wireless router to power up, and then return to PC1 to view the Signal/Noise meter.

Has the indicated signal strength changed? _____

Record the signal strength of the wireless router at the current location and include its distance from PC1:

_____

_____

_____

Task 4: Relocate the Wireless AP to a Secure Location

Step 1. Disconnect the power cord on the wireless router and move the device to a secure wiring closet, outside the classroom. This room should be able to be locked and also provide a power outlet for the wireless router power.

Step 2. Connect the wireless router power supply. While waiting for the wireless router to power up, close the wiring closet door, and return to PC1 to view the Signal/Noise meter.

Has the indicated signal strength changed?

_____

Step 3. Record the signal strength of the wireless router at the current location and include its distance from PC1.

Will the current placement of the wireless router be a good location to provide wireless access to other rooms within the area? Explain your answer.

_____

Judge how far away end devices can be placed from the wireless AP and determine the number of end devices that the AP could service.

_____

What obstructions tend to cause the largest drop in signal strength?

_____

Task 5: Clean Up

Return the wireless router to the classroom. For PC hosts that are normally connected to other networks (such as the school LAN or to the Internet), reconnect the appropriate cabling and restore the TCP/IP settings.

Challenge

Determine possible secure locations in your building topology that can contain wireless APs that will still provide usable signal strength:

_____

_____

_____

_____

Lab 3-9: Creating an Overall Project Goal (3.5.2)

Upon completion of this lab, you will be able to identify and record the goals of a new network design project.

Expected Results and Success Criteria

Before starting this lab, read through the tasks that you are expected to perform. What do you expect the result of performing these tasks will be?

_____

_____

_____

How is an understanding of a Project Goal statement useful in network administration?

_____

_____

_____

What do you think is the most important detail of the Project Goal statement?

_____

_____

_____

Background/Preparation

FilmCompany is an expanding, small advertising company moving into interactive advertising media, including video presentations. This company has just been awarded a large video support contract by the StadiumCompany. With this new contract, FilmCompany expects to see its business grow approximately 70 percent.

To facilitate this growth, the FilmCompany has decided to significantly upgrade its data network. You have the role of network design consultant. Your job is to develop network design and project documents for FilmCompany that will meet the requirements of this upgrade.

As part of the new network design requirements, an overall Project Goal statement has to be developed.

This section of the Network Design document states the overall goals of the upgrade and how this upgrade will help FilmCompany become more successful.

Task 1: Gather Information About the Company Goals That This Network Upgrade Will Facilitate

Consider what FilmCompany sees as benefits that the upgraded network will provide to their business in terms of their new stadium contract. These business benefits will not be the direct technical improvements that networking technicians and engineers may see. A business manager does not necessarily see the network in terms of bandwidth, latency, efficient protocols, or device operation. He is more likely to consider issues of profitability, flexibility, customer service, and reliability.

As a network designer, you take into account all the information obtained through interviewing the company managers and key members of the staff.

Step 1.   Draft informal notes of what you consider are the business benefits in this case.

Step 2.   Use word processing software to create a Project Goal document based on these notes.

Step 3.   Organize or group your informal notes and save these in your Project Goal document.

General headings could include the following:

- Financial Goals
- Job Management Goals
- Customer Communication Goals

Task 2: Summarize Important Goals in a List

Step 1.   Examine the general goals recorded and summarize these as three or four key points.

Begin each point with a verb, such as *provide, increase, improve,* or an equivalent word.

Try to include a measurable achievement if possible.

For example:

- Provide the stadium with a broadcast-quality, 30-minute highlight video package within 3 hours of the conclusion of an event.

Step 2.   Save the list of important goals in your Project Goal document.

Task 3: Develop an Overall Project Goal Statement

Step 1.   Write a single statement that introduces the summarized important goals.

For example:

The proposed network upgrade will enable FilmCompany to increase its share of the sports event video market through the following:

- Improved response times to customer requests
- Improved processing and delivery of video content across the network
- Improved communications access to customer facilities
- Ability for improved flexibility in meeting customer needs

Step 2.   Add this statement to your Project Goal document.

Task 4: Obtain Agreement from the Company on the Project Goal Statement

FilmCompany has to agree with your assessment of the project goal before you proceed further with the design. If this agreement is not obtained, the network you design might not meet the FilmCompany overall business requirements. An agreement provides clarification and acknowledgment of why the upgrade is to occur and what it is to achieve.

Step 1. Discuss your Project Goal document with another student and arrive at an agreed-upon project goal. It might be necessary to amend the statement and important goals before agreement is reached.

Step 2. Save your Project Goal document and retain it for the next stages of this network design case study.

Reflection

Consider the issue of communication between the network designer and a manager of the company considering an upgrade of the business network.

The network designer is trained in network operation and performance and how to optimize network resources and technologies to best provide network services. To the manager, the network is only one of a number of business tools that the company may use. The business manager probably wants to improve profitability and sees an enhanced network as a tool to help achieve that goal. A business manager is not likely to relate to a goal expressed solely in technical terms, such as an upgraded LAN with higher bandwidth, less latency, and maximized server utilization.

Although most designers may want to talk about network capabilities, the lifecycle approach is about customer requirements and enabling the business process.

Discuss some strategies that will enable clear communication between a network designer and a business manager so that the resulting Project Goal document represents business needs that ultimately can be met by a network design.

Lab 3-10: Creating a Scope Statement (3.5.3)

Upon completion of this lab, you will be able to identify and record the scope of a new network design project.

Expected Results and Success Criteria

Before starting this lab, read through the tasks that you are expected to perform. What do you expect the result of performing these tasks will be?

_____

_____

_____

How is an understanding of a Project Scope statement useful in network administration?

_____

_____

_____

Background/Preparation

FilmCompany is an expanding, small advertising company moving into interactive advertising media, including video presentations. This company has just been awarded a large video support contract by the StadiumCompany. With this new contract, FilmCompany expects to see its business grow approximately 70 percent.

To facilitate this growth, the FilmCompany has decided to significantly upgrade its data network. You have the role of network designer. Your job is to develop network design and project documents for FilmCompany that will meet the requirements of this upgrade.

As part of the new network design requirements, and based on the Project Goal statement, an overall Project Scope statement has to be developed.

This section of the Network Design document outlines the physical areas, applications, and user groups affected by the network upgrade. It can also list components of the network that are beyond the scope of the network upgrade, such as server or application updates.

Task 1: Consider How Meeting the Project Goals Will Impact the Existing Network

Step 1.   As the network designer, look at the existing network topology and the services that it provides. Consider how much of the network is affected or changed as a result of the project.

Step 2.   Record what areas of the existing network will have to change or will in some way be affected by meeting the project goals.

Draft informal descriptive notes of these possible changes. Organize these notes under headings such as these:

■ Access Layer

■ Distribution Layer

- Core Layer
- Data Center
- Network Services
- WAN Access

Step 3.   Use word processing software to create a Project Scope document based on these notes.

Task 2: Refine and Record the Proposed Changes to the Existing Network

Step 1.   Distinguish between possible upgrades to existing network resources, such as additional servers or VLANs, and completely new additional resources, such as QoS and WAN links.

Step 2.   Record which areas and users will be affected by these changes.

Step 3.   Include these network changes in your Project Scope document.

Task 3: Define the Areas of the Existing Network Not Covered by the Project

It is important to note the parts of the existing network that are not within the areas covered by the project. These out-of-scope areas are defined so that there is no misunderstanding between the NetworkingCompany and FilmCompany management.

In this case study, for example, providing IP telephony services may be a future consideration, but it is not within the scope of this project.

Clearly state these out-of-scope areas in your Project Scope document.

Task 4: Compile and Present the Project Scope Document

FilmCompany has to agree with your assessment of the project scope before you proceed further with the design. An agreement ensures that there is a common understanding about what is included in the network upgrade project and what is not included.

Step 1.   Discuss your project scope with another student to ensure that the issues you present are clear.

Step 2.   Save your Project Scope document and retain it for the next stages of this network design case study.

Reflection

It is important that a project have clearly defined boundaries so that all parties know what is included and what is not.

Consider the issues of ensuring that customer business and network needs are satisfied before the scope is broadened beyond what is feasible and required.

What strategies could be used to ensure that a project scope is developed that is clear and appropriate?

_____

_____

_____

_____

_____

_____

_____

_____

Lab 3-11: Developing Network Requirements (3.5.4)

Upon completion of this lab, you will be able to

- Identify and record the new business and technical requirements of a new network design project.
- Develop network requirements.

Expected Results and Success Criteria

Before starting this lab, read through the tasks that you are expected to perform. What do you expect the result of performing these tasks will be?

_____

_____

_____

How is an understanding of a Network Requirements document useful in network administration?

_____

_____

_____

How do business goals affect the Network Requirements document?

_____

_____

_____

Background/Preparation

FilmCompany is an expanding, small advertising company moving into interactive advertising media, including video presentations. This company has just been awarded a large video support contract by the StadiumCompany. With this new contract, FilmCompany expects to see its business grow approximately 70 percent.

To facilitate this growth, the FilmCompany has decided to significantly upgrade its data network. You have the role of network designer. Your job is to develop network design and project documents for FilmCompany that will meet the requirements of this upgrade.

As part of the new network design requirements, and based on the Project Goal statement and Project Scope documents, a Network Requirements document has to be developed.

This section of the Network Design document details the business goals, business constraints, technical requirements, user groups, and applications that influence the design of the new network.

Task 1: Record the Company Business Goals and Constraints That Will Influence the Network Design

As the network designer, you need to identify and prioritize the business goals of FilmCompany as defined in the Project Goals document. Develop your understanding of what these goals are from the FilmCompany case study information.

Step 1.   List these goals in order of priority.

Step 2.   Expand and consider the details of how these goals can be achieved using the network as a platform.

Step 3.   Note any constraints that these expanded goals may impose on the network design, such as retaining the current number of IT and network support staff.

Step 4.   Use word processing software to create a Network Requirements document.

Step 5.   Clearly state the business goals and constraints in the document.

Task 2: Record the Technical Requirements That Will Influence the Network Design

Step 1.   Evaluate each of the business goals and determine the technical requirements to meet the goals.

List these technical requirements under the following headings:

- Scalability

- Availability and Performance

- Security

- Manageability

Step 2.   Initially, list all technologies that may be able to meet these technical requirements.

Step 3.   Include these requirements in your Network Requirements document.

Task 3: Record the User Requirements That Will Influence the Network Design

Step 1.   Consider the types of users that will influence the network design. These users may be onsite, in the office, in the video-editing room, offsite (at the stadium), or mobile.

Which types of users generate the heaviest amount of network traffic? Which types generate the lightest traffic?

_____

_____

_____

_____

How might different types of users be grouped for access layer purposes?

_____

_____

Step 2.   Include these requirements in your Network Requirements document.

Task 4: Record the Application Requirements That Will Influence the Network Design

Step 1.   Consider the type of applications that will influence the network design.

What applications are essentially device based, with minimal network requirements?

_____

_____

_____

Which applications are network intensive?

_____

_____

_____

Which applications and services are delivered onsite, in the offices, and which may need to be delivered offsite over the WAN or to mobile users?

_____

_____

_____

Step 2.   Include these requirements in your Network Requirements document.

Task 5: Develop the Network Requirements

Step 1.   Refine the technical requirements of the network to match user and application requirements.

What compromises may have to be made to ensure that the project remains within the business constraints?

_____

_____

Step 2.   Finalize the technical requirements of the network that will meet the project goals.

Step 3.   Discuss and review your Technical Requirements document with another student to ensure it addresses all the business, user, and application requirements within the project scope and does not unnecessarily address out-of-scope requirements. Modify the document as necessary.

Step 4.   Save and retain your Technical Requirements document for the next stage of this network design case study.

Reflection

Developing the technical requirements of a network that meets the project goals, while remaining within scope, requires knowledge of the available and appropriate technologies and services.

Discuss strategies that will ensure that a network design team is current with networking technologies and their applications.

_____

_____

_____

_____

_____

_____

Lab 3-12: Analyzing an Existing Network (3.5.5)

Upon completion of this lab, you will be able to characterize the current network in relation to the identified business and technical requirements of a new network design project.

This lab contains skills that relate to the following 640-802 CCNA exam objectives:

- Describe the purpose and functions of various network devices.
- Interpret network diagrams.

Expected Results and Success Criteria

Before starting this lab, read through the tasks that you are expected to perform. What do you expect the result of performing these tasks will be?

_____

_____

_____

How can a network analysis be useful in network topology upgrades?

_____

_____

_____

Background/Preparation

FilmCompany is an expanding, small advertising company moving into interactive advertising media, including video presentations. This company has just been awarded a large video support contract by the StadiumCompany. With this new contract, FilmCompany expects to see its business grow approximately 70 percent.

To facilitate this growth, the FilmCompany has decided to significantly upgrade its data network. You have the role of network designer. Your job is to develop network design and project documents for FilmCompany that will meet the requirements of this upgrade.

As part of the new network design requirements, the current network has to be analyzed against the project technical requirements.

This section of the Network Design document describes what can be done to improve or eliminate the weaknesses and to build on the strengths of the existing network.

Task 1: Document and Confirm Existing Network Topology, Addressing, and Naming Schemes

Step 1.   Read the FilmCompany case study document in Appendix B and examine the existing network topology diagram (see Figure 3-14). Record the current addressing scheme in a table, and associate device names with addresses on the table.

Figure 3-14   Lab 3-12 FilmCompany Network Topology

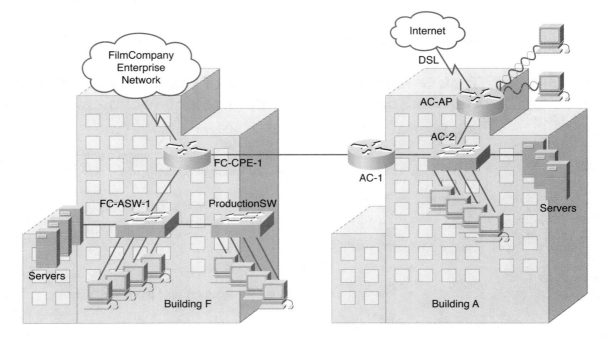

Step 2.   Highlight any inconsistencies in the naming and addressing schemes.

For example:

- Naming some devices by location and others by function

- Inconsistent or confusing use of abbreviations

- Some gateway addresses as the first address of a subnet, others as the last address

Step 3.   Use word processing software to create a Current Network document.

Task 2: Identify Those Parts of the Existing Network That Currently Meet the Project Technical Requirements

Step 1.   Examine the network topology and specifications.

Record which current features meet the technical requirements of the proposed network upgrade.

Examples include the following:

- Capacity (bandwidth, address ranges, VLANs)

- Redundant links

- Router and switch interfaces and ports

- Router and switch feature sets, memory, and processing capability

- WAN

- Wireless

- QoS

Step 2.   Include these strengths and capabilities in your Current Network document.

Task 3: Identify Those Parts of the Existing Network That Can Be Scaled to Meet the Project Technical Requirements

Step 1.   Examine the network topology and specifications.

Record which current features do not meet the technical requirements of the proposed network upgrade but can be scaled within the capacity of the network to do so.

Examples include the following:

- Capacity (bandwidth, address ranges, VLANs)

- Redundant links

- Router and switch interfaces and ports

- Router and switch feature sets, memory, and processing capability

- WAN

- Wireless

- QoS

Step 2.   Include these scalable features and capabilities in your Current Network document.

Task 4: Identify Those Parts of the Existing Network That Do Not Meet the Project Technical Requirements

Step 1.   Examine the network topology and specifications.

Record which current features do not meet the technical requirements of the proposed network upgrade and what additional networking resources are required.

Examples include the following:

- Capacity (bandwidth, address ranges, VLANs)

- Redundant links

- Router and switch interfaces and ports

- Router and switch feature sets, memory, and processing capability

- WAN

- Wireless

- QoS

Step 2.   Include these weaknesses and shortfalls in your Current Network document.

_____

_____

_____

_____

_____

_____

_____

_____

_____

_____

Task 5: Obtain Agreement and Authorization from the Company to Continue with the Network Upgrade Design

Step 1.   Finalize the Current Network document so that the strengths and shortfalls are clearly and precisely presented.

Step 2.   Discuss and review your Current Network document with another student to ensure that it clearly states which parts of the network meet the technical requirements of the upgrade project and which parts do not. Amend the document as necessary to clarify any areas that could be misunderstood. At this stage of the network design process, a meeting with the FilmCompany management would be held to obtain their agreement and authorization to continue with the design of the upgrade.

Step 3.   Save and retain your Current Network document so that it can be incorporated with the previous documents to complete this network design case study.

Reflection

Consider the resources and information that will facilitate the task of analyzing a current network.

_____

_____

_____

_____

_____

_____

_____

Identifying Application Impacts on Network Design: Labs

The lab exercises included in this chapter cover all the Chapter 4 online curriculum labs to ensure that you have mastered the practical, hands-on skills needed to identify how applications impact the performance of the network and what this means for network design. As you work through these labs, use Chapter 4 in Part I of this book or use the corresponding Chapter 4 in the Discovery Designing and Supporting Computer Networks online curriculum for assistance.

Lab 4-1: Characterizing Network Applications (4.1.2)

Upon completion of this lab, you will be able to configure NetFlow to observe how the network traffic flows.

Expected Results and Success Criteria

Before starting this lab, read through the tasks that you are expected to perform. What do you expect the result of performing these tasks will be?

_____

_____

_____

How is an understanding of traffic flow useful in network design and in network administration?

_____

_____

_____

Background/Preparation

Cisco IOS can include a feature called NetFlow that provides information about network users, network applications, peak usage times, and traffic routing. NetFlow can provide the following services:

- Network traffic accounting
- Usage-based network billing
- Network planning
- Security
- Denial-of-service monitoring capabilities
- Network monitoring

Cisco routers that have the NetFlow feature enabled generate NetFlow records. These details can be viewed using **show** commands or exported from the router and collected using a NetFlow collector.

Although initially implemented by Cisco, NetFlow is emerging as an IETF standard: Internet Protocol Flow Information eXport (IPFIX). See RFC 3954 at http://www.ietf.org/rfc/rfc3954.txt.

NetFlow defines a data flow as a unidirectional sequence of packets that includes all the following five values:

- Source IP address

- Destination IP address

- Source TCP port

- Destination TCP port

- IP protocol

In this lab, you will observe the results of configuring NetFlow. In later labs, you will see how the state of data flows across the current network can be established so that a network upgrade can be planned and implemented.

Task 1: Cable and Configure the Network

This lab will use the network topology shown in Figure 4-1, and the hostnames, addresses, and subnet masks given in Table 4-1.

Note: If the PCs used in this lab are also connected to your Academy LAN or to the Internet, ensure that you record the cable connections and TCP/IP settings so that these can be restored at the conclusion of the lab.

Figure 4-1   Lab 4-1 Network Topology

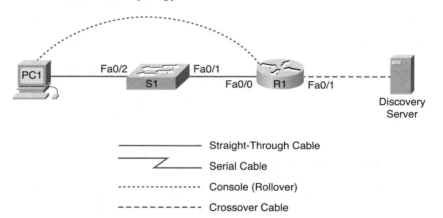

Table 4-1   Addressing Table for Lab 4-1

Device Designation	Device Name	Address	Subnet Mask
Discovery Server	Business Services	172.17.1.1	255.255.0.0
R1	FC-CPE-1	Fa0/1 172.17.0.1	255.255.0.0
		Fa0/0 10.0.0.1	255.255.255.0
S1	FC-ASW-1	—	—
PC1	Host 1	10.0.0.200	255.255.255.0

Step 1.   Connect and configure the devices in accordance with the topology shown in Figure 4-1 and the configuration details in Table 4-1.

For this lab, a PC workstation can substitute for a Discovery Server.

Step 2. Ping between Host 1 and Discovery Server to confirm network connectivity.

Troubleshoot and establish connectivity if the pings fail.

Task 2: Configure NetFlow on the Router Interfaces

NetFlow is configured to monitor data flows in or out of specific router interfaces. The **ingress** configuration option captures traffic that is being received by the interface. The **egress** option captures traffic that is being transmitted by the interface. In this lab, the traffic will be monitored on both router interfaces and in both directions from within the console session.

Step 1. From global configuration mode, issue the following commands:

```
FC-CPE-1(config)# interface fastethernet 0/0
FC-CPE-1(config-if)# ip flow ?
```

Record the two options available:

_____

_____

Which option captures traffic that is being received by the interface? _____

Which option captures traffic that is being transmitted by the interface? _____

Step 2. Complete the NetFlow configuration by issuing the following commands:

```
FC-CPE-1(config-if)# ip flow egress
FC-CPE-1(config-if)# ip flow ingress
FC-CPE-1(config-if)# interface fastethernet 0/1
FC-CPE-1(config-if)# ip flow ingress
FC-CPE-1(config-if)# ip flow egress
FC-CPE-1(config-if)# exit
FC-CPE-1(config)# end
```

Task 3: Verify the NetFlow Configuration

Step 1. From privileged EXEC mode, issue the **show running-configuration** command.

For each FastEthernet interface, what statement from the **running-configuration** command denotes that NetFlow is configured?

For interface FastEthernet 0/0:

_____

_____

For interface FastEthernet 0/1:

_____

_____

Step 2.   From privileged EXEC mode, issue the command:

FC-CPE-1# **show ip flow ?**

Note the three options available:

_____

_____

_____

Complete the command using the **interface** option:

FC-CPE-1# **show ip flow interface**

FastEthernet0/0

  ip flow ingress

  ip flow egress

FastEthernet0/1

  ip flow ingress

  ip flow egress

Confirm that the preceding output is displayed. Troubleshoot your configuration if this output is not displayed.

Task 4: Create Network Data Traffic

Step 1.   You can examine the captured data flow using the **show ip cache flow** command issued from privileged EXEC mode:

FC-CPE-1# **show ip cache flow**

Issuing this command before any data traffic has flowed should produce output similar to the following:

```
IP packet size distribution (0 total packets):
   1-32   64   96  128  160  192  224  256  288  320  352  384  416  448  480
   .000 .000 .000 .000 .000 .000 .000 .000 .000 .000 .000 .000 .000 .000 .000

    512  544  576 1024 1536 2048 2560 3072 3584 4096 4608
   .000 .000 .000 .000 .000 .000 .000 .000 .000 .000 .000

IP Flow Switching Cache, 0 bytes
  0 active, 0 inactive, 0 added
  0 ager polls, 0 flow alloc failures
  Active flows timeout in 30 minutes
  Inactive flows timeout in 15 seconds
  last clearing of statistics never
Protocol          Total    Flows   Packets Bytes  Packets Active(Sec) Idle(Sec)
--------          Flows     /Sec    /Flow  /Pkt     /Sec    /Flow        /Flow

SrcIf        SrcIPaddress   DstIf       DstIPaddress   Pr SrcP DstP  Pkts
```

Step 2.   List the eight highlighted column headings and consider what use this information may be in characterizing the network.

_____

_____

_____

_____

_____

_____

_____

_____

Step 3.   To ensure that flow cache statistics are reset, from privileged EXEC mode issue the following command:

```
FC-CPE-1#  clear ip flow stats
```

Step 4.   Ping the Business Server from Host 1 to generate a data flow.

From the command line of Host 1, issue the following command:

```
C:\>ping 172.17.1.1 -n 200
```

Task 5: View the Data Flows

Step 1.   At the conclusion of the data flow, you can view the details of the flow. From privileged EXEC mode, issue the following command:

```
FC-CPE-1# show ip cache flow
```

Output similar to the following will be displayed. Some values and details may be different in your lab.

```
IP packet size distribution (464 total packets):
   1-32   64   96  128  160  192  224  256  288  320  352  384  416  448  480
   .000 .900 .096 .000 .000 .000 .000 .002 .000 .000 .000 .000 .000 .000 .000

    512  544  576 1024 1536 2048 2560 3072 3584 4096 4608
   .000 .000 .000 .000 .000 .000 .000 .000 .000 .000 .000


IP Flow Switching Cache, 278544 bytes
  5 active, 4091 inactive, 48 added
  1168 ager polls, 0 flow alloc failures
  Active flows timeout in 30 minutes
  Inactive flows timeout in 15 seconds
IP Sub Flow Cache, 17416 bytes
  0 active, 1024 inactive, 0 added, 0 added to flow
  0 alloc failures, 0 force free
  1 chunk, 1 chunk added
  last clearing of statistics never
```

Protocol	Total Flows	Flows /Sec	Packets /Flow	Bytes /Pkt	Packets /Sec	Active(Sec) /Flow	Idle(Sec) /Flow
UDP-DNS	31	0.0	1	72	0.0	0.0	15.5
UDP-other	10	0.0	2	76	0.0	4.1	15.2
ICMP	2	0.0	200	60	0.3	198.9	15.3
Total:	43	0.0	10	61	0.3	10.2	15.5

```
SrcIf        SrcIPaddress    DstIf        DstIPaddress    Pr SrcP DstP  Pkts
< output omitted >
```

Step 2.   Examine your output and list details that indicate data flow:

_____

_____

_____

_____

_____

_____

_____

_____

_____

_____

Task 6: Stop the NetFlow Capture

Step 1.   To deactivate NetFlow capture, issue the **no ip flow** command at the interface configuration prompt:

```
FC-CPE-1(config)# interface fastethernet 0/0
FC-CPE-1(config-if)# no ip flow ingress
FC-CPE-1(config-if)# no ip flow egress
FC-CPE-1(config)# interface fastethernet 0/1
FC-CPE-1(config-if)# no ip flow ingress
FC-CPE-1(config-if)# no ip flow egress
```

Step 2.   To verify that NetFlow is deactivated, issue the **show ip flow interface** command from privileged EXEC mode:

```
FC-CPE-1# show ip flow interface
FC-CPE-1#
```

No output is displayed if NetFlow is off.

Task 7: Clean Up

Erase the configurations and reload the routers and switches. Disconnect and store the cabling. For PC hosts that are normally connected to other networks (such as the school LAN or the Internet), reconnect the appropriate cabling and restore the TCP/IP settings.

Reflection

Consider the possible range of data flow types across a network and how you could implement a tool like NetFlow to assist in analyzing those flows.

_____

_____

_____

_____

_____

Lab 4-2: Analyzing Network Traffic (4.2.3)

Upon completion of this activity, you will be able to identify and describe the network requirements to support file transfer and e-mail applications.

This lab contains skills that relate to the following 640-802 CCNA exam objectives:

- Select the components required to meet a network specification.

- Describe common networked applications, including web applications.

Expected Results and Success Criteria

Before starting this lab, read through the tasks that you are expected to perform. What do you expect the result of performing these tasks will be?

_____

_____

_____

What benefits are gained from designing a network to deliver services such as e-mail and FTP before implementing it?

_____

_____

_____

What problems could arise if e-mail and FTP services are provided without first planning and designing the network?

_____

_____

_____

Background/Preparation

FilmCompany is an expanding small advertising company moving into interactive advertising media, including video presentations. This company has just been awarded a large video support contract by the StadiumCompany. With this new contract, FilmCompany expects to see their business grow approximately 70 percent.

A part of this expansion requires consideration of the e-mail, and FTP services provided by the network. Users expect immediate access to their e-mails and to the files that they are sharing or updating.

In this lab, you will first consider the network design requirements for FTP and e-mail. Then you will generate some FTP and e-mail traffic on a network and use the Cisco IOS NBAR (Network-Based Application Recognition) feature to identify and examine that traffic.

Part 1: Design Network Access to FTP and E-mail Services

In this first part of the lab you will examine network considerations for FTP and e-mail services.

Task 1: FTP Network Considerations

File transfer traffic can put high-volume traffic onto the network. This traffic can have a greater effect on throughput than interactive end-to-end connections. Although file transfers are throughput-intensive, they typically have low response-time requirements.

As part of the initial characterization of the network, it is important to identify the level of FTP traffic that will be generated. From this information, the network designers can decide on throughput and redundancy requirements.

Step 1. List possible file transfer applications that would generate traffic on the FilmCompany network:

_____

_____

_____

_____

Step 2. List these applications by priority based on response time with the highest priority first and numbered "1" followed by applications in numbered descending order:

_____

_____

_____

_____

Step 3. List these applications by priority based on bandwidth requirements:

_____

_____

_____

_____

Task 2: E-mail Network Considerations

Although customers expect immediate access to their e-mails, they usually do not expect e-mails to have network priority over files that they are sharing or updating. Customers expect e-mails to be delivered reliably and accurately. Generally, e-mails are not throughput-intensive, except when there are enterprise-wide mail-outs or there is a denial-of-service attack.

List some e-mail policies that could control the volume of e-mail data and the bandwidth used:

_____

_____

_____

Part 2: Configure and Examine Network Traffic

In this part of the lab you will set up the network, configure NBAR, and generate and examine FTP and e-mail network traffic.

Task 1: Configure and Connect the Network

This lab will use the network topology shown in Figure 4-2, and the hostnames, addresses, and subnet masks given in Table 4-2.

Note: If the PCs used in this lab are also connected to your Academy LAN or to the Internet, ensure that you record the cable connections and TCP/IP settings so that these can be restored at the conclusion of the lab.

Figure 4-2   Lab 4-2 Network Topology

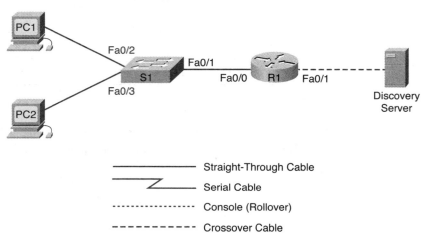

Straight-Through Cable
Serial Cable
Console (Rollover)
Crossover Cable

Table 4-2   Addressing Table for Lab 4-2

Device Designation	Device Name	Address	Subnet Mask
Discovery Server	Network Services	172.17.1.1	255.255.0.0
R1	FC-CPE-1	Fa0/1 172.17.0.1	255.255.0.0
		Fa0/0 10.0.0.1	255.255.255.0
PC1	Host1	10.0.0.200	255.255.255.0
PC2	Host2	10.0.0.201	255.255.255.0

Step 1.   Connect the devices in accordance with the network topology shown in Figure 4-2.

Note: Your instructor may substitute an equivalent server for Discovery Server for this lab.

Step 2.   Configure PC1 and PC2 in accordance with the address and subnet mask details in Table 4-2.

Step 3.   Establish a HyperTerminal, or other terminal emulation program, session from one of the PCs to R1. Configure R1 with the hostname, addresses, and subnet masks given in Table 4-2.

Step 4.   Ping between PC1, PC2, and Discovery Server to confirm network connectivity.

Troubleshoot and establish connectivity if the pings fail.

Task 2: Configure NBAR to Examine Network Traffic

NBAR can determine which protocols and applications are currently running on a network. NBAR includes the Protocol Discovery feature, which identifies the application protocols operating on an interface, so that appropriate QoS policies can be developed and applied. To enable Protocol Discovery to monitor selected protocols on a router interface, issue the following commands from the global configuration mode:

```
FC-CPE-1(config)# interface fastethernet 0/0
FC-CPE-1(config-if)# ip nbar protocol-discovery
```

Task 3: Confirm That Protocol Discovery Is Configured

From the privileged EXEC mode, issue the **show running-config** command and confirm that the following output appears under interface FastEthernet 0/0:

```
interface FastEthernet0/0
 ip address 10.0.0.1 255.255.255.0
 ip nbar protocol-discovery
```

If **protocol-discovery** is not confirmed, reissue the configuration commands for interface FastEthernet 0/0.

Task 4: Generate FTP Network Traffic

The Mozilla Thunderbird e-mail client program will be downloaded from Discovery Server as an example of FTP.

Step 1.   On PC1, launch a web browser and enter the URL ftp://server.discovery.ccna.

Alternatively, from the command line, enter ftp server.discovery.ccna.

If DNS is not configured, the IP address **172.17.1.1** must be used instead of the domain name.

Step 2.   Locate the file thunderbird_setup.exe in the pub directory of the Discovery FTP Server, download the file, and save it on PC1.

Step 3.   Repeat Steps 1 and 2 for PC2.

Task 5: Generate E-mail Network Traffic

If the Thunderbird, or other, e-mail client has previously been installed and e-mail accounts set up on both PC1 and PC2, proceed to Step 4. Otherwise, install and set up the e-mail client on PC1 and PC2 as described in Steps 1, 2, and 3.

Step 1.   Install the Thunderbird e-mail client on PC1 and PC2 by double-clicking the downloaded thunderbird_setup.exe file and accepting the default settings.

Step 2.   When the installation has completed, launch the program.

Step 3.   Configure e-mail accounts on PC1 and PC2 using settings as shown in Table 4-3.

Table 4-3   Thunderbird E-mail Client Settings

Field	Value
Account Name	The account name is based on the pod and host computer. A total of 20 accounts are configured on Discovery Server, labeled user[1..20]. The password for each account is cheetah[1..20].
Your Name	Use the same name selected for Account Name.
E-mail address	username@server.discovery.ccna
Type of incoming server you are using	POP
Incoming Server (SMTP)	172.17.1.1
Outgoing Server (SMTP)	172.17.1.1

On the Tools menu, select **Account Settings**. The layout of the configuration windows varies between versions, but the required Thunderbird Account Settings, Server Settings, and Outgoing Server Settings can be completed using the necessary details in Table 4-3.

Step 4.   Send and receive two e-mails between accounts on each PC.

Task 6: Display the NBAR Results

With Protocol Discovery enabled, any protocol traffic supported by NBAR, as well as the statistics associated with that protocol, can be discovered.

Step 1.   To display the traffic identified by NBAR, issue the **show ip nbar protocol-discovery command** from privileged EXEC mode:

```
FC-CPE-1# show ip nbar protocol-discovery
```

The output will have the following headings:

```
FastEthernet0/0
                    Input                     Output
                    - - - - -                 - - - - - -
        Protocol    Packet Count              Packet Count
                    Byte Count                Byte Count
                    5min Bit Rate (bps)       5min Bit Rate (bps)
                    5min Max Bit Rate (bps)   5min Max Bit Rate (bps)
- - - - - - - - - - - -   - - - - - - - - - - - - - - - -   - - - - - - - - - - - - - -
```

Step 2.   List each protocol identified and the input and output information:

Step 3.   Although the data traffic in this lab may not be sufficient to generate values for the **5min Bit rate (bps)** and **5min Max Bit Rate (bps)** fields, consider and discuss how these values would be applied to designing an FTP and e-mail network.

Task 7: Use NBAR to Monitor Other Data Traffic

NBAR can identify and monitor a range of network application traffic protocols.

From the privileged EXEC mode of the router, issue the command **show ip nbar port-map** and note the output displayed.

```
FC-CPE-1# show ip nbar port-map
```

List some protocols that you consider should be monitored and to which policies should be applied:

_____

_____

_____

_____

_____

_____

_____

_____

Task 8: Clean Up

Erase the configurations and reload the routers and switches. Disconnect and store the cabling. For PC hosts that are normally connected to other networks (such as the school LAN or the Internet), reconnect the appropriate cabling and restore the TCP/IP settings.

Challenge

This lab considered only the volume of FTP and e-mail data traffic and its impact on network design. Reliable access to servers is also important. Based on the topology shown in Figure 4-3, sketch a revised topology for this lab that would provide redundancy for these services at the Access Layer.

Figure 4-3   Student Lab 4-2 Challenge Network Topology

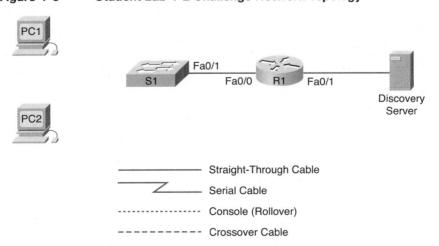

Lab 4-3: Prioritizing Traffic (4.3.3)

Upon completion of this lab, you will be able to explain where QoS can be implemented to affect traffic flow.

Expected Results and Success Criteria

Before starting this lab, read through the tasks that you are expected to perform. What do you expect the result of performing these tasks will be?

_____

_____

_____

Why is establishing quality of service on a network important?

_____

_____

_____

What issues would arise if the wrong priorities were assigned to network data traffic?

_____

_____

_____

Background/Preparation

In this lab, you analyze the information provided in the curriculum for the StadiumCompany case study, found in Appendix A of Part II of this Learning Guide, "StadiumCompany Story," and develop network data traffic priorities.

Task 1: Compile Data Traffic Information

Step 1.   Read through the StadiumCompany case study in Appendix A.

List the current types of data traffic carried by the StadiumCompany network as well as the types planned for the future:

_____

_____

_____

_____

_____

_____

_____

_____

_____

_____

_____

Step 2.   Refer to the stadium network topology in Figure 4-4 and the stadium facilities plan in Figure 4-5.

Figure 4-4   StadiumCompany Network Topology

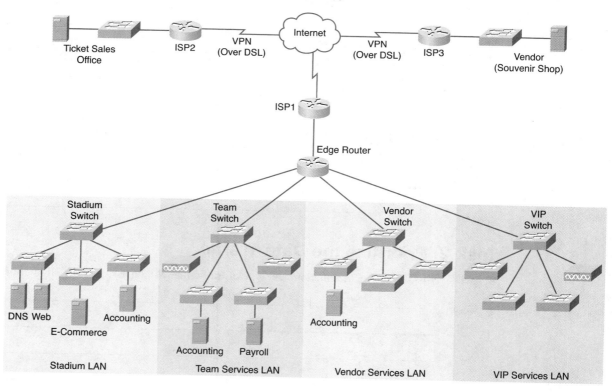

Figure 4-5   Stadium Facilities Plan

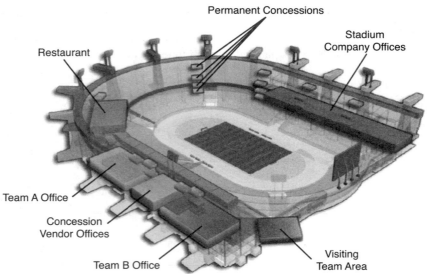

List the possible data sources and destinations on the StadiumCompany network. For example, there is likely to be data communications between the stadium management and the vendor management, but not between Team A and Team B.

_____

_____

_____

_____

_____

_____

_____

_____

_____

_____

Task 2: Prioritize the Data Traffic

Step 1.   List the source, destination, and type of traffic that will be assigned the High priority queue:

_____

_____

_____

_____

_____

_____

_____

_____

_____

_____

Step 2.   List the source, destination, and type of traffic that will be assigned the Medium priority queue:

_____

_____

_____

_____

_____

_____

_____

_____

_____

_____

Step 3.   List the source, destination, and type of traffic that will be assigned the Normal priority queue:

_____

_____

_____

_____

_____

_____

_____

_____

_____

Step 4. List the source, destination, and type of traffic that will be assigned the Low priority queue:

_____

_____

_____

_____

_____

_____

_____

_____

_____

_____

Task 3: Finalize the Data Priorities

Step 1. Discuss and review your data priority assignments with another student to ensure that it addresses all possible data. Modify your priorities as necessary.

Step 2. Highlight on the StadiumCompany topology diagram (Figure 4-4) the device or devices where data traffic priority policies are likely to be configured.

Reflection

Ideally, it may seem that all data traffic should be given the same priority and queued accordingly. Consider and discuss the potential for network performance to be negatively affected if this policy were implemented everywhere on the network.

_____

_____

_____

_____

_____

_____

Lab 4-4: Exploring Network QoS (4.3.4)

Upon completion of this lab, you will be able to explain where QoS can be implemented to affect traffic flow.

Expected Results and Success Criteria

Before starting this lab, read through the tasks that you are expected to perform. What do you expect the result of performing these tasks will be?

_____

_____

_____

Why is the establishing of priorities for different types of network traffic important?

_____

_____

_____

What information does a network administrator need to set QoS requirements on the network?

_____

_____

_____

Background/Preparation

FilmCompany is an expanding advertising company moving into interactive advertising media, including video presentations. This company has just been awarded a large video support contract by the StadiumCompany. With this new contract, FilmCompany expects to see their business grow approximately 70 percent.

The required network upgrade to support this growth in business will need to be able to carry a variety of data traffic types. Some of these data types may require priority access to network resources to ensure their useful and effective delivery.

In this lab, you will examine and apply some of the Cisco IOS commands to configure priority queuing on a router.

Task 1: Cable and Configure the Network

This lab will use the network topology shown in Figure 4-6, and the hostnames, addresses, and subnet masks given in Table 4-4.

Note: If the PCs used in this lab are also connected to your Academy LAN or to the Internet, ensure that you record the cable connections and TCP/IP settings so that these can be restored at the conclusion of the lab.

Figure 4-6   Lab 4-4 Network Topology

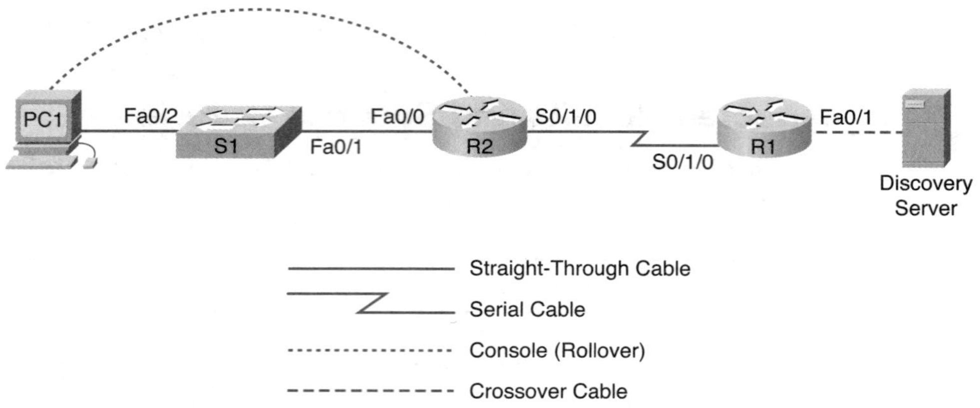

Table 4-4   Addressing Table for Lab 4-4

Device Designation	Device Name	Address	Subnet Mask
Discovery Server	Network Services	172.17.1.1	255.255.0.0
R1	ISP	Fa0/1 172.17.0.1	255.255.0.0
		S0/1/0 10.10.0.1	255.255.255.252
R2	FC-CPE-1	Fa0/0 10.0.0.1	255.255.255.0
		S0/1/0 10.10.0.2	255.255.255.252
S1	FC-ASW-1	—	—
PC1	Host1	10.0.0.200	255.255.255.0

Step 1.   Connect the devices in accordance with the network topology shown in Figure 4-6.

Note: Your instructor may substitute an equivalent server for Discovery Server for this lab.

Step 2.   Configure PC1 in accordance with the address and subnet mask details in Table 4-4.

Step 3.   Establish a HyperTerminal, or other terminal emulation program, session from PC1 to R1 and R2 in turn. Configure R1 and R2 with the hostname, addresses, and subnet masks given in Table 4-4.

Routing will have to be configured across the serial WAN link to establish data communications.

Configure Telnet access on each router.

Step 4.   Ping between PC1 and Discovery Server to confirm network connectivity.

Confirm Application Layer connectivity by telnetting from R2 to R1.

Troubleshoot and establish connectivity if the pings or Telnet fail.

Step 5.   After confirming the initial configurations, maintain a console terminal session connection with R2.

Task 2: Examine Priority Queue Commands

In this task, you define the required network priority lists and examine the Cisco IOS commands to implement these lists.

Configuring Priority Queueing

Configuring priority queueing (PQ) has two required steps and an optional third step:

Step 1.   Define the priority list (required).

Step 2.   Assign the priority list to an interface (required).

Step 3.   Monitor priority queueing lists (optional).

A priority list contains the definitions for a set of priority queues. The priority list specifies which queue a packet will be placed in and, optionally, the maximum length of the different queues. To perform queueing using a priority list, you must assign the list to an interface. The same priority list can be applied to multiple interfaces. Alternatively, you can create many different priority policies to apply to different interfaces.

Defining the Priority List

The priority list is defined by doing the following:

■ Assigning packets to priority queues

■ Specifying the maximum size of the priority queues (optional)

Packets are assigned to priority queues based on the protocol type and the interface where the packets enter the router.

The **priority-list** commands are read in order of appearance until a matching protocol or interface type is found. When a match is found, the packet is assigned to the appropriate queue and the search ends. Packets that do not match other assignment rules are assigned to the default queue.

The following global configuration mode commands are used to specify in which queue a packet is placed.

The command format is **priority-list** *list-number*

Use a list-number of **1** and note the options available.

Step 1.   Enter the following command and record the options available:

```
FC-CPE-1(config)# priority-list 1 ?
```

_____

_____

_____

_____

Step 2. Enter the following command and record some of the protocol options available:

FC-CPE-1(config)# `priority-list 1 protocol ?`

_____

_____

_____

_____

_____

_____

_____

_____

_____

_____

Step 3. Issue the following command and record the IP protocol options available:

FC-CPE-1(config)# `priority-list 1 protocol ip ?`

_____

_____

_____

_____

Step 4. Issue the following command and note the HTTP protocol options available:

FC-CPE-1(config)# `priority-list 1 protocol http ?`

_____

_____

_____

_____

Step 5. Issue the following command and note the IP protocol high-priority options available:

FC-CPE-1(config)# `priority-list 1 protocol ip high ?`

_____

_____

_____

_____

_____

_____

Step 6.   Issue the following command and note the IP protocol high-priority TCP options available:

FC-CPE-1(config)# `priority-list 1 protocol ip high tcp ?`

_____

_____

_____

_____

_____

_____

_____

_____

_____

_____

_____

_____

_____

Task 3: Configure an Example Priority Queue

From global configuration mode, issue the following commands:

FC-CPE-1(config)# `priority-list 1 protocol http high`

FC-CPE-1(config)# `priority-list 1 protocol ip normal tcp ftp`

FC-CPE-1(config)# `priority-list 1 protocol ip medium tcp telnet`

What do these commands establish?

_____

_____

Task 4: Assign the Priority List to an Interface

Step 1.   From global configuration mode, issue the following commands to assign the priority list to interface serial 0/1/0:

FC-CPE-1(config)# `int s0/1/0`

FC-CPE-1(config-if)# `priority-group 1`

Step 2.   Confirm the priority list configuration. From privileged EXEC mode, issue the **show running-config** command.

Which statements in the configuration show that the priority list has been configured and applied correctly?

Step 3.   Confirm that issuing the **show queueing priority** command from privileged EXEC mode produces the following output:

```
FC-CPE-1# show queueing priority
Current DLCI priority queue configuration:
Current priority queue configuration:


List    Queue   Args
1       high    protocol http
1       normal  protocol ip              tcp port ftp
1       medium  protocol ip              tcp port telnet
```

Task 5: Examine Priority Queue Operation

Step 1.   On Host1, launch a web browser and enter the URL **http://172.17.1.1** to access the web services configured on the server.

Step 2.   Use FTP to download a file. On Host1, launch a new web browser window and enter the URL **ftp://172.17.1.1**, or from the command line, issue **ftp 172.17.1.1**.

Step 3.   Download a large file from the server; for example, the Thunderbird setup program file.

Step 4.   From privileged EXEC mode, issue the following command:

```
FC-CPE-1# show queueing interface s0/1/0
```

You should see output similar to the following:

```
Interface Serial0/1/0 queueing strategy: priority


Output queue utilization (queue/count)
        high/94 medium/0 normal/106759 low/0
```

Note the packet count for each queue:

High _____ Medium _____ Normal _____ Low _____

Step 5.   Initiate a Telnet session from R2 to R1 and issue some **show** commands on R1.

Step 6.   Close the Telnet session.

Step 7.   Issue the following command from the R2 privileged EXEC mode:

```
FC-CPE-1# show queueing interface s0/1/0
```

Note the packet count for each queue:

High _____ Medium _____ Normal _____ Low _____

What is the significant difference when compared to the previous output from this command in Step 4?

Task 6: Determine Priority Queue Requirements

Step 1.   Using the FilmCompany case study, what would you expect the priority queue requirements to be?

Step 2.   Discuss and compare your priorities with other students:

_____

_____

_____

_____

_____

_____

_____

_____

Step 3.   Amend your priority list statements to include traffic associated with the proposed network upgrade:

_____

_____

_____

_____

_____

_____

_____

_____

_____

Task 7: Clean Up

Erase the configurations and reload the routers and switches. Disconnect and store the cabling. For PC hosts that are normally connected to other networks (such as the school LAN or the Internet), reconnect the appropriate cabling and restore the TCP/IP settings.

Challenge

The following privileged EXEC command displays the details of packets inside a queue for a particular interface:

```
show queue interface-type interface-number
```

However, in this lab, it is not likely that sufficient data traffic was generated at one time for the interface queues to hold packets long enough to be inspected.

Discuss how a network has to be load tested to ensure that all traffic priorities are met.

_____

_____

_____

_____

_____

_____

_____

_____

Lab 4-5: Investigating Video Traffic Impact on a Network (4.4.4)

Upon completion of this lab, you will be able to explain how voice and video traffic impacts the network design.

This lab contains skills that relate to the following 640-802 CCNA exam objectives:

- Select the components required to meet a network specification.

- Describe common networked applications, including web applications.

- Describe the impact of applications (Voice over IP and Video over IP) on a network.

Expected Results and Success Criteria

Before starting this lab, read through the tasks that you are expected to perform. What do you expect the result of performing these tasks will be?

_____

_____

_____

How could streaming video data affect the network performance?

_____

_____

_____

What possible actions could a network administrator take if network performance was noted to be deteriorating due to video?

_____

_____

_____

Background/Preparation

FilmCompany is an expanding advertising company moving into interactive advertising media, including video presentations. This company has just been awarded a large video support contract by the StadiumCompany. With this new contract, FilmCompany expects to see their business grow approximately 70 percent.

The required network upgrade to support this growth in business will need to be able to carry video data traffic from remote sites without degrading the performance of the network for other users.

In this lab, you will observe video streaming from Discovery Server across a serial connection and note the impact on other data traffic.

Task 1: Cable and Configure the Network

This lab will use the network topology shown in Figure 4-7, and the hostnames, addresses, and subnet masks given in Table 4-5.

Note: If the PCs used in this lab are also connected to your Academy LAN or to the Internet, ensure that you record the cable connections and TCP/IP settings so that these can be restored at the conclusion of the lab.

Figure 4-7   Lab 4-5 Network Topology

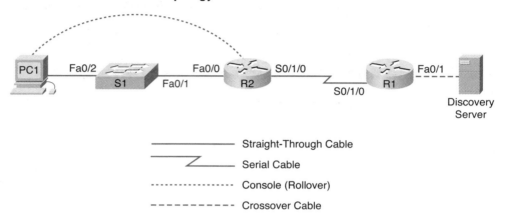

- ——————————— Straight-Through Cable
- ———/——— Serial Cable
- ················ Console (Rollover)
- ————— Crossover Cable

Table 4-5   Addressing Table for Lab 4-5

Device Designation	Device Name	Address	Subnet Mask
Discovery Server	Network Services	172.17.1.1	255.255.0.0
R1	ISP	Fa0/1 172.17.0.1	255.255.0.0
		S0/1/0 10.10.0.1	255.255.255.252
R2	FC-CPE-1	Fa0/0 10.0.0.1	255.255.255.0
		S0/1/0 10.10.0.2	255.255.255.252
S1	FC-ASW-1	—	—
PC1	Host1	10.0.0.200	255.255.255.0

Step 1.   Connect the devices in accordance with the network topology shown in Figure 4-7.

Note: Your instructor may substitute an equivalent server for Discovery Server for this lab.

Step 2.   Configure PC1 in accordance with the address and subnet mask details in Table 4-5.

Step 3.   Establish a HyperTerminal, or other terminal emulation program, session from PC1 to R1. Configure R1 with the hostname, addresses, and subnet masks given in Table 4-5.

Set the clock rate on the serial link to 56000.

Step 4.   Establish a HyperTerminal, or other terminal emulation program, session from PC1 to R2. Configure R2 with the hostname, addresses, and subnet masks given in Table 4-5.

Routing will have to be configured across the serial WAN link to establish data communications.

Step 5.   Ping between PC1 and Discovery Server to confirm network connectivity.

Troubleshoot and establish connectivity if the pings fail.

Task 2: Observe Data Traffic

In this task you will generate concurrent data traffic and observe the time the flows take.

Step 1.   From the Host1 command line, issue the command **ping 172.17.1 1 –n 500** to generate a large number of pings to Discovery Server.

Step 2.   While the pings are being generated on Host1, launch a web browser and enter the URL **http://server.discovery.ccna** or **http://172.17.1.1** to access the web services configured on the server.

Step 3.   Use FTP to download a file. On Host1, launch a new web browser window and enter the URL **ftp://server.discovery.ccna**, or issue **ftp server.discovery.ccna** from the command line. If DNS is not configured, the IP address 172.17.1.1 must be used instead of the domain name.

Step 4.   Download a large file from the server; for example, the Thunderbird setup program file.

Record the total time taken to complete the pings, access the web page, and download the file.

Task 3: Stream the Video File

Before beginning to stream the video. ensure that QuickTime Player is installed on Host1, and that the video streaming service has been enabled on Discovery Server version 2. See your instructor for advice if you are unsure.

Step 1.   Launch QuickTime Player. On the File menu, go to **Open URL**.

Step 2.   Enter the URL **rtsp://172.17.1.1/MWO.sdp**, or a URL as provided by the instructor.

Note the rate at which the video plays and record the video and sound quality.

_____

_____

What is RTSP and why is it used in this step?

_____

_____

_____

_____

Task 4: Observe Both Video and Data Traffic

Step 1.   From the Host1 command line, issue the command **ping 172.17.1 1 –n 500** to generate a large number of pings to Discovery Server.

Step 2.   While the pings are being generated, use QuickTime Player to access the streaming video URL again.

Step 3.   While the video is being played, launch a new web browser window on Host1 and enter the URL **http://server.discovery.ccna** or **http://172.17.1.1** to access the web services configured on the server.

Step 4.   On Host1, launch another web browser window and enter the URL **ftp://server.discovery.ccna**, or issue **ftp server.discovery.ccna** from the command line.

           If DNS is not configured, the IP address 172.17.1.1 must be used instead of the domain name.

Step 5.   Download a large file from the server; for example, the Thunderbird setup program file.

           Record the total time taken to complete the pings, access the web page, and download the file.

           _____

           Note the rate at which the video plays and record the video and sound quality.

           _____

           _____

Task 5: Observe Data Flows for Different Serial Link Clock Rates

Step 1.   Change the serial link clock rate to **250000** on the router with the DCE interface.

Step 2.   Repeat Task 4 and record your observations.

           Record the total time taken to complete the pings, access the web page, and download the file.

           _____

           Note the rate at which the video plays and record the video and sound quality.

           _____

           _____

Step 3.   Change the serial link clock rate to **2000000** on the router with the DCE interface.

Step 4.   Repeat Task 4 and record your observations.

           Record the total time taken to complete the pings, access the web page, and download the file.

           _____

           Note the rate at which the video plays and record the video and sound quality.

           _____

           _____

Task 6: Record Your General Observations

Compare the different download times and video quality.

_____

_____

_____

_____

_____

_____

_____

_____

Task 7: Clean Up

Erase the configurations and reload the routers and switches. Disconnect and store the cabling. For PC hosts that are normally connected to other networks (such as the school LAN or the Internet), reconnect the appropriate cabling and restore the TCP/IP settings.

Reflection

Consider and discuss how video and other data traffic can share network resources while maintaining acceptable performance.

_____

_____

_____

Lab 4-6: Identifying Traffic Flows (4.5.1)

Upon completion of this lab, you will be able to explain what is meant by application traffic flows.

This lab contains skills that relate to the following 640-802 CCNA exam objective:

- Use the OSI and TCP/IP models and their associated protocols to explain how data flows in a network.

Expected Results and Success Criteria

Before starting this lab, read through the tasks that you are expected to perform. What do you expect the result of performing these tasks will be?

_____

_____

_____

How is an understanding of traffic flow useful in network administration?

_____

_____

_____

How will a network administrator know if the network devices can handle the amount of traffic?

_____

_____

_____

Background/Preparation

FilmCompany is an expanding small advertising company moving into interactive advertising media, including video presentations. This company has just been awarded a large video support contract by the StadiumCompany. With this new contract, FilmCompany expects to see their business grow approximately 70 percent.

To facilitate this expansion, the state of data flow across the current network has to be established so that the network upgrade can be planned and implemented.

In this lab, you will use the Cisco routers IOS NetFlow feature capture and view data flow information.

Task 1: Cable and Configure the Network

This lab will use the network topology shown in Figure 4-8, and the hostnames, addresses, and subnet masks given in Table 4-6.

Note: If the PCs used in this lab are also connected to your Academy LAN or to the Internet, ensure that you record the cable connections and TCP/IP settings so that these can be restored at the conclusion of the lab.

Figure 4-8   Lab 4-6 Network Topology

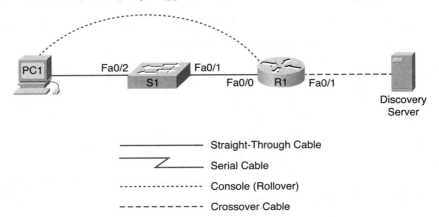

————————	Straight-Through Cable
———⟋———	Serial Cable
- - - - - - - - - - -	Console (Rollover)
– – – – – – – – –	Crossover Cable

Table 4-6   Addressing Table for Lab 4-6

Device Designation	Device Name	Address	Subnet Mask
Discovery Server	Business Services	172.17.1.1	255.255.0.0
R1	FC-CPE-1	Fa0/1 172.17.0.1	255.255.0.0
		Fa0/0 10.0.0.1	255.255.255.0
S1	FC-ASW-1	—	—
PC1	Host1	10.0.0.200	255.255.255.0

Step 1.   Connect the devices in accordance with the network topology shown in Figure 4-8.

Note: Your instructor may substitute an equivalent server for Discovery Server for this lab.

Step 2.   Configure PC1 in accordance with the address and subnet mask details in Table 4-6.

Step 3.   Establish a HyperTerminal, or other terminal emulation program, session from PC1 to R1. Configure R1 with the hostname, addresses, and subnet masks given in Table 4-6.

Step 4.   Ping between PC1 and Discovery Server to confirm network connectivity.

Troubleshoot and establish connectivity if the pings or Telnet fail.

Task 2: Configure NetFlow on the Interfaces

From global configuration mode of R1, issue the following commands to configure NetFlow:

```
FC-CPE-1(config)# interface fastethernet 0/0
FC-CPE-1(config-if)# ip flow egress
FC-CPE-1(config-if)# ip flow ingress
FC-CPE-1(config-if)# interface fastethernet 0/1
FC-CPE-1(config-if)# ip flow ingress
FC-CPE-1(config-if)# ip flow egress
FC-CPE-1(config-if)# end
```

Task 3: Verify the NetFlow Configuration

Step 1.   From privileged EXEC mode, issue the **show ip flow interface** command:

```
FC-CPE-1# show ip flow interface
FastEthernet0/0
  ip flow ingress
  ip flow egress
FastEthernet0/1
  ip flow ingress
  ip flow egress
```

Confirm that the preceding output is displayed. Troubleshoot your configuration if this output is not displayed.

Step 2.   From the privileged EXEC mode, issue the following command to ensure that flow cache statistics are reset:

```
FC-CPE-1# clear ip flow stats
```

Task 4: Create Network Data Traffic

A range of network application data flows is to be generated and captured. Generate as many of the data flows outlined in the list that follows as possible in your lab. Your instructor will advise you of the particular applications that are available to be used in this lab.

Step 1.   Ping the Discovery Server from Host1 to generate a data flow.

From the command line of Host1, issue the command **ping 172.17.1.1 -n 200**

Step 2.   Telnet to the Discovery Server from Host1.

If Discovery Server is being used, issue the command **telnet server.discovery.ccna** from the command prompt of Host1.

If Discovery Server is not being used, DNS is not configured , or if a terminal program such as HyperTerminal or TeraTerm is being used, telnet from Host1 to 172.17.1.1.

Step 3.   On Host1, launch a web browser and enter the URL **http://server.discovery.ccna**.

If Discovery Server is not being used or DNS is not configured, use **http://172.17.1.1** to access the web services configured on that server.

Step 4.   Use FTP to download a file.

On Host1, launch a web browser and enter the URL **ftp://server.discovery.ccna**, or issue **ftp server.discovery.ccna** from the command line. If DNS is not configured, use the IP address 172.17.1.1 instead of the domain name.

Download a file from the server.

Note: If an e-mail client program is not installed on Host1, download the Thunderbird setup program file for use in the next step.

Step 5.   If e-mail accounts have been configured using the POP3 and SMTP services on Discovery Server, send an e-mail using one of these accounts.

Note: If an e-mail client program is not installed on Host1, install the Thunderbird setup program file downloaded in the previous step. Lab 4-2 provides the Thunderbird e-mail client set up details.

Task 5: View the Data Flows

At the conclusion of the data flow, view the details by issuing the **show ip cache flow** command from privileged EXEC mode:

```
FC-CPE-1# show ip cache flow
```

You should see output similar to the following:

```
IP packet size distribution (3969 total packets):
   1-32   64   96  128  160  192  224  256  288  320  352  384  416  448  480
   .000 .351 .395 .004 .011 .001 .005 .009 .001 .002 .005 .001 .000 .000 .000

    512  544  576 1024 1536 2048 2560 3072 3584 4096 4608
   .000 .000 .013 .000 .195 .000 .000 .000 .000 .000 .000


IP Flow Switching Cache, 278544 bytes
  2 active, 4094 inactive, 1368 added
  22316 ager polls, 0 flow alloc failures
  Active flows timeout in 30 minutes
  Inactive flows timeout in 15 seconds
IP Sub Flow Cache, 17416 bytes
  0 active, 1024 inactive, 0 added, 0 added to flow
  0 alloc failures, 0 force free
  1 chunk, 0 chunks added
  last clearing of statistics 02:50:15
```

Protocol	Total Flows	Flows /Sec	Packets /Flow	Bytes /Pkt	Packets /Sec	Active(Sec) /Flow	Idle(Sec) /Flow
TCP-Telnet	9	0.0	13	47	0.0	5.2	10.8
TCP-FTP	28	0.0	7	62	0.0	0.8	10.4
TCP-WWW	64	0.0	7	138	0.0	0.3	2.1
TCP-other	16	0.0	75	840	0.1	0.0	4.1
UDP-DNS	878	0.0	1	72	0.0	0.0	15.4
UDP-other	347	0.0	3	88	0.1	4.5	15.5
ICMP	26	0.0	1	70	0.0	0.8	15.4
Total:	1368	0.1	2	318	0.3	1.2	14.6

```
< output omitted >
```

From your output, list the name of each protocol with the number of flows.

_____

_____

_____

_____

_____

_____

_____

_____

What was the total number of packets generated?

_____

Which protocol generated the most packets?

_____

Which protocol produced the most bytes per flow?

_____

Which protocol's flows were on the network the longest time?

_____

Which protocol used the longest amount of network time?

_____

Task 6: Clean Up

Erase the configurations and reload the routers and switches. Disconnect and store the cabling. For PC hosts that are normally connected to other networks (such as the school LAN or the Internet), reconnect the appropriate cabling and restore the TCP/IP settings.

Reflection

Create a projected applications document listing the applications planned to use the network.

Application Type	Application	Protocol	Priority	Comments

Lab 4-7: Diagramming Intranet Traffic Flows (4.5.2)

Upon completion of this lab, you will be able to diagram the flow of traffic to and from hosts and servers within the LAN.

This lab contains skills that relate to the following 640-802 CCNA exam objective:

- Use the OSI and TCP/IP models and their associated protocols to explain how data flows in a network.

Expected Results and Success Criteria

Before starting this lab, read through the tasks that you are expected to perform. What do you expect the result of performing these tasks will be?

_____

_____

_____

Why is diagramming traffic flow useful in network administration?

_____

_____

_____

What can be expected from diagramming traffic flows in a network?

_____

_____

_____

Background/Preparation

FilmCompany is an expanding advertising company moving into interactive advertising media, including video presentations. This company has just been awarded a large video support contract by the StadiumCompany. With this new contract, FilmCompany expects to see their business grow approximately 70 percent.

To facilitate this expansion, the state of data flow across the current network has to be established so that the network upgrade can be planned and implemented.

Developing a diagram of applications, devices, and traffic flow enables the designer to analyze the proposed design and identify where the network can be improved. The logical topology diagram shows that the servers are identified with the applications that will be used. Areas that require redundancy or increased security are also easier to identify. Redundant paths to the server and security measures, such as a hardware firewall, can be marked on the diagram. The logical design for the network must be aligned with the initial business goals and technical requirements of the customer. The diagram gives the designer and customer a visual idea of what is already on the network and helps to get a better view of what is still required.

In this lab, you will use NetFlow to diagram the flow of traffic from host to host and from host to server within a LAN segment of FilmCompany. Preparing this diagram requires you to identify the hardware (hosts, servers, and so on) and determine the traffic generated across the network from the hosts and from the server.

Task 1: Cable and Configure the Network

This lab will use the network topology shown in Figure 4-9, and the hostnames, addresses, and subnet masks given in Table 4-7.

Note: If the PCs used in this lab are also connected to your Academy LAN or to the Internet, ensure that you record the cable connections and TCP/IP settings so that these can be restored at the conclusion of the lab.

Figure 4-9   Lab 4-7 Network Topology

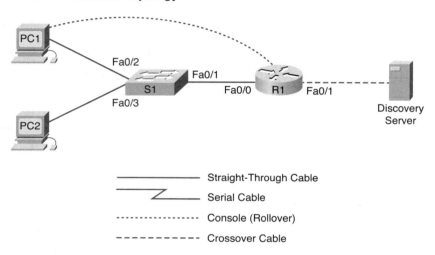

Table 4-7   Addressing Table for Lab 4-7

Device Designation	Device Name	Address	Subnet Mask
Discovery Server	Business Services	172.17.1.1	255.255.0.0
R1	FC-CPE-1	Fa0/1 172.17.0.1	255.255.0.0
		Fa0/0 10.0.0.1	255.255.255.0
S1	FC-ASW-1	—	—
PC1	Host1	10.0.0.200	255.255.255.0
PC2	Host2	10.0.0.201	255.255.255.0

Step 1.   Connect the devices in accordance with the network topology shown in Figure 4-9.

Note: Your instructor may substitute an equivalent server for Discovery Server for this lab.

Step 2.   Configure PC1 and PC2 in accordance with the address and subnet mask details in Table 4-7.

Step 3.   Establish a HyperTerminal, or other terminal emulation program, session from PC1 to R1. Configure R1 with the hostname, addresses, and subnet masks given in Table 4-7.

Step 4.   Ping between PC1 and Discovery Server to confirm network connectivity.

Troubleshoot and establish connectivity if the pings fail.

Task 2: Configure NetFlow on the Interfaces

From global configuration mode of R1, issue the following commands to configure NetFlow:

```
FC-CPE-1(config)# interface fastethernet 0/0
FC-CPE-1(config-if)# ip flow egress
FC-CPE-1(config-if)# ip flow ingress
FC-CPE-1(config-if)# interface fastethernet 0/1
FC-CPE-1(config-if)# ip flow ingress
FC-CPE-1(config-if)# ip flow egress
FC-CPE-1(config-if)# end
```

Task 3: Verify the NetFlow Configuration

Step 1.   From privileged EXEC mode, issue the **show ip flow interface** command:

```
FC-CPE-1# show ip flow interface
FastEthernet0/0
  ip flow ingress
  ip flow egress
FastEthernet0/1
  ip flow ingress
  ip flow egress
```

Confirm that you see the preceding output. Troubleshoot your configuration if this output is not displayed.

Step 2.   From privileged EXEC mode, issue the following command to ensure that flow cache statistics are reset:

```
FC-CPE-1# clear ip flow stats
```

Task 4: Create Network Data Traffic

A range of network application data flows between Host1, Host2, and the server is to be generated and captured. Generate as many of the data flows resulting from the following steps as possible in your lab. Your instructor will advise you of the particular applications that are available to be used in this lab.

Step 1.   On Host1, launch a web browser and enter the URL **http://server.discovery.ccna**.

If Discovery Server is not being used or DNS is not configured, use **http://172.17.1.1** to access the web services configured on that server.

Step 2.   On Host2, launch a web browser and enter the URL **http://server.discovery.ccna**.

If Discovery Server is not being used or DNS is not configured, use **http://172.17.1.1** to access the web services configured on that server.

Step 3. Use FTP to download a file.

On Host1, launch a web browser and enter the URL **ftp://server.discovery.ccna**, or issue **ftp server.discovery.ccna** from the command line. If DNS is not configured, use the IP address 172.17.1.1 instead of the domain name.

Download a file from the server.

Note: If an e-mail client program is not installed on Host1, download the Thunderbird setup program file for use in the next step.

Step 4. If e-mail accounts have been configured using the POP3 and SMTP services on Discovery Server, send an e-mail using one of these accounts.

Note: If an e-mail client program is not installed on Host1, install the Thunderbird setup program file downloaded in the previous step. Lab 4-2 provides the Thunderbird e-mail client setup details.

Step 5. Set up Windows file sharing between Host1 and Host2 and copy a file from one to the other.

Task 5: View the Data Flows

At the conclusion of the data flow, view the details by issuing the **show ip cache verbose flow** command from privileged EXEC mode.

FC-CPE-1# **show ip cache verbose flow**

Examine the output and record the different data flows.

Application Type	Source	Destination	Comments

Task 6: Clean Up

Erase the configurations and reload the routers and switches. Disconnect and store the cabling. For PC hosts that are normally connected to other networks (such as the school LAN or the Internet), reconnect the appropriate cabling and restore the TCP/IP settings.

Challenge

This lab simulates LAN data traffic. The LAN data flows of a production network would be much more extensive and recorded over a greater period of time, perhaps a full working week.

1. On the FilmCompany initial current network topology shown in Figure 4-10, add PC host and printer icons as listed for each VLAN described in the case study document found in Appendix B. Draw a circle that encloses the local LAN segments.

2. Using the data flows recorded in this lab as a starting point, use different colors to mark the different LAN data flows between hosts and the server.

Figure 4-10   Existing FilmCompany Network Topology

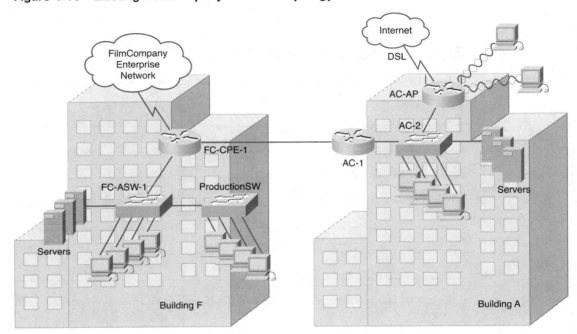

Lab 4-8: Diagramming Traffic Flows to and from Remote Sites (4.5.3)

Upon completion of this lab, you will be able to diagram the flow of traffic to and from remote sites.

This lab contains skills that relate to the following 640-802 CCNA exam objective:

- Use the OSI and TCP/IP models and their associated protocols to explain how data flows in a network.

Expected Results and Success Criteria

Before starting this lab, read through the tasks that you are expected to perform. What do you expect the result of performing these tasks will be?

_____

_____

_____

Why is diagramming remote network traffic flows useful in network administration?

_____

_____

_____

What can be learned from diagramming traffic flows to and from a remote network?

_____

_____

_____

Background/Preparation

FilmCompany is an expanding advertising company moving into interactive advertising media, including video presentations. This company has just been awarded a large video support contract by the StadiumCompany. With this new contract, FilmCompany expects to see their business grow approximately 70 percent.

To facilitate this expansion, the state of data flow across the current network has to be established so that the network upgrade can be planned and implemented.

Developing a diagram of applications, devices, and traffic flow enables the designer to analyze the proposed design and identify where the network can be improved. The logical topology diagram shows that the servers are identified with the applications that will be used. Areas that require redundancy or increased security are also easier to identify. Redundant paths to the server and security measures, such as a hardware firewall, can be marked on the diagram. The logical design for the network must be aligned with the initial business goals and technical requirements of the customer. The diagram gives the designer and customer a visual idea of what is already on the network and helps to get a better view of what is still required.

In this lab, you will use NetFlow to diagram the flow of traffic between a remote host at the stadium, the FilmCompany local network, and the data center. Preparing this diagram requires you to configure NetFlow on the three routers to determine the traffic generated across the network.

Task 1: Cable and Configure the Network

This lab will use the network topology shown in Figure 4-11, and the hostnames, addresses, and subnet masks given in Table 4-8.

Note: If the PCs used in this lab are also connected to your Academy LAN or to the Internet, ensure that you record the cable connections and TCP/IP settings so that these can be restored at the conclusion of the lab.

Figure 4-11   Lab 4-8 Network Topology

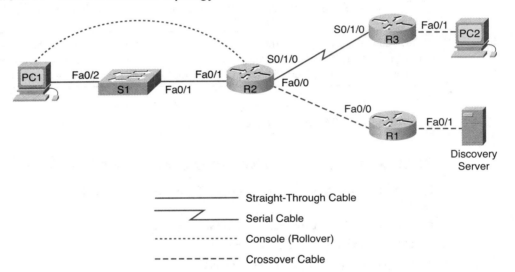

Table 4-8   Addressing Table for Lab 4-8

Device Designation	Device Name	Address	Subnet Mask
Discovery Server	Business Services	172.17.1.1	255.255.0.0
R1	FC-CPE-1	Fa0/1 172.17.0.1	255.255.0.0
		Fa0/0 10.10.0.1	255.255.255.252
R2	FC-CPE-2	Fa0/0 10.10.0.2	255.255.255.252
		Fa0/1 10.0.0.1	255.255.255.0
		S0/1/0 10.10.10.1	255.255.255.252
R3	ISP	Fa0/1 10.20.0.1	255.255.255.0
		S0/1/0 10.10.10.2	255.255.255.252
PC1	Local	10.0.0.200	255.255.255.0
PC2	Remote	10.20.0.200	255.255.255.0

Step 1.   Connect the devices in accordance with the network topology shown in Figure 4-11.

Note: Your instructor may substitute an equivalent server for Discovery Server for this lab.

Step 2. Configure PC1 and PC2 in accordance with the address and subnet mask details in Table 4-8.

Step 3. Establish a HyperTerminal, or other terminal emulation program, session from PC1 to R1. Configure R1 with the hostname, addresses, and subnet masks given in Table 4-8.

Step 4. Establish a HyperTerminal, or other terminal emulation program, session from PC1 to R2. Configure R2 with the hostname, addresses, and subnet masks given in Table 4-8.

Step 5. Establish a HyperTerminal, or other terminal emulation program, session from PC1 to R3. Configure R3 with the hostname, addresses, and subnet masks given in Table 4-8.

Step 6. Set a clock rate on the DCE interface of the serial link between R2 and R3. Routing will have to be configured on the three routers to establish data communications.

Note: You will need to use a terminal session to access all three routers during this lab. If the terminal program is running on PC1, it is suggested that you telnet from R2 to the other two routers. Alternately, PC2 could be used to maintain a terminal session with R3 and reduce the Telnet connections between routers to one.

Step 7. From PC1 and PC2, ping each other and the Discovery Server to confirm network connectivity. Troubleshoot and establish connectivity if the pings fail.

Task 2: Configure NetFlow on Router FC-CPE-1

From global configuration mode, issue the following commands to configure NetFlow on the router FC-CPE-1:

```
FC-CPE-1(config)# interface fastethernet 0/0
FC-CPE-1(config-if)# ip flow egress
FC-CPE-1(config-if)# ip flow ingress
FC-CPE-1(config-if)# interface fastethernet 0/1
FC-CPE-1(config-if)# ip flow ingress
FC-CPE-1(config-if)# ip flow egress
FC-CPE-2(config-if)# end
```

Task 3: Verify the NetFlow Configuration

Step 1. From privileged EXEC mode on router FC-CPE-1, issue the **show ip flow interface** command:

```
FC-CPE-1# show ip flow interface
FastEthernet0/0
  ip flow ingress
  ip flow egress
FastEthernet0/1
  ip flow ingress
  ip flow egress
```

Confirm that you see the preceding output. Troubleshoot your configuration if this output is not displayed.

Step 2.   From the privileged EXEC mode, issue the following command to ensure that flow cache statistics are reset:

```
FC-CPE-1# clear ip flow stats
```

Task 4: Configure NetFlow on Router FC-CPE-2

From global configuration mode, issue the following commands to configure NetFlow on the router FC-CPE-2:

```
FC-CPE-2(config)# interface fastethernet 0/0
FC-CPE-2(config-if)# ip flow egress
FC-CPE-2(config-if)# ip flow ingress
FC-CPE-2(config-if)# interface fastethernet 0/1
FC-CPE-2(config-if)# ip flow ingress
FC-CPE-2(config-if)# ip flow egress
FC-CPE-2(config-if)# interface serial 0/1/0
FC-CPE-2(config-if)# ip flow ingress
FC-CPE-2(config-if)# ip flow egress
FC-CPE-2(config-if)# end
```

Task 5: Verify the NetFlow Configuration

Step 1.   From privileged EXEC mode on router FC-CPE-2, issue the **show ip flow interface** command:

```
FC-CPE-2# show ip flow interface
FastEthernet0/0
  ip flow ingress
  ip flow egress
FastEthernet0/1
  ip flow ingress
  ip flow egress
Serial0/1/0
  ip flow ingress
  ip flow egress
```

Confirm that you see the preceding output. Troubleshoot your configuration if this output is not displayed.

Step 2.   From privileged EXEC mode, issue the following command to ensure that flow cache statistics are reset:

```
FC-CPE-2# clear ip flow stats
```

Task 6: Configure NetFlow on Router ISP

From global configuration mode, issue the following commands to configure NetFlow on the router ISP:

```
ISP(config)# interface fastethernet 0/1
ISP(config-if)# ip flow ingress
ISP(config-if)# ip flow egress
```

```
ISP(config-if)# interface serial 0/1/0
ISP(config-if)# ip flow ingress
ISP(config-if)# ip flow egress
ISP(config-if)# end
```

Task 7: Verify the NetFlow Configuration

Step 1.   From privileged EXEC mode on router ISP, issue the **show ip flow interface** command:

```
ISP# show ip flow interface
FastEthernet0/1
  ip flow ingress
  ip flow egress
Serial0/1/0
  ip flow ingress
  ip flow egress
```

Confirm that you see the preceding output. Troubleshoot your configuration if this output is not displayed.

Step 2.   From privileged EXEC mode, issue the following command to ensure that flow cache statistics are reset:

```
ISP# clear ip flow stats
```

Task 8: Create Network Data Traffic

A range of network application data flows between the remote site, the FilmCompany LAN, and the network server is to be generated and captured. Generate as many of the data flows outlined in the following steps as possible in your lab. Your instructor will advise you of the particular applications that are available to be used in this lab.

Step 1.   Access a web server.

On Host1 and Host2, launch a web browser and enter the URL **http://server.discovery.ccna**.

If Discovery Server is not being used or DNS is not configured, use **http://172.17.1.1** to access the web services configured on that server.

Step 2.   Use FTP to download a file.

On Host1 and Host2, launch a web browser and enter the URL **ftp://server.discovery.ccna**, or issue **ftp server.discovery.ccna** from the command line. If DNS is not configured use the IP address 172.17.1.1 instead of the domain name.

Download a file from the server to each PC.

Note: If an e-mail client program is not installed on the PCs, download the Thunderbird setup program file for use in the next step.

Step 3.   If e-mail accounts have been configured using the POP3 and SMTP services on Discovery Server, send an e-mail using one of these accounts.

Note: If an e-mail client program is not installed on the PCs, install the Thunderbird setup program file downloaded in the previous step. Lab 4-2 provides the Thunderbird e-mail client setup details.

Step 4.   To simulate data traffic between the two PCs, ping between them. Attempt to establish a Telnet session between the two PCs. If file sharing has been enabled, copy a file in both directions between the two.

Task 9: View the Data Flows

Step 1.   At the conclusion of the data flow, view the details by issuing the **show ip cache verbose flow** command from privileged EXEC mode on each router.

For router FC-CPE-1:

```
FC-CPE-1# show ip cache verbose flow
FC-CPE-2# show ip cache verbose flow
ISP# show ip cache verbose flow
```

Step 2.   Examine the output and record the different data flows for each router.

Router FC-CPE-1 Data Flows

Application Type	Source	Destination	Comments

Router FC-CPE-2 Data Flows

Application Type	Source	Destination	Comments

Router ISP Data Flows

Application Type	Source	Destination	Comments

Step 3.   Discuss and compare the data flows for each router. Particularly, consider how recording these flows can assist in understanding which network devices and resources are used for particular flows.

Task 10: Clean Up

Erase the configurations and reload the routers and switches. Disconnect and store the cabling. For PC hosts that are normally connected to other networks (such as the school LAN or the Internet), reconnect the appropriate cabling and restore the TCP/IP settings.

Challenge

This lab simulates the flow of traffic to and from FilmCompany remote sites. These data flows for a production network would be much more extensive and recorded over a greater period of time, perhaps a full working week. Additionally, remote access would most likely be established using VPNs (Virtual Private Networks) across the Internet or a WAN.

1. On the FilmCompany initial current network topology shown in Figure 4-12, add two remote site hosts attached to the "far" side of the Internet cloud icon. Draw a circle that encloses the remote access links to the FilmCompany network and servers in Building F. In this case study, initially, the FilmCompany remote sites access the network across the Internet.

2. One of the objects of this analysis is to establish the benefits of using a dedicated WAN link using Frame Relay for the stadium-based remote sites to directly access the FilmCompany network.

   Using the data flows recorded in this lab as a starting point, use different colors to mark on the diagram the different data flows between the remote hosts and devices on the FilmCompany network.

Figure 4-12   Existing FilmCompany Network Topology

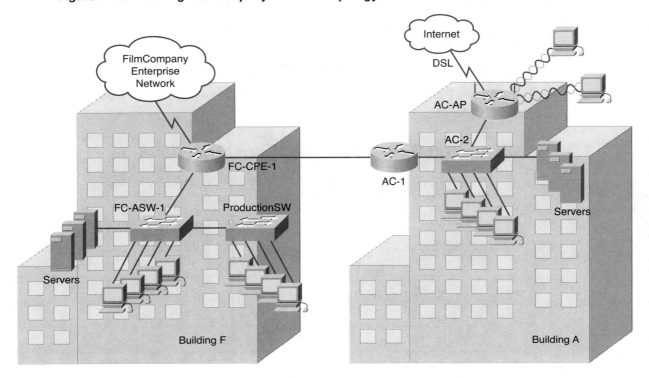

Lab 4-9: Diagramming External Traffic Flows (4.5.4)

Upon completion of this lab, you will be able to diagram traffic flows destined to the Internet gateway and incoming from the Internet to locally provided services.

This lab contains skills that relate to the following 640-802 CCNA exam objective:

- Use the OSI and TCP/IP models and their associated protocols to explain how data flows in a network.

Expected Results and Success Criteria

Before starting this lab, read through the tasks that you are expected to perform. What do you expect the result of performing these tasks will be?

_____

_____

_____

Why is diagramming Internet traffic flows useful in network administration?

_____

_____

_____

What can be learned from diagramming traffic flows to and from the Internet?

_____

_____

_____

Background/Preparation

FilmCompany is an expanding advertising company moving into interactive advertising media, including video presentations. This company has just been awarded a large video support contract by the StadiumCompany. With this new contract, FilmCompany expects to see their business grow approximately 70 percent.

To facilitate this expansion, the state of data flow across the current network has to be established so that the network upgrade can be planned and implemented.

Developing a diagram of applications, devices, and traffic flow enables the designer to analyze the proposed design and identify where the network can be improved. The logical topology diagram shows that the servers are identified with the applications that will be used. Areas that require redundancy or increased security are also easier to identify. Redundant paths to the server and security measures, such as a hardware firewall, can be marked on the diagram. The logical design for the network must be aligned with the initial business goals and technical requirements of the customer. The diagram gives the designer and customer a visual idea of what is already on the network and helps to get a better view of what is still required.

You will use NetFlow to identify the applications traffic that is destined for the Internet gateway and incoming traffic from the Internet to the local resources. Preparing this diagram requires you to configure NetFlow on the three routers to determine the traffic generated across the network. By determining the traffic flows associated with the Internet, internal or external, the designer can assess the need for redundancy and security to facilitate the traffic that is generated.

In this lab, PC2 represents a host on the Internet that communicates with the FilmCompany network.

Task 1: Cable and Configure the Network

This lab will use the network topology shown in Figure 4-13, and the hostnames, addresses, and subnet masks given in Table 4-9.

Note: If the PCs used in this lab are also connected to your Academy LAN or to the Internet, ensure that you record the cable connections and TCP/IP settings so that these can be restored at the conclusion of the lab.

Figure 4-13   Lab 4-9 Network Topology

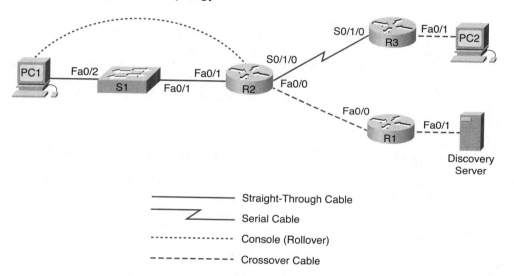

Table 4-9   Addressing Table for Lab 4-9

Device Designation	Device Name	Address	Subnet Mask
Discovery Server	Business Services	172.17.1.1	255.255.0.0
R1	FC-CPE-1	Fa0/1 172.17.0.1	255.255.0.0
		Fa0/0 10.10.0.1	255.255.255.252
R2	FC-CPE-2	Fa0/0 10.10.0.2	255.255.255.252
		Fa0/1 10.0.0.1	255.255.255.0
		S0/1/0 10.10.10.1	255.255.255.252
R3	ISP	Fa0/1 10.20.0.1	255.255.255.0
		S0/1/0 10.10.10.2	255.255.255.252
PC1	Local	10.0.0.200	255.255.255.0
PC2	Remote	10.20.0.200	255.255.255.0

Step 1.   Connect the devices in accordance with the network topology shown in Figure 4-13.

Note: Your instructor may substitute an equivalent server for Discovery Server for this lab.

Step 2.   Configure PC1 and PC2 in accordance with the address and subnet mask details in Table 4-9.

Step 3.   Establish a HyperTerminal, or other terminal emulation program, session from PC1 to R1. Configure R1 with the hostname, addresses, and subnet masks given in Table 4-9.

Step 4.   Establish a HyperTerminal, or other terminal emulation program, session from PC1 to R2. Configure R2 with the hostname, addresses, and subnet masks given in Table 4-9.

Step 5.   Establish a HyperTerminal, or other terminal emulation program, session from PC1 to R3. Configure R3 with the hostname, addresses, and subnet masks given in Table 4-9.

Step 6.   Set a clock rate on the DCE interface of the serial link between R2 and R3. Routing will have to be configured on the three routers to establish data communications.

Note: You will need to use a terminal session to access all three routers during this lab. If the terminal program is running on PC1, it is suggested that you telnet from R2 to the other two routers. Alternately, PC2 could be used to maintain a terminal session with R3 and reduce the Telnet connections between routers to one.

Step 7.   From PC1 and PC2, ping each other and the Discovery Server to confirm network connectivity. Troubleshoot and establish connectivity if the pings fail.

Task 2: Configure NetFlow on Router FC-CPE-1

From global configuration mode, issue the following commands to configure NetFlow on the router FC-CPE-1:

```
FC-CPE-1(config)# interface fastethernet 0/0
FC-CPE-1(config-if)# ip flow egress
FC-CPE-1(config-if)# ip flow ingress
FC-CPE-1(config-if)# interface fastethernet 0/1
FC-CPE-1(config-if)# ip flow ingress
FC-CPE-1(config-if)# ip flow egress
FC-CPE-1(config-if)# end
```

Task 3: Verify the NetFlow Configuration

Step 1.   From privileged EXEC mode on router FC-CPE-1, issue the **show ip flow interface** command:

```
FC-CPE-1# show ip flow interface
FastEthernet0/0
  ip flow ingress
  ip flow egress
FastEthernet0/1
  ip flow ingress
  ip flow egress
```

Confirm that you see the preceding output. Troubleshoot your configuration if this output is not displayed.

Step 2.   From privileged EXEC mode, issue the following command to ensure that flow cache statistics are reset:

```
FC-CPE-1# clear ip flow stats
```

Task 4: Configure NetFlow on Router FC-CPE-2

From global configuration mode, issue the following commands to configure NetFlow on the router FC-CPE-2:

```
FC-CPE-2(config)# interface fastethernet 0/0
FC-CPE-2(config-if)# ip flow egress
FC-CPE-2(config-if)# ip flow ingress
FC-CPE-2(config-if)# interface fastethernet 0/1
FC-CPE-2(config-if)# ip flow ingress
FC-CPE-2(config-if)# ip flow egress
FC-CPE-2(config-if)# interface serial 0/1/0
FC-CPE-2(config-if)# ip flow ingress
FC-CPE-2(config-if)# ip flow egress
FC-CPE-2(config-if)# end
```

Task 5: Verify the NetFlow Configuration

Step 1.   From privileged EXEC mode on router FC-CPE-2, issue the **show ip flow interface** command.

```
FC-CPE-2# show ip flow interface
FastEthernet0/0
  ip flow ingress
  ip flow egress
FastEthernet0/1
  ip flow ingress
  ip flow egress
Serial0/1/0
  ip flow ingress
  ip flow egress
```

Confirm that you see the preceding output. Troubleshoot your configuration if this output is not displayed.

Step 2.   From the privileged EXEC mode, issue the following command to ensure that flow cache statistics are reset:

```
FC-CPE-2# clear ip flow stats
```

Task 6: Configure NetFlow on Router ISP

From global configuration mode, issue the following commands to configure NetFlow on the router ISP:

```
ISP(config)# interface fastethernet 0/1
ISP(config-if)# ip flow ingress
ISP(config-if)# ip flow egress
ISP(config-if)# interface serial 0/1/0
```

```
ISP(config-if)# ip flow ingress
ISP(config-if)# ip flow egress
ISP(config-if)# end
```

Task 7: Verify the NetFlow Configuration

Step 1. From privileged EXEC mode on router ISP, issue the **show ip flow interface** command:

```
ISP# show ip flow interface
FastEthernet0/1
  ip flow ingress
  ip flow egress
Serial0/1/0
  ip flow ingress
  ip flow egress
```

Confirm that you see the preceding output. Troubleshoot your configuration if this output is not displayed.

Step 2. From privileged EXEC mode, issue the following command to ensure that flow cache statistics are reset:

```
ISP# clear ip flow stats
```

Task 8: Create Network Data Traffic

A range of Internet application data flows between PC2 (the Internet) and the FilmCompany network is to be generated and captured. Generate as many of the data flows outlined in the following steps as possible in your lab. Your instructor will advise you of the particular applications that are available and to be used in this lab.

Step 1. Access a web server.

On PC2 launch a web browser and enter the URL **http://server.discovery.ccna**.

If Discovery Server is not being used or DNS is not configured, use **http://172.17.1.1** to access the web services configured on that server.

Step 2. Use FTP to download a file.

On PC2 launch a web browser and enter the URL **ftp://server.discovery.ccna**, or issue **ftp server.discovery.ccna** from the command line. If DNS is not configured, use the IP address 172.17.1.1 instead of the domain name.

Download a file from the server to each PC.

Note: If an e-mail client program is not installed on the PC, download the Thunderbird setup program file for use in the next step.

Step 3. If e-mail accounts have been configured using the POP3 and SMTP services on Discovery Server, send an e-mail from PC2 using one of these accounts.

Note: If an e-mail client program is not installed on the PCs, install the Thunderbird set up program file downloaded in the previous step. Lab 4-2 provides the Thunderbird e-mail client setup details.

Task 9: View the Data Flows

Step 1. At the conclusion of the data flow, view the details by issuing the **show ip cache verbose flow** command from privileged EXEC mode on each router.

For router FC-CPE-1:

```
FC-CPE-1# show ip cache verbose flow
FC-CPE-2# show ip cache verbose flow
ISP# show ip cache verbose flow
```

Step 2. Examine the output and record the different data flows for each router.

Router FC-CPE-1 Data Flows

Application Type	Source	Destination	Comments

Router FC-CPE-2 Data Flows

Application Type	Source	Destination	Comments

Router ISP Data Flows

Application Type	Source	Destination	Comments

Step 3. Discuss and compare the data flows for each router. Particularly consider how these flows differ from those in Lab 4-8 and the implications of this difference in understanding which network devices and resources are used for particular flows.

Task 10: Clean Up

Erase the configurations and reload the routers and switches. Disconnect and store the cabling. For PC hosts that are normally connected to other networks (such as the school LAN or the Internet), reconnect the appropriate cabling and restore the TCP/IP settings.

Challenge

This lab simulates the flow of traffic to and from FilmCompany network and the Internet. These data flows for a production network would be much more extensive and recorded over a greater period of time, perhaps a full working week.

On the FilmCompany initial current network topology shown in Figure 4-14, highlight the network Internet link.

Using the data flows recorded in this lab as a starting point, use different colors to mark on the diagram the different possible data flows between the hosts and devices on the FilmCompany network to and from the Internet.

Figure 4-14   Existing FilmCompany Network Topology

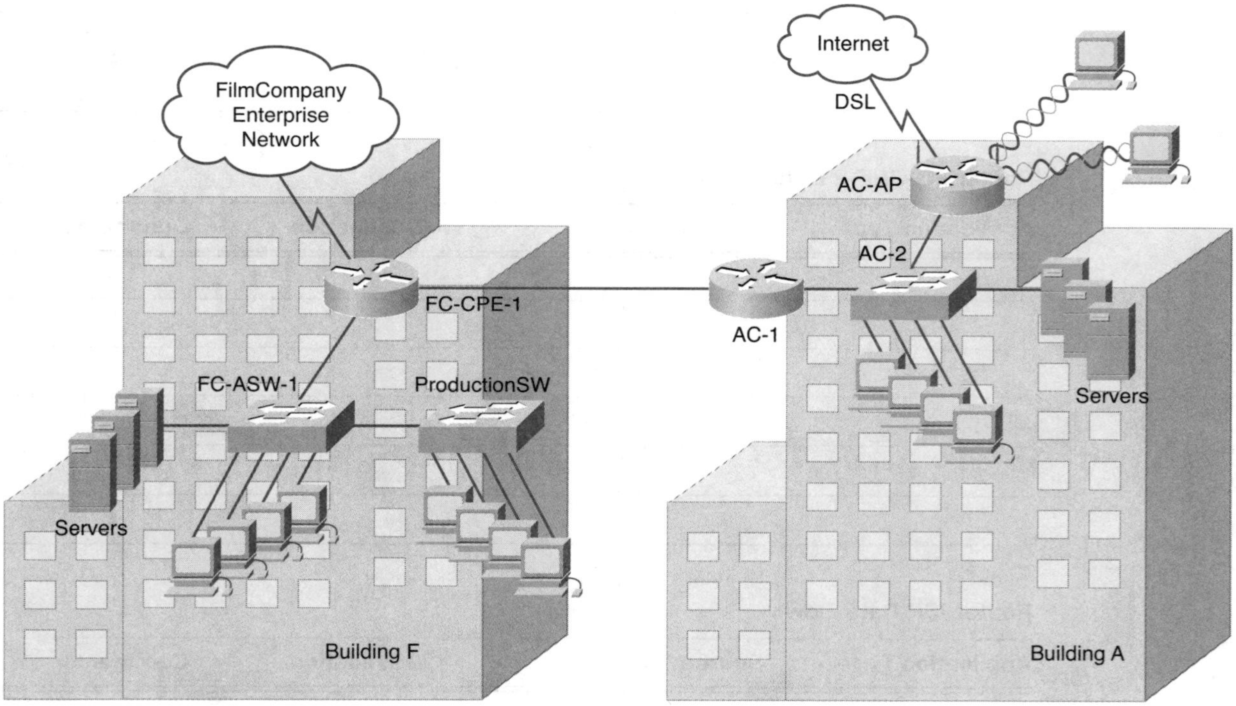

Lab 4-10: Diagramming Extranet Traffic Flows (4.5.5)

Upon completion of this lab, you will be able to use NetFlow to diagram FilmCompany Extranet traffic flows.

This lab contains skills that relate to the following 640-802 CCNA exam objective:

- Use the OSI and TCP/IP models and their associated protocols to explain how data flows in a network.

Expected Results and Success Criteria

Before starting this lab, read through the tasks that you are expected to perform. What do you expect the result of performing these tasks will be?

_____

_____

_____

Why is diagramming extranet traffic flows useful in network administration?

_____

_____

_____

What can be learned from diagramming traffic flows to and from the extranet?

_____

_____

_____

Background/Preparation

FilmCompany is an expanding advertising company moving into interactive advertising media, including video presentations. This company has just been awarded a large video support contract by the StadiumCompany. With this new contract, FilmCompany expects to see their business grow approximately 70 percent.

To facilitate this expansion, the state of data flow across the current network has to be established so that the network upgrade can be planned and implemented.

Developing a diagram of applications, devices, and traffic flow enables the designer to analyze the proposed design and identify where the network can be improved. The logical topology diagram shows that the servers are identified with the applications that will be used. Areas that require redundancy or increased security are also easier to identify. Redundant paths to the server and security measures, such as a hardware firewall, can be marked on the diagram. The logical design for the network must be aligned with the initial business goals and technical requirements of the customer. The diagram gives the designer and customer a visual idea of what is already on the network and helps to get a better view of what is still required.

In this lab, you will use NetFlow to diagram the flow of traffic to and from two trusted remote partners, or customers, at the stadium to the FilmCompany network. Preparing this diagram requires you to identify the remote hosts and determine the traffic generated across the network, both from the hosts and from the FilmCompany server.

In this lab, PC2 represents a host on the FilmCompany extranet that communicates with the FilmCompany network.

Task 1: Cable and Configure the Network

This lab will use the network topology shown in Figure 4-15, and the hostnames, addresses, and subnet masks given in Table 4-10.

Note: If the PCs used in this lab are also connected to your Academy LAN or to the Internet, ensure that you record the cable connections and TCP/IP settings so that these can be restored at the conclusion of the lab.

Figure 4-15   Lab 4-10 Network Topology

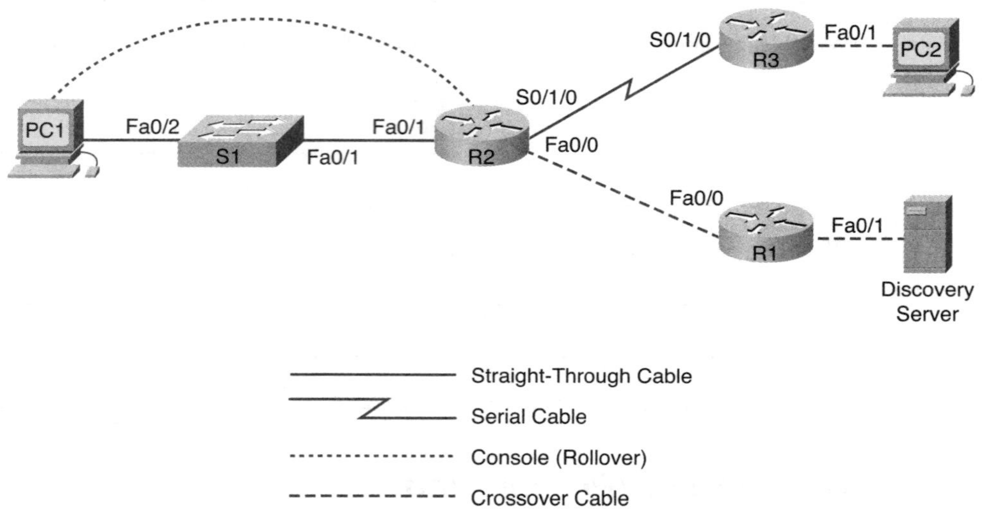

Table 4-10   Addressing Table for Lab 4-10

Device Designation	Device Name	Address	Subnet Mask
Discovery Server	Business Services	172.17.1.1	255.255.0.0
R1	FC-CPE-1	Fa0/1 172.17.0.1	255.255.0.0
		Fa0/0 10.10.0.1	255.255.255.252
R2	FC-CPE-2	Fa0/0 10.10.0.2	255.255.255.252
		Fa0/1 10.0.0.1	255.255.255.0
		S0/1/0 10.10.10.1	255.255.255.252
R3	ISP	Fa0/1 10.20.0.1	255.255.255.0
		S0/1/0 10.10.10.2	255.255.255.252
PC1	Video Workstation	10.0.0.200	255.255.255.0
PC2	Extranet Host	10.20.0.200	255.255.255.0

Step 1.   Connect the devices in accordance with the network topology shown in Figure 4-15.

Note: Your instructor may substitute an equivalent server for Discovery Server for this lab.

Step 2.   Configure PC1 and PC2 in accordance with the address and subnet mask details in Table 4-10.

Step 3.   Establish a HyperTerminal, or other terminal emulation program, session from PC1 to R1. Configure R1 with the hostname, addresses, and subnet masks given in Table 4-10.

Step 4.   Establish a HyperTerminal, or other terminal emulation program, session from PC1 to R2. Configure R2 with the hostname, addresses, and subnet masks given in Table 4-10.

Step 5.   Establish a HyperTerminal, or other terminal emulation program, session from PC1 to R3. Configure R3 with the hostname, addresses, and subnet masks given in Table 4-10.

Step 6.   Set a clock rate on the DCE interface of the serial link between R2 and R3. Routing will have to be configured on the three routers to establish data communications.

Note: You will need to use a terminal session to access all three routers during this lab. If the terminal program is running on PC1, it is suggested that you telnet from R2 to the other two routers. Alternately, PC2 could be used to maintain a terminal session with R3 and reduce the Telnet connections between routers to one.

Step 7.   From PC1 and PC2, ping each other and Discovery Server to confirm network connectivity. Troubleshoot and establish connectivity if the pings fail.

Task 2: Configure NetFlow on Router FC-CPE-1

From global configuration mode, issue the following commands to configure NetFlow on the router FC-CPE-1:

```
FC-CPE-1(config)# interface fastethernet 0/0
FC-CPE-1(config-if)# ip flow egress
FC-CPE-1(config-if)# ip flow ingress
FC-CPE-1(config-if)# interface fastethernet 0/1
FC-CPE-1(config-if)# ip flow ingress
FC-CPE-1(config-if)# ip flow egress
FC-CPE-1(config-if)# end
```

Task 3: Verify the NetFlow Configuration

Step 1.   From privileged EXEC mode on router FC-CPE-1, issue the show ip flow interface command:

```
FC-CPE-1# show ip flow interface
FastEthernet0/0
  ip flow ingress
  ip flow egress
FastEthernet0/1
  ip flow ingress
  ip flow egress
```

Confirm that you see the preceding output. Troubleshoot your configuration if this output is not displayed.

Step 2.   From privileged EXEC mode, issue the following command to ensure that flow cache statistics are reset:

```
FC-CPE-1# clear ip flow stats
```

Task 4: Configure NetFlow on Router FC-CPE-2

From global configuration mode, issue the following commands to configure NetFlow on the router FC-CPE-2:

```
FC-CPE-2(config)# interface fastethernet 0/0
FC-CPE-2(config-if)# ip flow egress
FC-CPE-2(config-if)# ip flow ingress
FC-CPE-2(config-if)# interface fastethernet 0/1
FC-CPE-2(config-if)# ip flow ingress
FC-CPE-2(config-if)# ip flow egress
FC-CPE-2(config-if)# interface serial 0/1/0
FC-CPE-2(config-if)# ip flow ingress
FC-CPE-2(config-if)# ip flow egress
FC-CPE-2(config-if)# end
```

Task 5: Verify the NetFlow Configuration

Step 1.   From privileged EXEC mode on router FC-CPE-2, issue the **show ip flow interface** command:

```
FC-CPE-2# show ip flow interface
FastEthernet0/0
  ip flow ingress
  ip flow egress
FastEthernet0/1
  ip flow ingress
  ip flow egress
Serial0/1/0
  ip flow ingress
  ip flow egress
```

Confirm that you see the preceding output. Troubleshoot your configuration if this output is not displayed.

Step 2.   From privileged EXEC mode, issue the following command to ensure that flow cache statistics are reset:

```
FC-CPE-2# clear ip flow stats
```

Task 6: Configure NetFlow on Router ISP

From global configuration mode, issue the following commands to configure NetFlow on the router ISP:

```
ISP(config)# interface fastethernet 0/1
ISP(config-if)# ip flow ingress
ISP(config-if)# ip flow egress
```

```
ISP(config-if)# interface serial 0/1/0
ISP(config-if)# ip flow ingress
ISP(config-if)# ip flow egress
ISP(config-if)# end
```

Task 7: Verify the NetFlow Configuration

Step 1.   From privileged EXEC mode on router ISP, issue the **show ip flow interface** command:

```
ISP# show ip flow interface
FastEthernet0/1
  ip flow ingress
  ip flow egress
Serial0/1/0
  ip flow ingress
  ip flow egress
```

Confirm that you see the preceding output. Troubleshoot your configuration if this output is not displayed.

Step 2.   From privileged EXEC mode, issue the following command to ensure that flow cache statistics are reset:

```
ISP# clear ip flow stats
```

Task 8: Create Network Data Traffic

Ideally, a range of network application data flows between the trusted extranet host PC2 and PC1 on the FilmCompany LAN should be generated and captured. Generate as many of the data flows resulting from the following steps as possible in your lab. Your instructor will advise you of the particular applications that are available and to be used in this lab.

To simulate data traffic between the two PCs:

Step 1.   Ping between them.

Step 2.   Attempt to establish a Telnet session between the two PCs.

Step 3.   If you have rights, enable file sharing and copy a file in both directions between the two PCs.

Task 9: View the Data Flows

Step 1.   At the conclusion of the data flow, view the details by issuing the **show ip cache verbose flow** command from privileged EXEC mode on each router.

For router FC-CPE-1:

```
FC-CPE-1# show ip cache verbose flow
FC-CPE-2# show ip cache verbose flow
ISP# show ip cache verbose flow
```

Step 2.   Examine the output and record the different data flows for each router.

Router FC-CPE-1 Data Flows

Application Type	Source	Destination	Comments

Router FC-CPE-2 Data Flows

Application Type	Source	Destination	Comments

Router ISP Data Flows

Application Type	Source	Destination	Comments

Step 3.   Discuss and compare the data flows for each router. Particularly consider how these flows differ from those in the previous labs and the implications of this difference in understanding which network devices and resources are used for particular flows.

Task 10: Clean Up

Erase the configurations and reload the routers and switches. Disconnect and store the cabling. For PC hosts that are normally connected to other networks (such as the school LAN or the Internet), reconnect the appropriate cabling and restore the TCP/IP settings.

Challenge

This lab simulates the flow of traffic to and from FilmCompany and from selected trusted partners and customers. These data flows for a production network would be much more extensive and recorded over a greater period of time, perhaps a full working week. Additionally, remote access from trusted sites would most likely be established using VPNs (Virtual Private Networks) across the Internet or a WAN.

On the FilmCompany initial current network topology shown in Figure 4-16, add two trusted remote site hosts attached to the "far" side of the Internet cloud icon. Draw a circle that encloses the remote access links to the FilmCompany network and server. In this case study, initially, the FilmCompany remote sites access its network across the Internet.

One of the objects of this analysis is to establish the benefits of using a dedicated WAN link using Frame Relay for the stadium-based remote sites to access the FilmCompany network.

Then, using the data flows recorded in this lab as a starting point, use different colors to mark on the diagram the different extranet data flows between the trusted remote hosts and devices on the FilmCompany network.

Diagram traffic flows to and from selected trusted partners, customers, and vendors.

Figure 4-16   Existing FilmCompany Network Topology

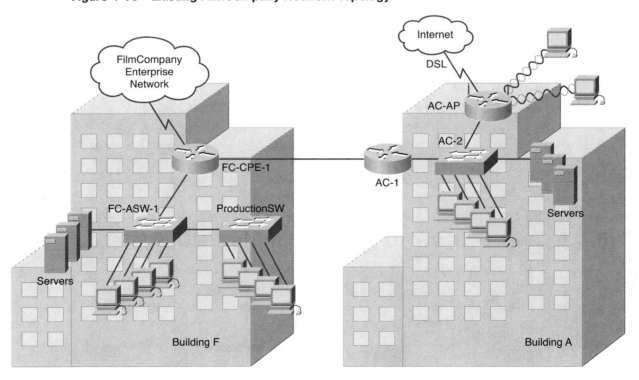

Creating the Network Design: Labs

The lab exercises included in this chapter cover all the Chapter 5 online curriculum labs to ensure that you have mastered the practical, hands-on skills needed to investigate and determine the business goals and technical requirements that will enable the creation of the network design. As you work through these labs, use Chapter 5 in Part I of this book or use the corresponding Chapter 5 in the Discovery Designing and Supporting Computer Networks online curriculum for assistance.

 ## Lab 5-1: Applying Design Constraints (5.1.1)

Upon completion of this lab, you will be able to analyze the business goals and technical requirements and apply the constraints to begin the design.

Expected Results and Success Criteria

Before starting this lab, read through the tasks that you are expected to perform. What do you expect the result of performing these tasks will be?

_____

_____

_____

Why is identifying the constraints that apply to a project an important part of the network design?

_____

_____

_____

Background/Preparation

FilmCompany is an expanding advertising company moving into interactive advertising media, including video presentations. This company has just been awarded a big video-support contract by the StadiumCompany. With this new contract, FilmCompany expects to see its business grow approximately 70 percent.

To facilitate this growth, the FilmCompany has decided to significantly upgrade its data network. You have the role of network design consultant. Your job is to develop network design and project documents for the FilmCompany that will meet the requirements of this upgrade.

This lab is one of a series of labs that explore the FilmCompany existing network and its upgrade requirements.

A comprehensive network project plan has to include details of constraints that apply to the project and potential trade-offs that need to be made. In this lab, you use the identified organizational constraints from the FilmCompany case study and adjust your design according to the trade-offs identified. These constraints will be used in the decision-making process for the proposed design.

Task 1: Identify Possible Project Constraints

Step 1.   Use word processing software to create a new Project Constraints document.

Step 2.   The identified constraints that set limits or boundaries on the network upgrade project should be entered into the Gathered Data field of the Project Constraints document. Brainstorm ideas with other students to identify additional constraints.

Classify each constraint as one of the following four types:

- Budget
- Policy
- Schedule
- Personnel

Task 2: Tabulate Comments Based on Identified Constraints

Step 1.   Using the list of constraints discovered from the FilmCompany case study, apply appropriate comments on how the constraints affect the design.

Step 2.   Enter the comments into Table 5-1.

Table 5-1   **FilmCompany Constraints**

Constraint	Gathered Data	Comments
Budget		
Policy		
Schedule		
Personnel		

Step 3.   Save your Project Constraints checklist.

Task 3: Identify Trade-Offs

Step 1.   Use word processing software to create an addition to the Project Constraints document.

Step 2.   The identified constraints that set limits or boundaries on the network upgrade project will require potential trade-offs. Discuss ideas about trade-offs for proposed designs with other students.

_____

_____

_____

_____

_____

_____

_____

Step 3.   Record the trade-offs in your Project Constraints checklist.

Step 4.   Save your Project Constraints checklist. Place a copy in your design project portfolio.

Reflection

The constraints imposed on this network design project are determined by the internal requirements of the FilmCompany. Consider and discuss the identified constraints and potential trade-offs. Do the trade-offs pose a significant obstacle to the design? Can alternative methods be used to achieve the success criteria without a significant budget increase?

_____

_____

_____

_____

_____

_____

_____

Lab 5-2: Identifying Design Strategies for Scalability (5.1.2)

Upon completion of this lab, you will be able to use the identified constraints and trade-offs to create design strategies for scalability.

Expected Results and Success Criteria

Before starting this lab, read through the tasks that you are expected to perform. What do you expect the result of performing these tasks will be?

_____

_____

_____

Why is identifying a design strategy that applies to a project an important part of the network design?

_____

_____

_____

How can developing multiple design strategies assist in the completion of the project?

_____

_____

_____

Background/Preparation

FilmCompany is an expanding advertising company moving into interactive advertising media, including video presentations. This company has just been awarded a big video-support contract by the StadiumCompany. With this new contract, FilmCompany expects to see its business grow approximately 70 percent.

To facilitate this growth, the FilmCompany has decided to significantly upgrade its data network. You have the role of network design consultant. Your job is to develop network design and project documents for the FilmCompany that will meet the requirements of this upgrade.

This lab is one of a series of labs that explore the FilmCompany existing network and its upgrade requirements.

A comprehensive network project plan has to include details of constraints that apply to the project and potential trade-offs that need to be made. In this lab, you use the identified organizational constraints from the FilmCompany case study and adjust your design according to the trade-offs identified. These constraints will be used in the decision-making process for the proposed design and allow the creation of design strategies that facilitate network scalability.

Task 1: Identify Useful Areas for a Design Strategy That Facilitates Scalability

Step 1.   Use word processing software to create a new document called Design Strategies.

Step 2.   Use the identified constraints that set limits or boundaries on the network upgrade project and the potential trade-offs to assist in the discussion with other students.

The strategy should cover the following areas:

- Access layer modules that can be added

- Expandable, modular equipment or clustered devices that can be easily upgraded

- Choosing routers or multilayer switches to limit broadcasts and filter traffic

- Planned redundancy

- An IP address strategy that is hierarchal and that supports summarization

- Identification of VLANs needed

Task 2: Create an Access Layer Module Design

Using the list developed from the group discussion, create an access layer module (design only).

Step 1.   Create your design using the existing equipment.

The FilmCompany network equipment includes the following:

- Two 1841 Routers (FC-CPE-1, FC-CPE-2)

- Three 2960 Switches (FC-ASW-1, FC-ASW-2, ProductionSW)

- Several servers

- One Linksys WRT300N wireless router (FC-AP)

- One ADSL modem for Internet access

Step 2.   Using the list of equipment, identify modules that can be added to the existing equipment to support new features and devices without requiring major equipment upgrades.

Step 3.   Save your Design Strategies documentation.

Task 3: Select Distribution Layer Devices

Step 1.   Use word processing software to create an addition to the Design Strategies document.

Step 2.   Use the identified access layer module design (created in Task 2) to create the distribution layer design. Equipment selected must include existing equipment. Use Layer 3 devices at the distribution layer to filter and reduce traffic to the network core.

Step 3.   With a modular Layer 3 distribution layer design, new access layer modules can be connected without requiring major reconfiguration. Using your documentation, identify which modules can be added to increase bandwidth.

Step 4.   Save your Design Strategies document. Place a copy in your design project portfolio.

Reflection

The constraints and trade-offs identified for the FilmCompany pose many challenges for the designer. What were some of the more difficult challenges you encountered?

_____

_____

_____

_____

Consider and discuss the identified strategies that will facilitate scalability. Do all the strategies designed accomplish the task the same way?

_____

_____

_____

Would one be less expensive or less time-consuming than the other?

_____

_____

_____

_____

Lab 5-3: Identifying Availability Strategies (5.1.3)

Upon completion of this lab, you will be able to use the identified availability strategies to assist in the design of a network.

Expected Results and Success Criteria

Before starting this lab, read through the tasks that you are expected to perform. What do you expect the result of performing these tasks will be?

_____

_____

_____

Why is identifying an availability strategy that applies to a project an important part of the network design?

_____

_____

_____

How can developing availability strategies assist in the completion of the project?

_____

_____

_____

Background/Preparation

FilmCompany is an expanding advertising company moving into interactive advertising media, including video presentations. This company has just been awarded a big video-support contract by the StadiumCompany. With this new contract, FilmCompany expects to see its business grow approximately 70 percent.

To facilitate this growth, the FilmCompany has decided to significantly upgrade its data network. You have the role of network design consultant. Your job is to develop network design and project documents for the FilmCompany that will meet the requirements of this upgrade.

This lab specifically considers design strategies that facilitate availability. It is one of a series of labs that explore the FilmCompany existing network and its upgrade requirements.

Task 1: Identify Areas Useful for a Design Strategy that Facilitates Availability

Step 1.   Use word processing software to create a new document called Availability Strategies.

Step 2.   Use the identified constraints that set limits or boundaries on the network upgrade project and the potential trade-offs to assist in brainstorming ideas with other students.

The strategy should cover the following areas:

Availability strategies for switches:

- Redundant power supplies and modules
- Hot-swappable cards and controllers
- Redundant links
- UPS and generator power

Availability strategies for routers:

- Redundant power supplies, UPS, and generator power
- Redundant devices
- Redundant links
- Out-of-band management
- Fast converging routing protocols

Availability strategies for Internet/enterprise edge:

- Dual ISP providers or dual connectivity to a single provider
- Co-located servers
- Secondary DNS servers

Task 2: Create Availability Strategies for Switches

Step 1.   Using the list developed from the brainstorming session, create a list of equipment that will be incorporated into the availability strategy.

_____

_____

_____

_____

_____

_____

Step 2.   Using the list of equipment, identify modules and redundant power supplies that will increase availability for the switches.

_____

_____

_____

Step 3.   Research and identify potential hot-swappable cards and controllers that can be used. Create a list that identifies each with cost and features.

_____

_____

Step 4.   Using Figure 5-1 as a base, develop a diagram that shows potential redundant switch links that can be incorporated into the network design.

Figure 5-1   Potential Topology with Redundant Switch Links

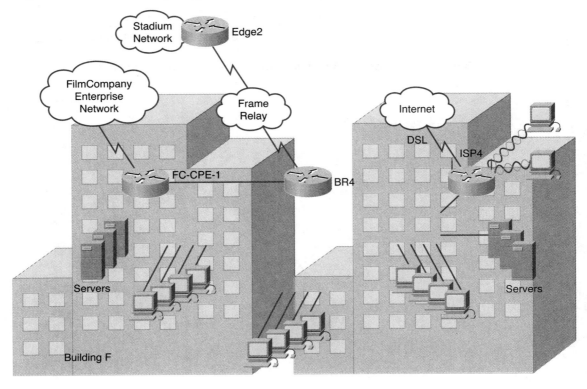

Step 5.   Use an Internet search engine to research and identify at least two possible UPS devices suitable for networking devices that can be incorporated into the design. Create a list that identifies features such the cost, specifications, and performance of each.

_____

_____

Step 6.   Save your Availability Strategies document.

Task 3: Create Availability Strategies for Routers

Step 1.   Use word processing software to create an addition to the Availability Strategies document.

Step 2.   Using the list of equipment, identify redundant power supplies that will increase availability for the routers.

_____

_____

_____

Step 3. Identify potential redundant routers and links that can be used. Research and create a list of the devices with identified features and, if possible, the local price.

_____

_____

Step 4. Using Figure 5-2 as a base, create a diagram that displays the redundant router connections.

Figure 5-2   Potential Topology with Redundant Router Links

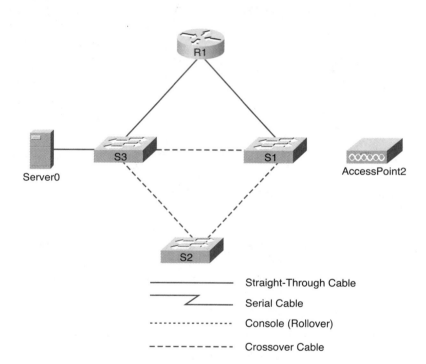

Step 5. Develop a list of potential routing protocols that will facilitate fast convergence times.

Step 6. Save your Availability Strategies document.

Task 4: Create Availability Strategies for Internet/Enterprise Edge

Step 1. Use word processing software to create an addition to the Availability Strategies document.

Step 2. Identify provider options available that would allow for dual ISP or dual connectivity to a single provider.

Step 3. Using Figure 5-3 as a base, create a topology design that will co-locate the servers to allow for redundancy and ease of maintenance.

Figure 5-3   Potential Topology with Redundant Edge/Internet Links

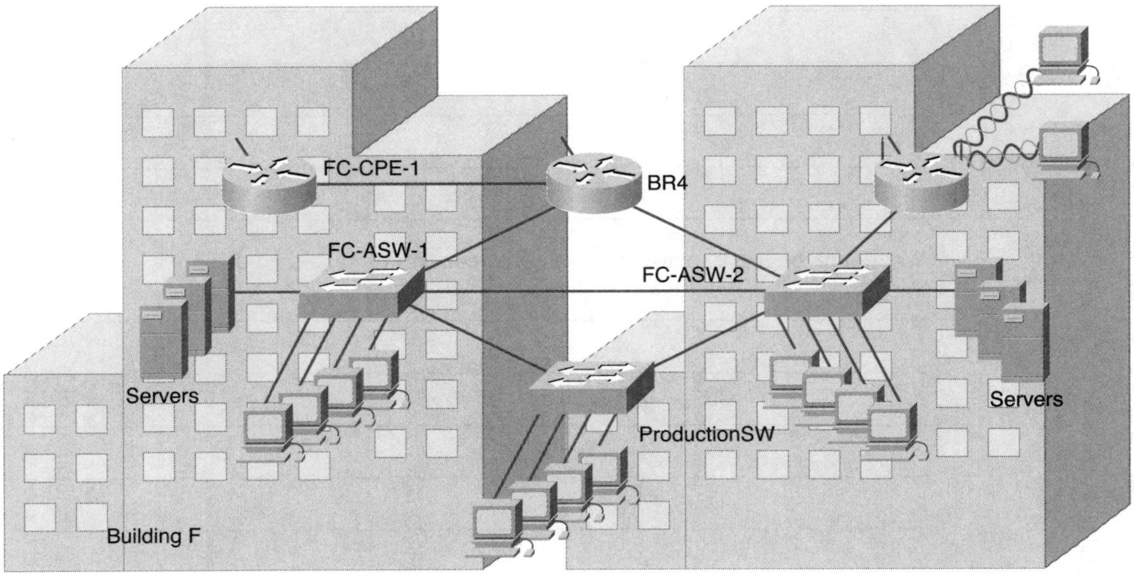

Step 4.   Save your Availability Strategies document. Place a copy in your design project portfolio.

Reflection

The creation of availability strategies poses many challenges for the designer. What were some of the more difficult challenges you encountered?

_____

_____

_____

_____

_____

_____

Consider and discuss the identified strategies. Do all the strategies designed accomplish the task the same way?

_____

_____

_____

_____

_____

_____

Would one be less expensive or less time-consuming than the other?

_____

_____

_____

_____

_____

_____

Lab 5-4: Identifying Security Requirements (5.1.5)

Upon completion of this lab, you will be able to

- Research different security options and make a recommendation.
- Select an appropriate design strategy to meet the requirements

This lab contains skills that relate to the following 640-802 CCNA exam objectives:

- Explain general methods to mitigate common security threats to network devices, hosts, and applications.
- Describe recommended security practices, including initial steps to secure network devices.

Expected Results and Success Criteria

Before starting this lab, read through the tasks that you are expected to perform. What do you expect the result of performing these tasks will be?

_____

_____

_____

How is an understanding of the potential security threats beneficial to the network design?

_____

_____

_____

How will a network administrator know whether the security recommendations are adequate?

_____

_____

_____

Background/Preparation

FilmCompany is an expanding, small advertising company moving into interactive advertising media, including video presentations. This company has just been awarded a big video-support contract by the StadiumCompany. With this new contract, FilmCompany expects to see its business grow approximately 70 percent.

To facilitate this growth, the FilmCompany has decided to significantly upgrade its data network. You have the role of network design consultant. Your job is to develop network design and project documents for the FilmCompany that will meet the requirements of this upgrade.

This lab specifically considers design strategies that identify security requirements. It is one of a series of labs that explore the FilmCompany existing network and its upgrade requirements.

Task 1: Identify Potential Security Weaknesses of the FilmCompany Topology

Step 1. Use word processing software to create a new document called Security Strategies.

Step 2. Using the documents created in previous labs and the existing topology shown in Figure 5-4, identify and record potential weaknesses in the proposed design:

_____

_____

_____

_____

Figure 5-4   Proposed FilmCompany Network Topology

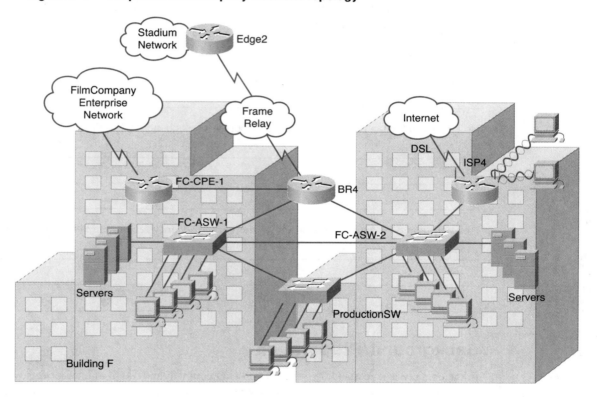

Step 3. Create a list of security practices that would reduce, or possibly eliminate, the recorded potential security weaknesses in the FilmCompany network.

_____

_____

Step 4. Save your Security Strategies document.

Task 2: Create a Security Practices List

Step 1.   Discuss and compare your list of potential security practices with another student. From this discussion, create and record a finalized list of recommended security practices for the FilmCompany.

_____

_____

_____

_____

_____

_____

_____

_____

_____

_____

_____

_____

_____

_____

_____

_____

_____

Step 2.   Identify and record what devices and software will need to be purchased to facilitate the recommended security practices:

_____

_____

_____

_____

Step 3.   Save your Security Strategies document.

Task 3: Create a Security Strategy

Step 1.   Use word processing software to create an addition to the Security Strategies document.

Step 2.   Using the list of identified equipment, develop and record a chart of costs and features of the recommended devices:

_____

_____

_____

_____

_____

Step 3.   Using the list of identified software needed, develop a chart of costs and features of the recommended software:

_____

_____

_____

_____

_____

Step 4.   Save your Security Strategies document.

Task 4: Create a Security Design

Step 1.   Use word processing software to create an addition to the Securities Strategies document.

Step 2.   Identify and record which types of access to the network should be secured by incorporating VPNs.

_____

_____

Step 3.   Identify and record methods for controlling physical network security at the FilmCompany building and at the stadium.

_____

_____

_____

Step 4.   Identify potential ACLs that can be created to filter unwanted traffic from entering the network:

_____

_____

_____

Step 5.   Identify and record methods for securing the wireless access points. Determine the best method for the FilmCompany network:

_____

_____

_____

Step 6.   Save your Security Strategies document. Place a copy in your design project portfolio.

Reflection

The creation of a security strategy creates many challenges for the designer. What were some of the more difficult challenges you encountered?

_____

_____

_____

Consider and discuss the identified challenges. Do all the proposed strategies accomplish the task the same way?

_____

_____

_____

Would one be less expensive or less time-consuming than the other?

_____

_____

_____

_____

How could implementing a physical security plan into an existing company be difficult?

_____

_____

_____

_____

Lab 5-5: Designing the Core Layer (5.2.3)

Upon completion of this lab, you will be able to design requirements for the core layer network.

This lab contains skills that relate to the following 640-802 CCNA exam objectives:

- Describe the purpose and functions of various network devices.
- Select the components required to meet a network specification.

Expected Results and Success Criteria

Before starting this lab, read through the tasks that you are expected to perform. What do you expect the result of performing these tasks will be?

_____

_____

_____

What are the advantages of diagramming the core layer devices?

_____

_____

_____

What benefit can be gained from diagramming a topology before it is implemented?

_____

_____

_____

Background/Preparation

FilmCompany is an expanding advertising company moving into interactive advertising media, including video presentations. This company has just been awarded a big video-support contract by the StadiumCompany. With this new contract, FilmCompany expects to see its business grow approximately 70 percent.

To facilitate this expansion, the state of data flow across the current network has to be established so that the network upgrade can be planned and implemented.

Developing a diagram of the core layer enables the designer to analyze the proposed design and identify where the network can be improved. The logical topology diagram shows that each router is identified by name and has a unique address. Redundant paths to the internal network should be planned and implemented when applicable. The logical design for the core layer must be aligned with the initial business goals and technical requirements of the customer. The diagram gives the designer and customer a visual idea of what is already on the network and helps to get a better view of what is still required.

In this lab, you create a diagram of the core layer topology design. You can draw the design diagram by hand or use Packet Tracer, or a graphics program such as Microsoft PowerPoint, Visio, or Diag (a network diagramming tool available on Discovery Server).

Task 1: Identify Core Layer Requirements

Step 1.   Use word processing software to create a new document called Core Layer diagram.

Step 2.   Use the identified topology and associated equipment to determine core layer design requirements, including the following:

- High-speed connectivity to the distribution layer switches

- 24 hours, 7 days a week availability

- Routed interconnections between core devices

- High-speed redundant links between core switches and between the core and distribution layer devices

Step 3.   Discuss with other students to identify areas that might have been omitted in the initial requirements document.

Task 2: Create a Core Layer Module Design

Using the list developed from the group discussion, design the requirements of the core layer module.

Step 1.   Create your design using the existing equipment.

The FilmCompany network equipment includes:

- Two 1841 Routers (FC-CPE-1, FC-CPE-2)

- Three 2960 Switches (FC-ASW-1, FC-ASW-2, ProductionSW)

- One ADSL Modem for Internet Access

Step 2.   Using the list of equipment, identify modules that can be added to the existing equipment to support new features, such as redundancy.

_____

_____

Step 3.   Save your Core Layer Diagram document.

Task 3: Select Core Layer Devices

Step 1.   Use word processing software to create an addition to the Core Layer Diagram document.

Step 2.   The identified core layer module diagram will be used to adjust the distribution layer design. Equipment selected must include existing equipment. Use Layer 3 devices at the core layer in a redundant configuration.

Step 3.   Save your Core Layer Diagram document.

Task 4: Design Redundancy

Step 1.   Use word processing software to create an addition to the Core Layer Diagram document.

Step 2.   Design a redundancy plan that combines multiple Layer 3 links to increase available bandwidth.

Step 3.   Create a design that incorporates redundancy similar to that shown in Figure 5-5.

Figure 5-5   Proposed FilmCompany Core Layer Redundant Links

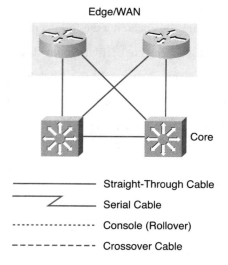

Step 4.   Save your Core Layer Diagram document. Place a copy in your design project portfolio.

Task 5: Reflection/Challenge

The design strategies for the FilmCompany pose many challenges for the designer. What were a few of the more difficult challenges you encountered?

_____

_____

_____

_____

_____

_____

Consider and discuss the identified strategies. Do all of the strategies designed accomplish the task the same way?

_____

_____

_____

_____

_____

Would one be less expensive or less time-consuming than the other?

_____

_____

Lab 5-6: Creating a Diagram of the FilmCompany LAN (5.2.4)

Upon completion of this lab, you will be able to design and diagram the new FilmCompany LAN.

Expected Results and Success Criteria

Before starting this lab, read through the tasks that you are expected to perform. What do you expect the result of performing these tasks will be?

_____

_____

_____

What are the benefits of designing and diagramming a LAN before installation begins?

_____

_____

_____

What advantages and disadvantages are there to using the existing network equipment?

_____

_____

_____

Background/Preparation

FilmCompany is an expanding advertising company moving into interactive advertising media, including video presentations. This company has just been awarded a large video support contract by the StadiumCompany. With this new contract, FilmCompany expects to see its business grow approximately 70 percent.

As a member of the network design team, the student will investigate the FilmCompany existing network and will plan, design, and prototype the upgrades necessary to enable the network to cope with this growth in business.

Developing a diagram of the LAN enables the designer to analyze the proposed design and identify where the network can be improved. The logical topology diagram shows that the switches are identified; each computer should have a unique address. Redundant paths from the switches should be planned and implemented when applicable. The logical design for the LAN must be aligned with the initial business goals and technical requirements of the customer. The diagram gives the designer and customer a visual idea of what is already on the network and helps to get a better view of what is still required.

In this lab, you create both a written document and a diagram of the core layer topology design. You can draw the design diagram by hand or use Packet Tracer, or a graphics program such as MS PowerPoint, MS Visio, or Diag, a network diagramming tool available on Discovery Server.

Task 1: Identify LAN Requirements

Step 1.   Use word processing software to create a new document called "LAN Diagram."

Step 2.   Use the identified topology and associated equipment to determine LAN design requirements.

- Design requirements for the LAN include the following:

- High-speed connectivity to the access layer switches

- 24 hours, 7 days a week availability

- High-speed redundant links between switches on the LAN and the access layer devices

- Identifying available hardware for the LAN

Step 3.   Discuss with other students to identify areas that may have been omitted in the initial requirements document.

Task 2: Determine Equipment Features

Using the list developed from the class discussions, create a LAN based on technical requirements (design only).

Step 1.   Create your design using the existing equipment.

The FilmCompany network equipment includes the following:

- Three 1841 Routers (FC-CPE-1, FC-CPE-2)

- Three 2960 switches (FC-ASW-1, FC-ASW-2, ProductionSW)

- One ADSL modem for Internet access

Step 2.   Using the list of equipment, identify modules that can be added to the existing equipment to support new features, such as redundancy.

_____

_____

Step 3.   Save your LAN Diagram document.

Task 3: Select LAN Devices

Step 1.   Use word processing software to create an addition to the LAN Diagram document.

Step 2.   The identified LAN diagram will be used to adjust the access layer design. Equipment selected must include existing equipment.

Step 3.   Save your LAN Diagram document.

Task 4: Design Redundancy

Step 1.   Use word processing software to create an addition to the LAN Diagram document.

Step 2.   Design a redundancy plan that combines multiple Layer 2 links to increase available bandwidth.

Step 3. Create a design that incorporates redundancy.

Step 4. Using drawing software, or by hand, create a diagram of the LAN design based on Figure 5-6.

Figure 5-6 **Potential FilmCompany LAN**

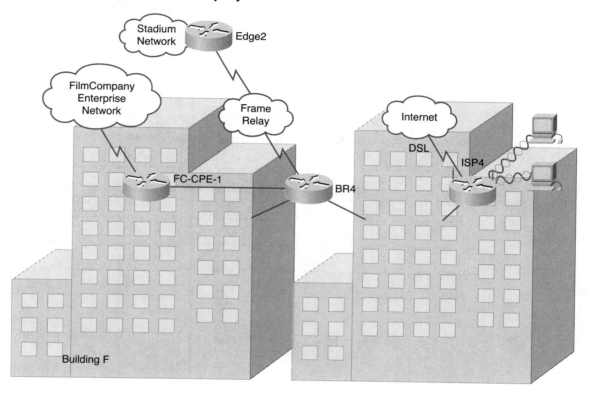

Step 5. Save your LAN Diagram document and file a copy in your project portfolio.

Reflection/Challenge

The design strategies for the FilmCompany LAN pose many challenges for the designer. What were a few of the more difficult challenges you encountered?

_____

_____

_____

_____

Consider and discuss the identified strategies. Do all the strategies designed accomplish the task the same way?

_____

_____

_____

_____

_____

_____

Would one be less expensive or less time-consuming than the other?

_____

Would the chosen LAN design allow for future growth and the addition of the WLAN?

_____

_____

_____

_____

Lab 5-7: Selecting Access Points (5.4.2)

Upon completion of this lab, you will be able to

- Evaluate an existing access point placement.

- Select appropriate access points for a new WLAN design.

This lab contains skills that relate to the following 640-802 CCNA exam objective:

- Select the components required to meet a network specification.

Expected Results and Success Criteria

Before starting this lab, read through the tasks that you are expected to perform. What do you expect the result of performing these tasks will be?

_____

_____

_____

What are the inherent risks of using wireless in a network?

_____

_____

_____

What are several methods to limit the security risks of wireless LANs?

_____

_____

_____

Background/Preparation

FilmCompany is an expanding advertising company moving into interactive advertising media, including video presentations. This company has just been awarded a big video-support contract by the StadiumCompany. With this new contract, FilmCompany expects to see its business grow approximately 70 percent.

As a member of the network design team, the student will investigate the Film Company existing network and will plan, design, and prototype the upgrades necessary to enable the network to cope with this growth in business.

A small wireless LAN is currently used occasionally by a few project managers with laptops and by guests at Building F. The FilmCompany believes that the WLAN might be used more regularly when the StadiumCompany contract work starts and mobile and contract workers will require network access. The FilmCompany plans to consolidate all their personnel and resources in one building.

Task 1: Identify WLAN Requirements

Step 1.   Use word processing software to create a new document called WLAN Diagram.

Step 2.   Use the identified topology and associated equipment to determine WLAN design requirements.

Design requirements for the WLAN include the following:

- Scalability
- Availability
- Security
- Manageability

Step 3.   Discuss with other students to identify areas that might have been missed in the initial requirements document.

Task 2: Determine Equipment Features

Using the list developed from the discussions, create a WLAN based on technical requirements (design only).

Step 1.   Begin by creating your design using the existing equipment.

Step 2.   Using the list of equipment, identify the model of wireless router. Identify the features and range of the device. Identify whether upgrades can be made to extend the range, security, and existing features.

Step 3.   Create a list of features and potential upgrades and compare them to other models of wireless router. Determine the device that can easily meet the technical requirements of the WLAN.

Step 4.   With the preceding list, estimate the range of coverage available with the existing wireless router. Using the FilmCompany floor plans as a guide (see Figure 5-7), determine whether the wireless router can provide thorough coverage of the work area. Determine whether standalone access points or wireless controllers are needed for the design.

Figure 5-7   FilmCompany Floor Plan

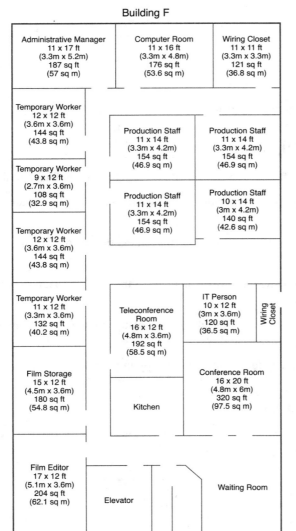

Step 5.   Save your WLAN Diagram document.

Task 3: Select WLAN Devices

Step 1.   Use word processing software to create an addition to the WLAN Diagram document.

Step 2.   The identified WLAN diagram will be used to determine the type of wireless device that will be included into the proposed network.

Step 3.   Ensure that the chosen wireless equipment meets the following WLAN requirements:

- Scalability
- Availability
- Security
- Manageability

Step 4.   Save your WLAN Diagram document.

Task 4: Design the WLAN

Step 1.   Use word processing software to create an addition to the WLAN Diagram document.

Step 2.   Design a WLAN that provides scalability. Annotate on the WLAN Diagram document how the design provides scalability.

Step 3.   Design a WLAN that provides availability. Annotate on the WLAN Diagram document how the design provides availability.

Step 4.   Design a WLAN that provides security. Annotate on the WLAN Diagram document how the design provides security.

Step 5.   Design a WLAN that provides manageability. Annotate on the WLAN Diagram document how the design provides manageability.

Step 6.   Save your WLAN Diagram document. Place a copy in your design project portfolio.

Reflection/Challenge

The design strategies for the FilmCompany WLAN pose many challenges for the designer. What were a few of the more difficult challenges you encountered?

_____

_____

_____

Consider and discuss the identified strategies. Do all the strategies designed or hardware identified accomplish the task the same way?

_____

_____

Would one be less expensive or less time-consuming than the other?

_____

_____

Would the current topology allow for future growth and the addition of the WLAN?

_____

_____

_____

_____

_____

_____

Lab 5-8: Developing ACLs to Implement Firewall Rule Set (5.5.3)

Upon completion of this lab, you will be able to

- Interpret a security policy to define firewall rules.

- Create ACL statements to implement firewall rules.

- Configure and test ACLs.

This lab contains skills that relate to the following 640-802 CCNA exam objectives:

- Describe the purpose and types of ACLs.

- Configure and apply ACLs based on network filtering requirements, including CLI/SDM.

- Configure and apply ACLs to limit Telnet and SSH access to the router using SDM/CLI.

- Verify and monitor ACLs in a network environment.

- Troubleshoot ACL issues.

Expected Results and Success Criteria

Before starting this lab, read through the tasks that you are expected to perform. What do you expect the result of performing these tasks will be?

_____

_____

_____

What are the inherent risks of not using an ACL to secure network traffic?

_____

_____

_____

What are several methods to limit the flow of traffic in to and out of LANs or WANs?

_____

_____

_____

Background/Preparation

The FilmCompany provides services to branch offices such as the one located at the stadium. This office has some minor security and performance concerns. These concerns will require the network designer to incorporate several ACLs to secure the network. The ACLs need to be implemented as a simple and effective tool to control traffic.

Given a security policy for the FilmCompany, create a firewall rule set and implement named extended ACLs to enforce the rule set.

The security policy for the FilmCompany has a section that relates to access from remote sites. Here is the text from the security policy:

Security Policy

Users accessing the network from remote locations, including remote branch offices, require the following access to the on-site network resources:

(1)   Remote users must be able to access the Production Server to view their schedules over the web and to enter new orders.

(2)   Remote users must be able to FTP files to and from the Production Server.

(3)   Remote users can use the Production Server to send and retrieve e-mail using IMAP and SMTP protocols.

(4)   Remote users must not be able to access any other services available on the Production Server.

(5)   No traffic is permitted from individual workstations at the main office to remote worker workstations. Any files that need to be transferred between the two sites must be stored on the Production Server and retrieved via FTP.

(6)   No traffic is permitted from workstations at the remote site to workstations at the main site.

(7)   No Telnet traffic is permitted from the remote site workstations to any devices, except their local switch.

Task 1: Cable and Configure the Network

This lab uses the network topology shown in Figure 5-8, and the hostnames, addresses, and subnet masks given in Table 5-2.

Note: If the PCs used in this lab are also connected to your Academy LAN or to the Internet, ensure that you record the cable connections and TCP/IP settings so that these can be restored at the conclusion of the lab.

Figure 5-8   Lab 5-8 Network Topology

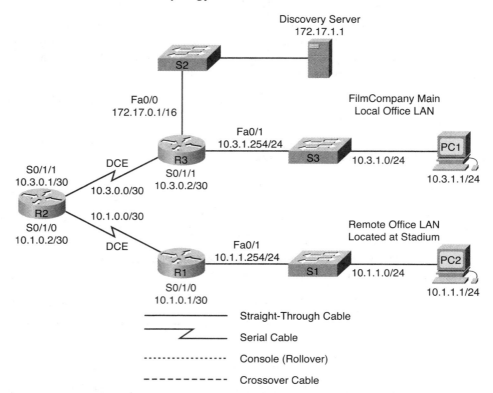

Table 5-2   Addressing Table for Lab 5-8

Device Designation	Device Name	Interface	IP Address
S1	SFC-ASW	VLAN 1	10.1.1.253/24
R1	SR1	Fa0/1	10.1.1.254/24
		S0/1/0	10.1.0.1/30
R2	Edge2	S0/1/0	10.1.0.2/30
		S0/1/1	10.3.0.1/30
R3	BR4	S0/1/1	10.3.0.2/30
		Fa0/0	172.17.0.1/16
		Fa0/1	10.3.1.254/24
S2	FC-ASW-2	VLAN 1	172.17.1.25/16
S3	FC-ASW-1	VLAN 1	10.3.1.253/24
PC1	PC1	–	10.1.1.1/24
PC2	PC2	–	10.3.1.1/24
Discovery Server	Production Server	–	172.17.1.1/16

Step 1.   Connect the devices in accordance with the network topology shown in Figure 5-8.

Note: Your instructor may substitute Discovery Server with an equivalent server for this lab.

Step 2.   Referring to the lab topology diagram in Figure 5-8, connect the console (or rollover) cable to the console port on the router and the other cable end to the host computer with a DB-9 or DB-25 adapter to the COM 1 port. Ensure that power has been applied to both the host computer and router.

Step 3.   Establish a HyperTerminal or other terminal emulation program connection to the router.

Step 4.   Configure the devices in accordance with Table 5-2 and the following requirements:

- Configure the hostnames on each device.

- Configure an EXEC mode password of **class.**

- Configure a password of **cisco** for console connections.

- Configure a password of **cisco** for vty connections.

- Configure IP addresses on all devices.

- Enable EIGRP on all routers and configure each to advertise all of the connected networks.

Step 5.   Verify full IP connectivity using the **ping** command.

Step 6.   Confirm application layer connectivity by telnetting to all routers. Troubleshoot and establish connectivity if the pings or Telnet fail.

Task 2: Create Firewall Rule Sets and Access List Statements

Using the security policy information for the FilmCompany remote access, create the firewall rules that must be implemented to enforce the policy. After the firewall rule is documented, create the access list statement that will implement the firewall rule. There may be more than one statement necessary to implement a rule.

An example of one of the firewall rules is as follows:

Security policy 1: Remote users must be able to access the Production Server to view their schedules over the web and to enter new orders.

Firewall rule: Permit users on the 10.1.1.0/24 access to the Production Server (172.17.1.1) on TCP port 80.

Access list statement(s): permit tcp 10.1.1.0 0.0.0.255 host 172.17.1.1 eq 80

Access list placement: Inbound on router SR1 Fa0/1 (remember that extended ACLs should be placed close as possible to the source of the traffic)

For each of the following security policies

1.   Create a firewall rule.

2.   Create an access list statement.

3.   Determine the access list placement to implement the firewall rule.

Security policy 2: Remote users must be able to FTP files to and from the Production Server.

Firewall rule:

_____

_____

Access list statement(s):

_____

_____

Access list placement:

_____

_____

Security policy 3: Remote users can use the Production Server to send and retrieve e-mail using IMAP and SMTP protocols.

Firewall rule:

_____

_____

Access list statement(s):

_____

_____

Access list placement:

_____

_____

Security policy 4: Remote users must not be able to access any other services available on the Production Server.

Firewall rule:

_____

_____

Access list statement(s):

_____

_____

Access list placement:

_____

_____

Security policy 5: No traffic is permitted from individual workstations at the main office to remote worker workstations. Any files that need to be transferred between the two sites must be stored on the Production Server and retrieved via FTP.

Firewall rule:

_____

_____

Access list statement(s):

_____

_____

Access List placement:

_____

_____

Security policy 6: No traffic is permitted from workstations at the remote site to workstations at the main site.

Firewall rule:

_____

_____

Access list statement(s):

_____

_____

Access list placement:

_____

_____

Security policy 7: No Telnet traffic is permitted from the remote site workstations to any devices, except their local switch.

Firewall rule:

_____

_____

Access list statement(s):

_____

_____

Access list placement:

_____

_____

Task 3: Create Extended ACLs

Step 1.   Review the ACL placement information that you created to implement each of the FilmCompany security policies. List each of the different access list placements that you noted previously.

_____

_____

Based on the placement information, how many access lists do you have to create?

On Router SR1 ___

On Router Edge2 ___

On Router BR4 ___

Step 2.   Based on the access list statements you developed in Task 2, create each ACL that is needed to implement the security policies. When creating access lists, remember the following principles:

- Only one access list can be applied per Layer 3 protocol, per direction on each interface.

- Access list statements are processed sequentially from first to last.

- Once a packet matches an access list statement, the statement is applied to that packet and no further statements are tested.

- Once an access list is created and applied on an interface, all traffic that does not match any access list statement is dropped.

Step 3.   Use a text editor to create the access lists, or write them here. Evaluate each access list statement to ensure that it will filter traffic as intended.

_____

_____

_____

_____

_____

_____

_____

_____

_____

_____

_____

Why is the order of access list statements important?

_____

_____

Task 4: Configure and Test Access Lists

Step 1.   Configure the access lists on the appropriate routers and apply them to the correct interfaces. Name the access lists with representative names, like RemoteOffice or FilterRemote.

Access list names:

_____

_____

Step 2.   Test the access lists and their placement by performing the following tests:

- Using Host1, open a browser and attempt to view a web page located on the Production Server using the http://172.17.1.1 address.

  Should this be successful? _____

  Was this successful? _____

- Using Host1, open a browser and attempt to connect to the Production Server using ftp://172.17.1.1.

  Should this be successful? _____

  Was this successful? _____

- Using Host1, attempt to telnet to any address on any of the routers or switches.

  Should this be successful? _____

  Was this successful? _____

- Using Host1, attempt to ping Host2.

  Should this be successful? _____

  Was this successful? _____

- Using Host2, attempt to ping Host1.

  Should this be successful? _____

  Was this successful? _____

Step 3.   Did your ACLs perform as you expected?

Correct and retest any ACLs, including their placement within the network that did not perform as expected.

Task 5: Document the Router Configurations

Copy and save the running configuration outputs from all routers into a word processing document to view their configurations. Place a copy of each configuration in your design project portfolio.

Reflection

The design strategies for the FilmCompany LAN pose many challenges for the designer. What were a few of the more difficult challenges of creating an ACL you encountered?

_____

_____

_____

_____

Consider and discuss the identified strategies. Do all the strategies designed or hardware identified accomplish the task the same way?

_____

_____

_____

Would one ACL work better than another?

_____

_____

_____

Would the chosen ACL design allow for future growth and the addition of more hosts on the LAN segment?

_____

_____

_____

_____

_____

_____

Using IP Addressing in the Network Design: Labs

The lab exercises included in this chapter cover all the Chapter 6 online curriculum labs to ensure that you have mastered the practical, hands-on skills needed to design an organized, hierarchical IP addressing plan that will scale, applies summarization, and uses logical and secure device names. As you work through these labs, use Chapter 6 in Part I of this book or use the corresponding Chapter 6 in the Discovery Designing and Supporting Computer Networks online curriculum for assistance.

Lab 6-1: Using CIDR to Ensure Route Summarization (6.1.4)

Upon completion of this lab, you will be able to do the following:

- Configure routers, including EIGRP routing protocol

- Configure EIGRP for manual CIDR route summarization

- Verify EIGRP default operation and with manual summarization

- Test and verify full connectivity

- Reflect upon and document the network implementation

This lab covers skills that relate to the following 640-802 CCNA exam objectives:

- Determine the appropriate classless addressing scheme using VLSM and summarization to satisfy addressing requirements in a LAN/WAN environment.

- Perform and verify routing configuration tasks for a static or default route given specific routing requirements.

- Configure, verify, and troubleshoot EIGRP.

Expected Results and Success Criteria

Before starting this lab, read through the tasks that you are expected to perform. What do you expect the result of performing these tasks will be?

_____

_____

_____

What are the expected benefits of route summarization?

_____

_____

_____

What could prevent effective route summarization?

_____

_____

_____

Background/Preparation

In this lab activity, you will configure and examine the operation of routes to take advantage of Classless Interdomain Routing (CIDR). You will configure the routers and observe the default operation of EIGRP with automatic summarization. Then you will configure manual summarization to create a supernet. The following individual network routes on R1 and R2 will be summarized: 172.16.0.0, 172.17.0.0, 172.18.0.0, and 172.19.0.0.

Task 1: Cable the Network and Configure the PCs

This lab will use the network topology shown in Figure 6-1, and the hostnames, addresses, and subnet masks given in Table 6-1.

Note: If the PCs used in this lab are also connected to your Academy LAN or to the Internet, ensure that you record the cable connections and TCP/IP settings so that these can be restored at the conclusion of the lab.

Figure 6-1   Lab 6-1 Network Topology

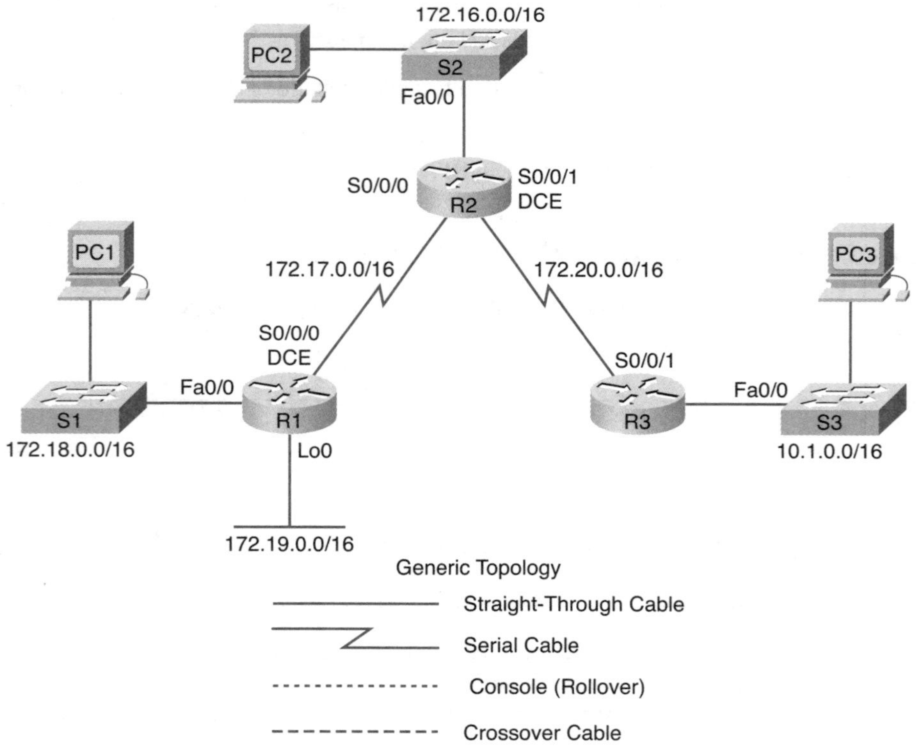

Table 6-1   Addressing Table for Lab 6-1

Device	Interface	IP Address	Subnet Mask	Default Gateway
R1	Fa0/0	172.18.0.1	255.255.0.0	N/A
	S0/0/0	172.17.0.1	255.255.0.0	N/A
	Lo0	172.19.0.1	255.255.0.0	N/A
R2	Fa0/0	172.16.0.1	255.255.0.0	N/A
	S0/0/0	172.17.0.2	255.255.0.0	N/A
	S0/0/1	172.20.0.2	255.255.0.0	N/A
R3	Fa0/0	10.1.0.1	255.255.0.0	N/A
	S0/0/1	172.20.0.1	255.255.0.0	N/A
PC1	NIC	172.18.0.254	255.255.0.0	172.18.0.1
PC2	NIC	172.16.0.254	255.255.0.0	172.16.0.1
PC3	NIC	10.1.0.254	255.255.0.0	10.1.0.1

Step 1.   Connect the devices in accordance with the network topology shown in Figure 6-1.

Step 2.   Configure PC1, PC2, and PC3 in accordance with the address and subnet mask details in Table 6-1.

Task 2: Perform Basic Router Configurations

Establish a HyperTerminal (or other terminal emulation program) session from PC1 to each of the three routers in turn and perform the following configuration functions:

Step 1.   Clear any existing configurations on the routers.

Step 2.   Configure the router hostname.

Step 3.   Disable DNS lookup.

Step 4.   Configure an EXEC mode password.

Step 5.   Configure a message-of-the-day banner.

Step 6.   Configure a password for console connections.

Step 7.   Configure a password for vty connections.

Step 8.   Configure all the interfaces on the three routers with the IP addresses given in Table 6-1.

Step 9.   Save the running configuration to the NVRAM of the router.

Task 3: Verify Connectivity of Routers

Step 1.   Verify that each router can ping each of the neighboring routers across the WAN links.

You should *not* have connectivity between end devices yet. However, you can test connectivity between two routers and between an end device and its default gateway.

Step 2.   Troubleshoot if connectivity is not achieved.

Task 4: Verify Connectivity of Host PCs

Step 1.   Verify that PC1, PC2, and PC3 can ping their respective default gateways.

Step 2.   Troubleshoot if connectivity is not achieved.

Task 5: Configure EIGRP Routing on Router R1

Consider the networks that need to be included in the EIGRP updates that are sent out by the R1 router.

What directly connected networks exist on R1?

_____

_____

_____

What commands are required to enable EGIRP and include the connected networks in the routing updates?

_____

_____

_____

_____

Are there any router interfaces that do not need to have EIGRP updates sent out?

_____

If yes, which ones?

_____

What command is used to disable EIGRP updates on these interfaces?

_____

Task 6: Configure EIGRP on Router R2

Consider the networks that need to be included in the EIGRP updates that are sent out by the R2 router.

What directly connected networks exist on R2?

_____

_____

_____

What commands are required to enable EGIRP and include the connected networks in the routing updates?

_____

_____

_____

_____

Are there any router interfaces that do not need to have EIGRP updates sent out?

_____

If yes, which ones?

_____

What command is used to disable EIGRP updates on these interfaces?

_____

Task 7: Configure EIGRP Routing on the Router R3

Consider the networks that need to be included in the EIGRP updates that are sent out by the R3 router. What directly connected networks exist on R3?

_____

_____

What commands are required to enable EGIRP and include the connected networks in the routing updates?

_____

_____

_____

Are there any router interfaces that do not need to have EIGRP updates sent out?

_____

If yes, which ones?

_____

What command is used to disable EIGRP updates on these interfaces?

_____

Task 8: Verify the Configurations

Ping between devices to confirm that each router can reach each device on the network and that there is connectivity between all the PCs.

If any of the pings failed, check your physical connections and configurations. Troubleshoot until connectivity is achieved.

Task 9: Display the EIGRP Routing Table for Each Router

Are there summary routes in any of the routing tables?

_____

_____

Are there any summary routes for the 172.x.0.0 networks?

_____

_____

_____

Sample output from the **show ip route** command for each router:

```
R1# show ip route
Codes: C - connected, S - static, R - RIP, M - mobile, B - BGP
       D - EIGRP, EX - EIGRP external, O - OSPF, IA - OSPF inter area
       N1 - OSPF NSSA external type 1, N2 - OSPF NSSA external type 2
       E1 - OSPF external type 1, E2 - OSPF external type 2
       i - IS-IS, su - IS-IS summary, L1 - IS-IS level-1, L2 - IS-IS level-2
       ia - IS-IS inter area, * - candidate default, U - per-user static route
       o - ODR, P - periodic downloaded static route


Gateway of last resort is not set


C    172.17.0.0/16 is directly connected, Serial0/0/0
D    172.16.0.0/16 [90/2172416] via 172.17.0.2, 01:36:51, Serial0/0/0
C    172.19.0.0/16 is directly connected, Loopback0
C    172.18.0.0/16 is directly connected, FastEthernet0/0
D    172.20.0.0/16 [90/2681856] via 172.17.0.2, 01:29:07, Serial0/0/0
D    10.0.0.0/8 [90/2684416] via 172.17.0.2, 01:29:04, Serial0/0/0
```

```
R2# show ip route
Codes: C - connected, S - static, R - RIP, M - mobile, B - BGP
       D - EIGRP, EX - EIGRP external, O - OSPF, IA - OSPF inter area
       N1 - OSPF NSSA external type 1, N2 - OSPF NSSA external type 2
       E1 - OSPF external type 1, E2 - OSPF external type 2
       i - IS-IS, su - IS-IS summary, L1 - IS-IS level-1, L2 - IS-IS level-2
       ia - IS-IS inter area, * - candidate default, U - per-user static route
       o - ODR, P - periodic downloaded static route


Gateway of last resort is not set


C    172.17.0.0/16 is directly connected, Serial0/0/0
C    172.16.0.0/16 is directly connected, FastEthernet0/0
D    172.19.0.0/16 [90/2172416] via 172.17.0.1, 01:38:10, Serial0/0/0
D    172.18.0.0/16 [90/2172416] via 172.17.0.1, 01:38:10, Serial0/0/0
C    172.20.0.0/16 is directly connected, Serial0/0/1
D    10.0.0.0/8 [90/2172416] via 172.20.0.1, 01:30:24, Serial0/0/1
```

```
R3# show ip route
Codes: C - connected, S - static, R - RIP, M - mobile, B - BGP
       D - EIGRP, EX - EIGRP external, O - OSPF, IA - OSPF inter area
```

```
        N1 - OSPF NSSA external type 1, N2 - OSPF NSSA external type 2
        E1 - OSPF external type 1, E2 - OSPF external type 2
        i - IS-IS, su - IS-IS summary, L1 - IS-IS level-1, L2 - IS-IS level-2
        ia - IS-IS inter area, * - candidate default, U - per-user static route
        o - ODR, P - periodic downloaded static route

Gateway of last resort is not set

D    172.17.0.0/16 [90/2681856] via 172.20.0.2, 00:02:57, Serial0/0/1
D    172.16.0.0/16 [90/2172416] via 172.20.0.2, 00:02:57, Serial0/0/1
D    172.19.0.0/16 [90/2684416] via 172.20.0.2, 00:02:57, Serial0/0/1
D    172.18.0.0/16 [90/2684416] via 172.20.0.2, 00:02:57, Serial0/0/1
C    172.20.0.0/16 is directly connected, Serial0/0/1
     10.0.0.0/8 is variably subnetted, 2 subnets, 2 masks
D       10.0.0.0/8 is a summary, 01:31:34, Null0
C       10.1.0.0/16 is directly connected, FastEthernet0/0
```

Task 10: Remove Automatic Summarization

On each of the three routers, remove automatic summarization to force EIGRP to report all subnets. A sample command is given for R1:

```
R1(config)# router eigrp 1
R1(config-router)# no auto-summary
```

Task 11: Configure Manual Summarization on R2

On R2, configure manual summarization so that EIGRP summarizes the four networks 172.16.0.0/16, 172.17.0.0/16, 172.18.0.0/16, and 172.19.0.0/16 as one CIDR route, or 172.16.0.0/14.

You are summarizing multiple classful networks, which creates a supernet, and results in a classless (/14) network address being advertised.

From the global configuration mode issue the following commands:

```
R2(config)# interface s0/0/1
R2(config-if)# ip summary-address eigrp 1 172.16.0.0 255.252.0.0
```

Task 12: Confirm R2 Is Advertising a CIDR Summary Route

Examine the routing table of each router using the **show ip route** command.

Sample output from **show ip route** command for each router:

```
R1# show ip route
Codes: C - connected, S - static, R - RIP, M - mobile, B - BGP
       D - EIGRP, EX - EIGRP external, O - OSPF, IA - OSPF inter area
       N1 - OSPF NSSA external type 1, N2 - OSPF NSSA external type 2
       E1 - OSPF external type 1, E2 - OSPF external type 2
       i - IS-IS, su - IS-IS summary, L1 - IS-IS level-1, L2 - IS-IS level-2
```

```
        ia - IS-IS inter area, * - candidate default, U - per-user static route
        o - ODR, P - periodic downloaded static route


Gateway of last resort is not set


C     172.17.0.0/16 is directly connected, Serial0/0/0
D     172.16.0.0/16 [90/2172416] via 172.17.0.2, 02:13:05, Serial0/0/0
C     172.19.0.0/16 is directly connected, Loopback0
C     172.18.0.0/16 is directly connected, FastEthernet0/0
D     172.20.0.0/16 [90/2681856] via 172.17.0.2, 02:05:21, Serial0/0/0
      10.0.0.0/16 is subnetted, 1 subnets
D        10.1.0.0 [90/2684416] via 172.17.0.2, 00:04:25, Serial0/0/0
```

R2# **show ip route**

```
Codes: C - connected, S - static, R - RIP, M - mobile, B - BGP
       D - EIGRP, EX - EIGRP external, O - OSPF, IA - OSPF inter area
       N1 - OSPF NSSA external type 1, N2 - OSPF NSSA external type 2
       E1 - OSPF external type 1, E2 - OSPF external type 2
       i - IS-IS, su - IS-IS summary, L1 - IS-IS level-1, L2 - IS-IS level-2
       ia - IS-IS inter area, * - candidate default, U - per-user static route
       o - ODR, P - periodic downloaded static route


Gateway of last resort is not set


C     172.17.0.0/16 is directly connected, Serial0/0/0
C     172.16.0.0/16 is directly connected, FastEthernet0/0
D     172.19.0.0/16 [90/2172416] via 172.17.0.1, 02:14:37, Serial0/0/0
D     172.18.0.0/16 [90/2172416] via 172.17.0.1, 02:14:37, Serial0/0/0
C     172.20.0.0/16 is directly connected, Serial0/0/1
      10.0.0.0/16 is subnetted, 1 subnets
D        10.1.0.0 [90/2172416] via 172.20.0.1, 00:05:57, Serial0/0/1
D     172.16.0.0/14 is a summary, 00:11:55, Null0
```

R3# **show ip route**

```
Codes: C - connected, S - static, R - RIP, M - mobile, B - BGP
       D - EIGRP, EX - EIGRP external, O - OSPF, IA - OSPF inter area
       N1 - OSPF NSSA external type 1, N2 - OSPF NSSA external type 2
       E1 - OSPF external type 1, E2 - OSPF external type 2
       i - IS-IS, su - IS-IS summary, L1 - IS-IS level-1, L2 - IS-IS level-2
       ia - IS-IS inter area, * - candidate default, U - per-user static route
       o - ODR, P - periodic downloaded static route


Gateway of last resort is not set


C     172.20.0.0/16 is directly connected, Serial0/0/1
```

```
        10.0.0.0/16 is subnetted, 1 subnets
C          10.1.0.0 is directly connected, FastEthernet0/0
D       172.16.0.0/14 [90/2172416] via 172.20.0.2, 00:13:32, Serial0/0/1
```

Which router has a summarized route to the 172.x.0.0 networks in its routing table?

_____

_____

Task 13: Clean Up

Erase the configurations and reload the routers. Disconnect and store the cabling. For PC hosts that are normally connected to other networks (such as the school LAN or the Internet), reconnect the appropriate cabling and restore the TCP/IP settings.

Reflection

In this lab, initially automatic summarization was used. Discuss the advantages of using route summarization. Consider whether route summarization could still be applied if more effective use of the IPv4 address space had been made by using VLSM for those networks requiring fewer addresses, such as the serial links between routers,

_____

_____

_____

Lab 6-2: Determining an IP Addressing Scheme (6.2.1)

Upon completion of this lab, you will be able to determine an appropriate IP addressing strategy for the FilmCompany network.

This lab contains skills that relate to the following 640-802 CCNA exam objectives:

- Describe the operation and benefits of using private and public IP addressing.
- Implement static and dynamic addressing services for hosts in a LAN environment.

Expected Results and Success Criteria

Before starting this lab, read through the tasks that you are expected to perform. What do you expect the result of performing these tasks will be?

_____

_____

_____

What issues would you expect to arise if an IP addressing scheme was not thoroughly planned for a network before implementation?

_____

_____

_____

Background/Preparation

This lab is part of a series of labs in which you design the IP addressing scheme for the new FilmCompany network. This series includes this lab, Determining an IP Addressing Scheme (Lab 6-2); Determining the Number of IP Networks (Lab 6-3); and Creating an Address Allocation Spreadsheet (Lab 6-4).

In this lab, you will start to plan an IP addressing scheme that satisfies the new network design of the branch office of FilmCompany. This scheme will be applied to the network over the following two labs.

The IP address scheme has to meet the network requirements to support scalability and a hierarchical design model.

With the acquisition of AnyCompany and the new contract with the StadiumCompany, the network infrastructure of this branch office of FilmCompany needs to change significantly.

To begin planning the addressing scheme, you will examine the topology in conjunction with the different user types and traffic types. The different users and services will be grouped into VLANs and subnets. The IP addressing scheme will then be applied to the subnets.

Task 1: Consider VLAN Issues

The initial step in determining the required VLANs is to group users and services into VLANs. Each of these VLANs will represent an IP subnet.

A VLAN can be considered to be a group of switch ports assigned to a broadcast domain. Grouping the switch ports confines broadcast traffic to specified hosts so that bandwidth is not unnecessarily consumed in unrelated VLANs. Therefore, it is a recommended best practice to assign only one IP network or subnetwork to each VLAN.

When determining how to group users and services, consider the following issues:

- **Flexibility**: The employees and hardware of the former AnyCompany will move into the building with the FilmCompany in the near future. The network from this newly acquired company needs to be tightly integrated with the FilmCompany network and a structure put in place to enhance the security of the network.

  To support this integration, with improvements in security and performance, additional VLANs need to be created on the network. These VLANs will also allow the personnel to move to the buildings without additional network changes or interruption in network services.

- **Security:** Security can be better enforced *between* VLANs than *within* VLANs:

    - Access control lists can be applied to the Distribution Layer router subinterfaces that interconnect the VLANs to enforce this security.

    - The interfaces on the switches can be assigned to VLANs as appropriate to support the network for the connected device.

    - Additional Layer 2 security measures can also be applied to these switch interfaces.

- **WANs and VPNs:** The contract with StadiumCompany adds a number of new requirements. Some FilmCompany personnel will be located at the stadium. Additional personnel and contract workers will also be present at the stadium during live events. These employees will use laptops and the wireless LAN at the FilmCompany branch as well as the wireless LAN at the stadium. To provide network connectivity for these laptops, they will be in their own VLAN. At the stadium, the FilmCompany laptop users will connect to a secure wireless VLAN and use a VPN over the Frame Relay connection between stadium and the FilmCompany branch. With this connection, the laptop users can be attached to the internal FilmCompany network regardless of physical location.

  To support the video feeds, FilmCompany will need resources available at the stadium. Some of the servers providing these resources will be located at the stadium. Other servers will be located at the branch office of the FilmCompany. For security and performance reasons, these servers, regardless of location, will be on secured VLANs. A separate VPN over the Frame Relay link will be created to connect the servers at the stadium to the servers located at the FilmCompany office.

What are the advantages and disadvantages of using a VPN to extend the wireless and video server networks over the Frame Relay connection from FilmCompany to the stadium?

Advantages:

_____

_____

Disadvantages:

_____

_____

- **Redundancy**: The VLAN structure will support load balancing and redundancy, which are major needs of this new network design. With such a large portion of the FilmCompany operations and revenues dependent on the network operation, a network failure could be devastating. The new VLAN arrangement allows the FC-ASW1 and FC-ASW2 switches to share the load of the traffic and be backups for each other.

This redundancy is accomplished by sharing the RSTP primary and secondary root duties for the traffic for the different VLANs:

- FC-ASW1 will be the primary root for approximately one-half of the VLAN traffic (not necessarily one-half of the VLANs), and FC-ASW2 will be the secondary root for these VLANs.

- The remaining VLANs will have FC-ASW2 as the primary root and FC-ASW1 as the secondary root.

Task 2: Group Network Users and Services

Examine the planned network topology. Applying the issues considered in Task 1, list all the possible groupings of users and services that may require separate VLANs and subnets.

_____

_____

_____

_____

_____

_____

_____

_____

_____

_____

_____

_____

_____

_____

_____

_____

_____

_____

Task 3: Tabulating the Groupings

The new addressing design needs to be scalable to allow easy inclusion of future services, such as voice.

The current addressing scheme does not allow for managed growth. Correcting this scheme will mean that most devices will be placed on new VLANs and new subnets. In some cases, it may be impossible to change a device address; for example, some of the servers have software registered to their IP addresses. In such cases, the server VLAN will keep its current addressing even though it may not be consistent with the remaining addressing scheme. Other addresses that cannot be changed are the addresses used with the WAN links and the addresses for NAT pool used to access the Internet.

Table 6-2 shows a possible grouping and addressing scheme. The number of hosts required for the FilmCompany branch office, including growth, has been determined. Assigning one subnet to each VLAN, the host count for each has been rounded up to the next logical network size supported by the binary patterns used in the subnet mask. Rounding up prevents underestimating the total number of host addresses required.

Table 6-2   **FilmCompany VLAN Design**

VLAN Number	Network Name	Number of Host Addresses	Predetermined Network Address	Description
1	Default	14		Default VLAN for the Layer 2 devices
10	Voice	254		Voice VLAN to support Voice over IP
20	Management	14		Management hosts and secure peripherals (payroll printer)
30	Administrative	62		Administrative hosts
40	Support	126		Support hosts
50	Production	126		High-performance production workstations (stationary)
60	Mobile	62		Mobile production hosts
70	Net_admin	14		Network support
80	servers	65534	172.17.0.0 /16	Servers to support video services and storage
90	Peripherals	62		Peripherals for general use (printers, scanners)
100	Web_access	14		VLAN for servers that are publicly accessible
120	Future	126		VLAN for future services
999	Null	126		VLAN for terminating unwanted or suspicious traffic

continues

Table 6-2   FilmCompany VLAN Design   *continued*

VLAN Number	Network Name	Number of Host Addresses	Predetermined Network Address	Description
NA	NAT_pool	6	209.165.200.224 /29	Addresses for NAT pool for BR4 or interface to ISP4
NA	DSL_Link	2	192.0.2.40 /30	DSL link to the ISP
NA	Frame_Link	2	172.18.0.16/30	Address of the FR link to the stadium

Note: For this exercise, VLANs 60 and 80 have been extended over VPNs to support hosts and services to the stadium. As discussed in Task 1, this may not be an optimal solution.

Task 4: Determine Total Number of Hosts

To determine the block of addresses to be used, count the number of hosts. To calculate the addresses, count only the hosts that will receive addresses from the new block. Use the information in Table 6-2 in Task 3 to complete Table 6-3 to calculate the total number of hosts in the new FilmCompany network requiring addresses.

Table 6-3   FilmCompany VLAN Names and Size

Network/VLAN Name	Number of host addresses

What is the smallest address block size that can potentially satisfy the FilmCompany network needs?

Note: Often, when you add the total number of addresses needed, the total count may not accurately reflect the number of addressing blocks required. This discrepancy can occur when the host counts for the networks have not been rounded up to the next logical network size. Because the individual counts represent rounded values, you can be confident that this block size can satisfy the network requirements.

File this information in your design portfolio for use in the next lab.

Reflection/Challenge

This lab provided a step-by-step process for determining an addressing scheme for a corporate network. Discuss and consider the issues that would arise if the required information for this planning process were not available. Consider also how this lack of information could be overcome.

Lab 6-3: Determining the Number of IP Networks (6.2.2)

Upon completion of this lab, you will be able to do the following:

- Define an addressing block scheme to support summarization.

This lab contains skills that relate to the following 640-802 CCNA exam objectives:

- Describe the operation and benefits of using private and public IP addressing.
- Implement static and dynamic addressing services for hosts in a LAN environment.

Expected Results and Success Criteria

Before starting this lab, read through the tasks that you are expected to perform. What do you expect the result of performing these tasks will be?

_____

_____

_____

Consider possible future issues that could arise if the number of IP networks is incorrectly designed.

_____

_____

_____

Background/Preparation

This lab is part of a series of labs in which you design the IP addressing scheme for the new FilmCompany network. This series includes Determining an IP Addressing Scheme (Lab 6-2); this lab, Determining the Number of IP Networks (Lab 6-3); and Creating an Address Allocation Spreadsheet (Lab 6-4).

With the acquisition of AnyCompany and the new contract with StadiumCompany, the network infrastructure of this branch office of FilmCompany needs to change significantly.

In this lab, you will design an IPv4 addressing plan that satisfies the requirements of the addressing scheme developed for the new FilmCompany network in Lab 6-2. This plan will be applied to the network in the next lab.

Task 1: Review Address Block Size

Review and record the total number of hosts to be addressed.

Complete Table 6-4 using the information determined in Lab 6-2.

Table 6-4   FilmCompany VLAN Names and Size

Network/VLAN Name	Number of Host Addresses

What is the smallest address block size that can potentially satisfy the FilmCompany network needs?

Task 2: Choose or Obtain an Address Block

Step 1.   Choose either public or private addresses.

A block of addresses needs to be acquired to support the addressing scheme. This block of addresses could be private space addresses (also known as RFC 1918 addresses) or public addresses. In most cases, the network users require only outbound connections to the Internet. Only a few hosts, such as web servers, require public addresses. These often exist on the local LAN with private addresses and have static NAT entries on the border router to translate to public addresses. Public addresses, however, are expensive and often difficult to justify.

Can you make a justification of the use of public addresses in this network?

If so, write this justification to forward to the ISP:

Step 2.   Ensure that the private space addresses do not conflict.

Although you are allowed to use private space addresses any way you choose, you must make sure that the addresses used do not conflict with another private space address to which this network will be connected. You must identify other networks to which you are connected and make sure that you are not using the same private addresses. In this case, you need to examine the addresses used by the StadiumCompany.

What address private space block does the StadiumCompany use?

_____

What address blocks are used by the WAN links?

_____

_____

What are the other devices or connections that need to be excluded from use?

_____

What address block is this?

_____

Step 3.   Ensure that the private space addresses are consistent with policy.

The company should have a network policy and method of allocating addresses. This is true even when using private addresses. You should contact the FilmCompany network administrators to request a block of addresses. In this case, ask your instructor if there is a preferred set of addresses to use.

Did your instructor assign a block of addresses?

_____

If so, what block?

_____

If your instructor does not assign addresses, you may choose any private space block that does not conflict.

What block of addresses are you using for this FilmCompany Branch?

_____

Task 3: Allocate Addresses for the Network

When assigning addresses to the different networks, start the assignments with the subnet that requires the largest address block and progress to the network that requires the smallest.

Step 1.   Order the networks from largest to smallest in Table 6-5.

Using the information from Lab 6-2, list the networks in order of size, from the network that requires the largest address block to the network that requires the smallest block.

Table 6-5   FilmCompany VLANs in Descending Size

Network/VLAN Name	Number of Host Addresses

Step 2.   Assign address blocks to the networks.

From the address block chosen in the previous task, begin calculating and assigning the address blocks to these networks. Use Table 6-6 to record your design. You should use contiguous blocks of addresses when making these assignments.

Table 6-6   FilmCompany VLAN Address Blocks

Network/VLAN Name	Number of Host Addresses	Network Address
Voice	254	
Support	126	
Production	126	
Future	126	
Null	126	

Network/VLAN Name	Number of Host Addresses	Network Address
Administrative	62	
Mobile	62	
Peripherals	62	
Web_access	14	
Default	14	
Management	14	
Net_admin	14	

Step 3.   Complete the address planning table.

Using the addresses you calculated in the previous step, complete Table 6-7. This plan will be used in future labs.

Table 6-7   FilmCompany VLAN Address Plan

VLAN	Network/ VLAN Name	Number of Host Addresses	Network Address	Description
1	Default	14		Default VLAN for the Layer 2 devices
10	Voice	254		Voice VLAN to support Voice over IP
20	Management	14		Management hosts and secure peripherals (payroll printer)
30	Administrative	62		Administrative hosts
40	Support	126		Support hosts
50	Production	126		High-performance production workstations (stationary)
60	Mobile	62		Mobile production hosts
70	Net_admin	14		Network support
80	Servers	65534		Servers to support video services and storage
90	Peripherals	62		Peripherals for general use (printers, scanners)
100	Web_access	14		VLAN for servers that are publicly accessible
120	Future	126		VLAN for future services
999	Null	126		VLAN for terminating unwanted or suspicious traffic
NA	NAT_pool	6		Addresses for NAT pool for BR4 or interface to ISP4
NA	DSL_Link	2		DSL link to the ISP
NA	Frame_link	2		Address of the FR link to the stadium

File this information in your design portfolio for use in the next lab.

Reflection/Challenge

This lab specifically used private IPv4 addresses. Discuss the issues to be considered if it was decided to use public IPv4 addresses throughout the network. Are there any situations that would require this?

_____

_____

_____

_____

_____

_____

Lab 6-4: Creating an Address Allocation Spreadsheet (6.2.5)

Upon completion of this lab, you will be able to document the address assignment within the FilmCompany network.

This lab contains skills that relate to the following 640-802 CCNA exam objectives:

- Calculate and apply an addressing scheme, including VLSM IP addressing design, to a network.

- Implement static and dynamic addressing services for hosts in a LAN environment.

- Determine the appropriate classless addressing scheme using VLSM and summarization to satisfy addressing requirements in a LAN/WAN environment.

Expected Results and Success Criteria

Before starting this lab, read through the tasks that you are expected to perform. What do you expect the result of performing these tasks will be?

_____

_____

_____

What are some problems that you think could arise if network address planning and allocation is not performed thoroughly?

_____

_____

_____

Background/Preparation

This lab is the third of a series of labs in which you design the IP addressing scheme for the new FilmCompany network. This series includes Determining an IP Addressing Scheme (Lab 6-2), Determining the Number of IP Networks (Lab 6-3), and Creating an Address Allocation Spreadsheet (Lab 6-4), which is this lab.

Based on the addressing plan you created in Labs 6-2 and 6-3, you will create a spreadsheet showing the VLSM addressing allocation for the networks. This information will be placed in the IP Network Requirements table to show the size of the IPv4 address blocks that are needed for each area of the network. You should group areas that have similar requirements, to reduce the number of different subnet masks that must be supported.

By reducing the number of subnet combinations, the designer simplifies the configurations. This makes it easier for the existing FilmCompany network staff to support and troubleshoot. The design requires the support of four different subnet masks.

Task 1: Create a Spreadsheet Showing VLSM Addresses and Assignment

Use a spreadsheet program to create a spreadsheet with columns for each of the network addressing requirements based on Table 6-8. Using a spreadsheet to create a table similar to Table 6-8 can make the allocation of addresses easier to plan and visualize. You can also use the spreadsheet to record where each block of addresses is implemented in the network. This helps to avoid overlapping address blocks.

For this task, first list the block you have chosen and then show the allocation of this block into the subnets. Begin with the largest block and work to the smallest.

Note: You may want to use a pencil to complete this table so that you can make changes until it is complete and final.

Table 6-8   FilmCompany Address Allocation Table

FilmCompany Network Block	Networks with 254 Hosts	Networks with 126 Hosts	Networks with 62 Hosts	Networks with 14 Hosts	Network Names

Step 1.   Record the network address block.

In the first column, record the address block used for the entire FilmCompany network chosen in the previous lab.

Step 2.   Define the 254-host networks.

Based on the requirements for the FilmCompany network, the address block is divided into 12 separate networks using four different masks.

In the second column of Table 6-8, record the network blocks that will support 254 hosts per network.

In the last column, record the names of the networks that need to be assigned to these blocks.

Note: Use only as many blocks as required to meet the address assignments.

The CIDR notation mask for the 254-host network is /24. What is the dotted decimal equivalent mask?

Step 3.   Define the 126-host networks.

In the third column of Table 6-8, choose the first unused 254-host address block to subdivide into 126-host networks.

In the last column, record the names of the networks assigned to these 126-host blocks.

Note: Use only as many blocks as required to meet the address assignments.

The CIDR notation mask for the 126-host network is /25. What is the dotted decimal equivalent mask?

Note: As you further divide these networks, you may need to move the networks around in the table to make room to show the further subnetting of these blocks.

Step 4.   Define the 62-host networks.

In the fourth column of Table 6-8, choose the first unused 126-host address block to subdivide into 62-host networks.

In the last column, record the names of the networks assigned to these 62-host blocks.

Note: Use only as many blocks as required to meet the address assignments.

The CIDR notation mask for the 62-host network is /26. What is the dotted decimal equivalent mask?

Step 5.   Define the 14-host networks.

In the fifth column of Table 6-8, choose the first unused 62-host address block to subdivide into 14-host networks.

In the last column, record the names of the networks assigned to these 14-host blocks.

Note: Use only as many blocks as required to meet the address assignments.

The CIDR notation mask for the 14-host network is /28. What is the dotted decimal equivalent mask?

Note: This FilmCompany branch office does not require any 30-host networks.

Task 2: Define the Host Address Assignments

For each network, determine and document the host addresses and broadcast addresses. Use Table 6-9 to document these networks and host information.

Step 1. Record the network names and addresses in the addressing table.

In Table 6-9, record the network names for the FilmCompany in the first column and the corresponding network address in the second column.

Step 2. Calculate the lowest host address in the addressing table.

The lowest address for a network is one greater than the address of the network. Therefore, to calculate the lowest host address, add a 1 to the network address. For each of these networks, calculate and record the lowest host address in the second column of Table 6-9.

Step 3. Calculate the broadcast address for each network in Table 6-9.

The broadcast address uses the highest address in the network range. This is the address in which the bits in the host portion are all 1s. To calculate the broadcast for each of the networks listed, convert the last octet of the network address into binary. Then fill the remaining host bits with 1s. Finally, convert the binary back to decimal. For each of these networks, calculate and record the broadcast address in the last column.

Step 4. Calculate the highest host address in the addressing table.

The highest address for a network is one less than the broadcast address for that network. Therefore, to calculate the highest host address, subtract a 1 from the broadcast address. For each of these networks, calculate and record the highest host address in the second column.

Table 6-9   FilmCompany Network Address Range Table

Network Names	Network Address	Lowest Host Address	Highest Host Address	Broadcast Address

Task 3: Examine Address Blocks for Overlapping Addresses

One of the major issues of planning network addresses is overlapping addresses. This is especially true when using VLSM addressing. Examine Table 6-9 to ensure that each network has a unique address range.

Confirm that there are no overlapping addresses in the networks.

If there are any overlapping addresses, recalculate the addressing plan for the FilmCompany network.

Important: File this information in your design portfolio; it is an essential part of your design documentation.

Reflection/Challenge

Examine the network Address Allocation table (Table 6-8) in Task 1. Discuss how it may be used to determine address summarization. Also, consider how these summarizations might be used.

_____

_____

_____

_____

_____

_____

_____

_____

_____

Lab 6-5: Designing a Naming Scheme (6.2.6)

Upon completion of this lab, you will be able to diagram selected portions of the new FilmCompany network, including devices, device names, and IP addressing.

This lab contains skills that relate to the following 640-802 CCNA exam objectives:

- Describe security recommended practices including initial steps to secure network devices.

Expected Results and Success Criteria

Before starting this lab, read through the tasks that you are expected to perform. What do you expect the result of performing these tasks will be?

_____

_____

_____

What issues could arise if devices are not named effectively and with consistency?

_____

_____

_____

Background/Preparation

Network device names are sometimes assigned without a unified plan. Without a good network naming scheme, the network can become difficult to manage.

However, it must also be recognized that device names that display their function and location can present a security issue.

In this lab, you will develop a naming convention and apply labels using this convention to selected devices. You should use the planning information from the previous three labs to complete this lab. The naming scheme will be documented in the topology shown in Figure 6-2 and, based on device name codes compiled in Table 6-10, entered in Table 6-11.

Task 1: Identify the Appropriate VLAN

In the previous labs, you identified VLANs and subnets to be used in the FilmCompany network expansion. For each device listed in Table 6-11, assign each host the appropriate VLAN based on its description. Record these VLAN assignments in the third column of Table 6-11.

Task 2: Assign Addresses to the Devices

In the previous lab, an address range was established for each subnet and VLAN. Using these established ranges and the VLAN assignments to the devices in the previous step, assign a host address to each of the selected hosts. Record this information in the last column of Table 6-11 in Task 5 of this lab.

Task 3: Define the Codes for Device Naming

From the device information, develop and apply a naming convention for the hosts.

A good naming scheme follows these guidelines:

- Keep the names as short as possible; using fewer than 12 characters is recommended.
- Indicate the device type, purpose, and location with codes, rather than words or abbreviations.
- Maintain a consistent scheme. Consistent naming makes it easier to sort and report on the devices, and to set up management systems.
- Document the names in the IT department files and on the network topology diagrams.
- Avoid names that make it easy to find protected resources.

For each naming criteria, assign a code for type. You will use these codes in different combinations to create device names. In Table 6-10, create codes for the elements of the device names. Use as many or as few codes as needed.

Table 6-10   FilmCompany Device Name Codes

Device Type	Type Code	Device Purpose	Purpose Code	Device Location	Location Code

Task 4: Establish the Naming Convention

Based on the device name codes entered into Table 6-10, the naming convention could include the fields

- device-type
- location
- device-purpose
- device-number

Laptop number 7 belonging to Production on the 3rd Floor would have the device name:

LT_3FLR_PROD_7

Task 5: Apply the Naming Convention

For each of the 12 devices shown in Table 6-11, apply the naming convention. Then add these device names in the appropriate numbered boxes in the topology shown in Figure 6-2.

Table 6-11   FilmCompany Device Names

Number	Device Name	VLAN	Description	IP Address
1			Server for capturing raw video feeds from stadium	
2			Server for storing finished (post-production) video	
3			Public web server for on demand video access	
4			Branch manager's computer	
5			Live event production worker (switched)	
6			Human resource clerk	
7			Payroll Manager	
8			Live event mobile worker (audio producer)	
9			Live event mobile worker (camera coordinator)	
10			Receptionist's computer	
11			Financial Manager's computer	
12			Information Technology Manager's computer	

Figure 6-2   Proposed FilmCompany Physical Layout

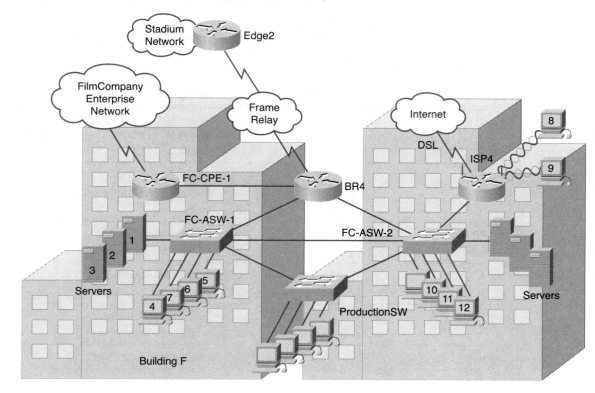

Important: File this information in your design portfolio; it is an essential part of your design documentation.

Reflection/Challenge

If you developed additional criteria to add to the naming convention, discuss why these criteria were used. If you did not use additional criteria, discuss what other criteria might need to be used and why they would be used.

_____

_____

_____

_____

Prototyping the Campus Network: Labs

The lab exercises included in this chapter cover all the Chapter 7 online curriculum labs to ensure that you have mastered the practical, hands-on skills needed to design and prototype a campus network using test plans. As you work through these labs, use Chapter 7 in Part I of this book or use the corresponding Chapter 7 in the Discovery Designing and Supporting Computer Networks online curriculum for assistance.

Lab 7-1: Analyzing a Test Plan and Performing a Test (7.1.6)

Upon completion of this lab, you will be able to

- Analyze a sample test plan to determine the following:
    - The subject of the test
    - The methods and tools for testing
    - The potential results
- Perform the test using the lab equipment.

This lab contains skills that relate to the following 640-802 CCNA exam objectives:

- Perform and verify initial switch configuration tasks, including remote-access management.
- Verify network status and switch operation using basic utilities (including the following: ping, traceroute, Telnet, SSH, arp, ipconfig) and **show** and **debug** commands.
- Describe how VLANs create logically separate networks and the need for routing between them.
- Configure, verify, and troubleshoot VLANs.

Expected Results and Success Criteria

Before starting this lab, read through the tasks that you are expected to perform. What do you expect the result of performing these tasks will be?

_____

_____

_____

How is an understanding of the ability to analyze a test plan important in network prototyping?

_____

_____

_____

How will a network administrator know whether the test was successful?

_____

_____

_____

Background/Preparation

This lab demonstrates the analysis of a standardized test plan to determine the nature of the test to be performed, the methods and tools to be used, and the potential results.

First, you analyze and answer questions regarding the test plan given in the first section of this lab.

The test plan structure and format is standardized and is also used in the labs that follow in this chapter and in Chapter 8, "Prototyping the WAN." This format is similar to that used by the Cisco Customer Proof-of-Concept Labs.

After reviewing the test plan, you then carry out and document the results of the specified tests given in the lab tasks.

The configuration output used in this lab matches that of a 2960 switch and 1841 series router. The same commands can be used with other Cisco switches and routers but might produce slightly different output.

[Begin Test Plan]

ıı|ıı|ı.
CISCO™

Example Test Plan

Table of Contents

Introduction

> **INSTRUCTIONS: Explain briefly what the purpose of the test is and what should be observed. Include a brief description of testing goals. List all tests that you intend to run.**

The purpose of this prototype is to demonstrate how the individual access layer VLANs can be configured to separate traffic from the end devices, IP telephones, and video cameras. The intent is to demonstrate that computers on VLAN 10 cannot access devices on the voice VLAN unless inter-VLAN routing is configured.

Test 1: Basic VLAN Connectivity Test

- Verify physical and IP connectivity between devices on the prototype network.

- Demonstrate IP connectivity between devices on the same VLANs.

- Demonstrate lack of IP connectivity between devices on different VLANs.

Test 2: VLAN Routing Test

- Demonstrate routing of traffic between separate VLANs, unrestricted.

Equipment

> **INSTRUCTIONS: List all the equipment needed to perform the tests. Be sure to include cables, optional connectors or components, and software.**

Table 7-1   Test Plan Equipment List

Qty. Rqd	Model	Additional Options or Software Required	Substitute	IOS Software Rev
1	2960 Layer 2 switch	None	Any 2950 or 2960 model switch	12.2 or later
1	37xx multilayer switch	None	Any multilayer switch or router with minimum 1 Fast Ethernet port.	12.2 or later
2	Personal computer end devices	Fast Ethernet NIC	At least one PC and any other IP end device (camera, printer, etc.).	Windows, Mac, or Linux operating system
3	Cat 5 or above straight-through patch cables	None	None	N/A

Design and Topology Diagram

> **INSTRUCTIONS: Place a copy of the prototype network topology in this section. This is the network as it should be built to be able to perform the required tests. If this topology duplicates a section of the actual network, include a reference topology showing the location within the existing or planned network. Initial configurations for each device must be included in the Appendix.**
>
> **Add a description about this design here that is essential to provide a better understanding of the testing or to emphasize any aspect of the test network to the reader.**

Network Topology

Figure 7-1   Lab 7-1 Test Plan Network Topology

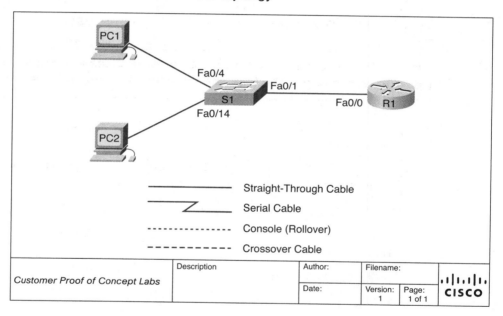

Customer Proof of Concept Labs	Description	Author:	Filename:	CISCO
		Date:	Version: 1	Page: 1 of 1

IP Address Plan

Table 7-2   Test Plan Address Plan

Device Designation	Device Name	Fast Ethernet Address	Subnet Mask	Default Gateway
R1	FC-CPE-1	Fa0/0.1–10.0.1.1		
		Fa0/0.10–10.0.10.1		
		Fa0/0.20–10.0.20.1	255.255.255.0	
S1	FC-ASW-1	VLAN1 10.0.1.2	255.255.255.0	10.0.1.1
PC1	Host1	10.0.10.2	255.255.255.0	10.0.10.1
PC2	Host2	10.0.20.2	255.255.255.0	10.0.20.1

VLAN Plan

Table 7-3   Test Plan VLAN Plan

Switch	VLAN Names and IDs	IP Address Range	Group	Switch Ports
S1	VLAN1 management	10.0.1.2	Network Management	Fa0/1
S1	VLAN10 main-net	10.0.10.0 / 24	Network Users	Fa0/2–12
S1	VLAN20 voice	10.0.20.0 / 24	IP Phones	Fa0/13–24

Note: In Test 1, each of the two PCs is to be attached to a different VLAN on the switch. In Test 2, the switch is connected to the router with a trunk link, and the router will be configured with subinterfaces to route between the two PCs.

Test 1. Description: Basic VLAN Connectivity Test

INSTRUCTIONS: For each test to be performed, state the goals of the test, the data to record during the test, and the estimated time required to perform the test.

Goals of Test:

The goal of the basic connectivity test is to verify that the proper physical connections are made, that the topology is up, and that devices are correctly configured.

Data to Record:

Switch and PC configurations

Ping test results

Estimated Time:

60 minutes

Test 1. Procedures

> **INSTRUCTIONS: Itemize the procedures to follow to perform the test.**

Step 1. Console into the switch and if available set the terminal program to capture the entered commands and output. Issue the **show running-config** and **show vlans** commands from the switch so these outputs are captured. Save the captured terminal screen output. (Alternatively, select, copy, and paste the screen output to a text file.)

Step 2. Verify that VLANs are correctly configured. Record any anomalies.

Step 3. Verify the IP configurations of the PCs.

Step 4. Test IP connectivity between host devices on the same VLAN.

Step 5. Test IP connectivity between host devices on different VLANs.

Test 1. Expected Results and Success Criteria

> **INSTRUCTIONS: List all the expected results. Specific criteria that must be met for the test to be considered a success should be listed. An example of specific criteria is: "A requirement that ping response times cannot exceed 100 ms."**

Step 1. Hosts on a VLAN can ping successfully to other hosts on the same VLAN.

Step 2. Hosts on different VLANs are unable to ping successfully.

Test 1. Results and Conclusions

> **INSTRUCTIONS: Record the results of the tests and the conclusions that can be drawn from the results.**

When Hosts 1 and 2 are in the same VLAN and with compatible IP addresses, they can communicate. When they are in different VLANs, they cannot.

Test 2. Description: VLAN Routing Test

Goals of Test:

The goal of the VLAN routing test is to verify that the host on one VLAN and subnetwork can communicate with a host on another VLAN and subnetwork, using the router.

Data to Record:

Configurations

Routing Tables

Ping Test Results

Estimated Time:

60 minutes

Test 2. Procedures

Step 1.   Console into the switch and ping all router subinterfaces and other devices in the test topology. Record any anomalies.

Step 2.   Ping the switch and the router default gateway from each PC. Record any anomalies.

Step 3.   Telnet from each PC to the switch and the router.

Step 4.   Capture and save the **show running-config** outputs from both the switch and router. Capture and save the **show vlan** output from the switch and the **show ip route** output from the router.

Step 5.   Test IP connectivity between host devices on the same VLAN.

Step 6.   Test IP connectivity between host devices on different VLANs.

Test 2. Expected Results and Success Criteria

Step 1. All networking devices are connected and accessible through ping and Telnet.

Step 2. Hosts on a VLAN can ping successfully to other hosts on the same VLAN.

Step 3. Hosts on different VLANs are able to ping successfully using the router.

Test 2. Results and Conclusions

When hosts are in different VLANs, they can communicate via the router.

[End Test Plan]

Part 1: Analyze the Test Plan

Analyze the test plan and answer the following questions:

1. What are the four main sections of the test plan?

    _____

    _____

    _____

    _____

    _____

    _____

    _____

    _____

    _____

    _____

2. How many tests are defined within the test plan in this lab? ___

3. In which testing subsection would you find the types of commands or analysis tools used to determine whether the test was successful?

    _____

4. In which main test plan section would you find a description of the devices and cabling used to build the prototype for the test plan?

    _____

5. In which main testing section would you find an overall description of the tests to be performed and the reasons why they are being specified in the test plan?

    _____

Part 2: Configure PCs and Switch VLANs and Perform Test 1

This lab uses the network topology shown in Figure 7-1 and the hostnames, addresses, and subnet masks given in Tables 7-2 and 7-3.

Note: If the PCs used in this lab are also connected to your Academy LAN or to the Internet, ensure that you record the cable connections and TCP/IP settings so these can be restored at the conclusion of the lab.

Task 1: Connect Devices and Configure PC IP addresses

Step 1.   Connect the switch to the router as shown in the Figure 7-1.

Step 2.   Connect the PC1 and PC2 hosts to the switch using the ports indicated in Table 7-3.

Step 3.   Using the IP address information from Table 7-2, configure PC1 and PC2.

Task 2: Prepare Switch for Configuration

Step 1.   Connect a PC with a console cable to the switch to perform configurations using a terminal emulation program.

Step 2.   Confirm that the switch is ready for lab configuration by ensuring that all existing VLAN and general configurations are removed. Refer to the section "Erasing and Reloading the Switch" in Appendix C, "Lab Equipment Interfaces and Initial Configuration Restoration," of Part II of this Learning Guide for these instructions.

Task 3: Configure VLANs on Switch S1

Step 1.   Configure switch S1 with a hostname and passwords:

```
Switch(config)# hostname FC-ASW-1
FC-ASW-1(config)# enable password cisco
FC-ASW-1(config)# enable secret class
FC-ASW-1(config)# line console 0
FC-ASW-1(config-line)# password cisco
FC-ASW-1(config-line)# login
FC-ASW-1(config-line)# line vty 0 15
FC-ASW-1(config-line)# password cisco
FC-ASW-1(config-line)# login
FC-ASW-1(config-line)# exit
FC-ASW-1(config)#
```

Step 2.   Configure switch S1 with the VLAN 1 IP address of 10.0.1.2/24:

```
FC-ASW-1(config)# interface vlan1
FC-ASW-1(config-if)# ip address 10.0.1.2 255.255.255.0
FC-ASW-1(config-if)# no shutdown
FC-ASW-1(config-if)# exit
FC-ASW-1(config)#
```

Step 3.   Configure switch S1 with the default gateway address of 10.0.1.1:

```
FC-ASW-1(config)# ip default-gateway 10.0.1.1
FC-ASW-1(config)#
```

Step 4.   Create VLAN 10 named **main-net** and VLAN 20 named **voice**:

```
FC-ASW-1(config)# vlan 10
FC-ASW-1(config-vlan)# name main-net
FC-ASW-1(config-vlan)# exit
FC-ASW-1(config-vlan)# vlan 20
FC-ASW-1(config-vlan)# name voice
FC-ASW-1(config-vlan)# exit
FC-ASW-1(config)#
```

Step 5.   Assign interface range Fa0/2 through Fa0/12 to VLAN 10:

```
FC-ASW-1(config)# interface range fa0/2 - 12
FC-ASW-1(config-if-range)# switchport mode access
FC-ASW-1(config-if-range)# switchport access vlan 10
```

```
FC-ASW-1(config-if-range)# exit
FC-ASW-1(config)#
```

Step 6.   Assign interface range Fa0/13 through Fa0/24 to VLAN 20:

```
FC-ASW-1(config)# interface range fa0/13 - 24
FC-ASW-1(config-if-range)# switchport mode access
FC-ASW-1(config-if-range)# switchport access vlan 20
FC-ASW-1(config-if-range)# end
FC-ASW-1#
```

Task 4: Perform Test 1—Determine Whether Hosts Can Communicate Between VLANs

Step 1.   Issue the **show running-config** commands from the switch and verify all basic configuration settings.

Step 2.   Issue the **show vlan brief** command on the switch to verify what ports are in which VLANs.

Sample output:

```
FC-ASW-1# show vlan brief

VLAN Name                   Status     Ports
---- -------------------- --------- ------------------------------
1    default                active    Fa0/1, Gi0/1, Gi0/2
10   main-net               active    Fa0/2, Fa0/3, Fa0/4, Fa0/5
                                      Fa0/6, Fa0/7, Fa0/8, Fa0/9
                                      Fa0/10, Fa0/11, Fa0/12
20   voice                  active    Fa0/13, Fa0/14, Fa0/15, Fa0/16
                                      Fa0/17, Fa0/18, Fa0/19, Fa0/20
                                      Fa0/21, Fa0/22, Fa0/23, Fa0/24

<*** output omitted ***>
```

Which switch ports are in VLAN 1?

_____

Which switch ports are in VLAN 10?

_____

Which switch ports are in VLAN 20?

_____

Step 3.   With PC1 connected to switch port 4 and PC2 attached to port 14, attempt to ping from PC1 to PC2.

Do you expect the ping to be successful? _____

Why or why not?

_____

_____

Step 4. Change the IP address of PC2 to 10.0.10.5 so that the two PCs are on the same network and ping again.

Do you expect the ping to be successful? _____

Why or why not?

Step 5. Move the cable for PC2 to a port that is in the VLAN 10 range (Fa0/2 to Fa0/12) and ping again.

Do you expect the ping to be successful? _____

Why or why not?

Step 6. Change the IP address for PC2 back to 10.0.20.2 and move the cable back to Fa0/14 in VLAN 20.

This test demonstrates that the PCs from the main-net VLAN cannot communicate with the PCs on the voice VLAN without assistance from a Layer 3 device.

Part 3: Configure Switch and Router for VLAN Routing and Perform Test 2

This part of the lab continues using the same network topology (shown in Figure 7-1) and the hostnames, addresses, and subnet masks (given in Tables 7-2 and 7-3) as used in Part 2.

Task 1: Configure VLAN Trunking on Switch S1

Note: The default trunking encapsulation for the Cisco C2900XL switch is Inter-Switch Link (ISL). If using this switch model, configure dot1q encapsulation by issuing the following additional command from interface configuration mode on the trunk interface:

```
Switch(config-if)# switchport trunk encapsulation dot1q
```

Configure trunking between switch S1 and the router with 802.1Q encapsulation on both devices:

```
FC-ASW-1(config)# int fa0/1
FC-ASW-1(config-if)# switchport mode trunk
FC-ASW-1(config-if)# end
```

Task 2: Perform Basic Configuration of the Router

Step 1. Connect a PC to the console port of the router to perform configurations using a terminal emulation program.

Step 2. Confirm that the router is ready for lab configuration by ensuring that all existing configurations are removed. Refer to the "Erasing and Reloading the Router" section in Appendix C for these instructions.

Step 3. Configure router R1 with a hostname and console, Telnet, and privileged passwords:

```
Router(config)# hostname FC-CPE-1
FC-CPE-1(config)# line con 0
```

```
FC-CPE-1(config-line)# password cisco
FC-CPE-1(config-line)# login
FC-CPE-1(config-line)# line vty 0 4
FC-CPE-1(config-line)# password cisco
FC-CPE-1(config-line)# login
FC-CPE-1(config-line)# exit
FC-CPE-1(config)# enable password cisco
FC-CPE-1(config)# enable secret class
FC-CPE-1(config)# no ip domain lookup
FC-CPE-1(config)# end
```

Task 3: Configure VLAN Trunking on the Router

Step 1. Configure router R1 Fa0/0 interface to trunk for VLAN 1, VLAN 10, and VLAN 20 with IEEE 802.1Q encapsulation:

```
FC-CPE-1(config)# interface fa0/0
FC-CPE-1(config-if)# no shutdown
FC-CPE-1(config-if)# interface fa0/0.1
FC-CPE-1(config-subif)# encapsulation dot1Q 1
FC-CPE-1(config-subif)# ip address 10.0.1.1 255.255.255.0
FC-CPE-1(config-subif)# exit
FC-CPE-1(config)# interface fa0/0.10
FC-CPE-1(config-subif)# encapsulation dot1Q 10
FC-CPE-1(config-subif)# ip address 10.0.10.1 255.255.255.0
FC-CPE-1(config-subif)# exit
FC-CPE-1(config)# interface fa0/0.20
FC-CPE-1(config-subif)# encapsulation dot1Q 20
FC-CPE-1(config-subif)# ip address 10.0.20.1 255.255.255.0
FC-CPE-1(config-subif)# end
FC-CPE-1#
```

Step 2. On the router, issue the command **show vlan**.

Sample output:

```
FC-CPE-1# show vlans
Virtual LAN ID:  1 (IEEE 802.1Q Encapsulation)

   vLAN Trunk Interface:   FastEthernet0/0.1

 This is configured as native Vlan for the following interface(s) :
FastEthernet0/0

      Protocols Configured:   Address:     Received:      Transmitted:
               IP             10.0.1.1     21             43
             Other                        0              138
```

```
        396 packets, 67954 bytes input
        181 packets, 51149 bytes output


Virtual LAN ID:  10 (IEEE 802.1Q Encapsulation)

   vLAN Trunk Interface:   FastEthernet0/0.10

   Protocols Configured:   Address:      Received:       Transmitted:
            IP             10.0.10.1     94              25
          Other                         0               12


   94 packets, 15324 bytes input
   37 packets, 3414 bytes output


Virtual LAN ID:  20 (IEEE 802.1Q Encapsulation)

   vLAN Trunk Interface:   FastEthernet0/0.20

   Protocols Configured:   Address:      Received:       Transmitted:
            IP             10.0.20.1     9781            113
          Other                         0               14


  9781 packets, 939660 bytes input
  127 packets, 9617 bytes output
```

What information is displayed?

Step 3.   From switch S1, issue the command **show interfaces trunk**.

Sample output:

FC-ASW-1# **show interfaces trunk**

```
Port        Mode            Encapsulation  Status      Native vlan
Fa0/1       on              802.1q         trunking    1


Port        Vlans allowed on trunk
Fa0/1       1-4094


Port        Vlans allowed and active in management domain
Fa0/1       1,10,20


Port        Vlans in spanning tree forwarding state and not pruned
Fa0/1       1,10,20
```

What interface on switch S1 is in trunking mode?

_____

Which VLANs are allowed and active in the management domain?

_____

Task 4: Perform Test 2—Determine Whether the Hosts Can Communicate Between VLANs

This test confirms the operation of inter-VLAN routing by the router.

Step 1.   Issue the **show running-config** commands from the switch and verify all basic configuration settings.

Step 2.   Ping from the switch to the router default gateway for VLAN 1.

Was the ping successful? _____

Step 3.   Telnet from the switch to the router.

Was the Telnet successful? _____

Step 4.   With PC1 connected to switch port 4 and PC2 attached to port 14, attempt to ping from PC1 to PC2.

Do you expect the ping to be successful? _____

Why or why not?

_____

_____

_____

Step 5.   Telnet from PC1 to the switch and the router.

Do you expect the Telnet to be successful? _____

Why or why not?

_____

_____

_____

Step 6.   Issue the **show ip route** command on the router to display the routing table.

Sample output:

```
FC-CPE-1# show ip route
Codes: C - connected, S - static, R - RIP, M - mobile, B - BGP
       D - EIGRP, EX - EIGRP external, O - OSPF, IA - OSPF inter area
       N1 - OSPF NSSA external type 1, N2 - OSPF NSSA external type 2
       E1 - OSPF external type 1, E2 - OSPF external type 2
       i - IS-IS, su - IS-IS summary, L1 - IS-IS level-1, L2 - IS-IS level-2
       ia - IS-IS inter area, * - candidate default, U - per-user static route
       o - ODR, P - periodic downloaded static route
```

```
Gateway of last resort is not set

    10.0.0.0/24 is subnetted, 3 subnets
C      10.0.10.0 is directly connected, FastEthernet0/0.10
C      10.0.1.0 is directly connected, FastEthernet0/0.1
C      10.0.20.0 is directly connected, FastEthernet0/0.20
```

How many subnet routes are there?

_____

_____

This test demonstrates that the PCs from the main-net VLAN require Layer 3 routing to communicate with the PCs on the voice VLAN.

Reflection

Why is it important to develop a test plan and prototype network behavior?

_____

_____

_____

_____

_____

Lab 7-2: Creating a Test Plan for the Campus Network (7.2.2)

Upon completion of this lab, you will be able to create a test plan for a prototype LAN test.

This lab contains skills that relate to the following 640-802 CCNA exam objectives:

- Interpret network diagrams.

- Determine the path between two hosts across a network.

- Select the components required to meet a network specification.

- Select the appropriate media, cables, ports, and connectors to connect switches to other network devices and hosts.

- Perform and verify initial switch configuration tasks, including remote-access management.

- Verify network status and switch operation using basic utilities (including ping, traceroute, Telnet, SSH, arp, ipconfig) and **show** and **debug** commands.

- Describe enhanced switching technologies (including VTP, RSTP, VLAN, PVSTP, 802.1Q).

- Describe how VLANs create logically separate networks and the need for routing between them.

- Configure, verify, and troubleshoot VLANs.

- Configure, verify, and troubleshoot trunking on Cisco switches.

- Configure, verify, and troubleshoot inter-VLAN routing.

- Implement static and dynamic addressing services for hosts in a LAN environment.

- Select the appropriate media, cables, ports, and connectors to connect routers to other network devices and hosts.

- Access and use the router to set basic parameters, including CLI/SDM.

- Connect, configure, and verify operation status of a device interface.

- Verify device configuration and network connectivity using ping, traceroute, Telnet, SSH, or other utilities.

- Perform and verify routing configuration tasks for a static or default route given specific routing requirements.

Expected Results and Success Criteria

Before starting this lab, read through the tasks that you are expected to perform. What do you expect the result of performing these tasks will be?

_____

_____

_____

Why do you think it is important to create a test plan before beginning a prototype test?

_____

_____

_____

Why do you think it is important to perform prototype tests before implementing a proposed design?

_____

_____

_____

Background/Preparation

This lab takes you through the steps required for creating a test plan to test the FilmCompany LAN design. To prepare for this lab, you need information from the results of earlier labs that you saved in your portfolio. The required information can be found in these labs:

- The topology diagram created in Lab 5-6
- The IP address spreadsheet created in Lab 6-4

Task 1: Review the Supporting Documentation

Step 1.   Refer to the proposed LAN Design Network Topology diagram (Figure 5-6) you prepared in Lab 5-6 and filed in your portfolio.

List all the necessary equipment and cables required to build the LAN portion of the proposed network design.

_____

_____

_____

_____

List all the VLANs required to implement the design.

_____

_____

_____

_____

_____

Step 2.   Review the proposed IP Address Allocation spreadsheet (Table 6-8) created in Lab 6-4.

This includes determining the appropriate IP addressing for the devices identified in Lab 6-4 and an appropriate IP address range for each identified VLAN.

_____

_____

Task 2: Create the LAN Design Test Plan

The format used to create the test plans may vary. The format used for this, and subsequent labs, is similar to the document used by the Cisco Customer Proof-of-Concept Labs. It is divided into sections to make it easier to read and understand.

The test plan is a formal document that can be included in a proposal. It verifies that the design functions as expected. Many times, customer representatives are invited to view the prototype tests. In these cases, customers can review the design and see for themselves that the network meets the requirements.

Step 1.   Review the contents of the test plan document.

Review the LAN Design Test Plan found on the CD-ROM in the LAN_Design_Test_Plan.pdf file. If possible, print out this file so that it is more convenient to refer to while doing this lab.

Record a description of each section and what types of information each section requires you to enter.

Introduction:

_____

_____

_____

_____

Equipment:

_____

_____

_____

_____

Design and Topology:

_____

_____

_____

_____

Test Description:

_____

_____

_____

_____

_____

_____

Test Procedures:

_____

_____

_____

_____

Test Expected Results and Success Criteria:

_____

_____

_____

_____

Test Results and Conclusions:

_____

_____

_____

_____

Appendix:

_____

_____

_____

_____

Step 2.   Complete the Introduction section of the test plan.

In this example test plan, much of the information has already been entered.

Enter the purpose of the test.

Think about why you want to test the LAN portion of the design.

Enter what functions of the LAN design you intend to test.

Three tests are entered for you to use with this test plan.

- Test 1: Basic connectivity

- Test 2: VLAN configuration

- Test 3: VLAN routing

Step 3.   Complete the Equipment section of the test plan.

Using the information you recorded in Task 1, Step 1, complete the Equipment section of the chart. List all network devices and cables. Two personal computers are already listed to assist in the testing of the design.

Note: If your Academy lab does not include the required equipment for the design, discuss possible substitute models with your instructor.

Step 4.   Complete the Design and Topology section of the test plan:

- Copy the LAN topology from the diagram created previously in Lab 5-6 to the test topology area.

- Enter the IP addressing information recorded in Task 1, Step 2, in the test plan IP Address Plan chart.

- Enter the VLAN names and IDs recorded in Task 1, Steps 1 and 2, in the test plan VLAN plan.

- Enter any additional information that you want the technician performing the test to be aware of before the test begins.

Step 5.   Complete the Test Description section of the test plan.

In the Test Description section, enter the goals for each of the three tests that you plan to perform. Test 1 is completed as an example of how to fill in the information.

Step 6.   Complete the Procedures section of the test plan.

In the Test Procedures section, enter the steps necessary to perform each planned test.

Step 7.   Complete the Expected Results section of the test plan

In the Expected Results and Success Criteria section, enter what you expect the results to be if all the steps in the Test Procedures section are followed correctly. Determine what results need to be observed for the test to be considered a success.

Step 8.   Save the LAN Design Test Plan in your portfolio.

Note: Do not complete the Test Results and Conclusions section or the Appendix section. These will be completed in a later lab.

Lab 7-3: Testing the FilmCompany Network (7.2.5)

Upon completion of this lab, you will be able to use a test plan to test the design of a LAN.

This lab contains skills that relate to the following 640-802 CCNA exam objectives:

- Interpret network diagrams.

- Determine the path between two hosts across a network.

- Select the components required to meet a network specification.

- Select the appropriate media, cables, ports, and connectors to connect switches to other network devices and hosts.

- Perform and verify initial switch configuration tasks, including remote-access management.

- Verify network status and switch operation using basic utilities (including ping, traceroute, Telnet, SSH, arp, ipconfig) and **show** and **debug** commands.

- Describe enhanced switching technologies (including VTP, RSTP, VLAN, PVSTP, 802.1Q).

- Describe how VLANs create logically separate networks and the need for routing between them.

- Configure, verify, and troubleshoot VLANs.

- Configure, verify, and troubleshoot trunking on Cisco switches.

- Configure, verify, and troubleshoot inter-VLAN routing.

- Implement static and dynamic addressing services for hosts in a LAN environment.

- Select the appropriate media, cables, ports, and connectors to connect routers to other network devices and hosts.

- Access and use the router to set basic parameters, including CLI/SDM.

- Connect, configure, and verify operation status of a device interface.

- Verify device configuration and network connectivity using ping, traceroute, Telnet, SSH, or other utilities.

- Perform and verify routing configuration tasks for a static or default route given specific routing requirements.

Expected Results and Success Criteria

Before starting this lab, read through the tasks that you are expected to perform. What do you expect the result of performing these tasks will be?

_____

_____

_____

How do you think having a test plan will help you test the design of the network using a prototype?

_____

_____

_____

Background/Preparation

Network designers build and test prototype networks to ensure that the elements they have included in their designs work as expected and meet the objectives of their customers. Using a test plan is one way to organize the testing and ensure that all the design elements are tested in a way that is appropriate. Using the LAN Design Test Plan that you completed in Lab 7-2, you will perform the following tests:

- **Test 1: Baseline connectivity test**
    - Verify physical and IP connectivity between devices on the prototype network.
    - Document operation.
- **Test 2: VLAN configuration test**
    - Demonstrate multiple VLANs, vty, and port security.
    - Verify that members of the same VLAN can communicate successfully and that members of different VLANs are not able to communicate successfully.
    - Demonstrate 802.1Q trunk links between devices.
    - Verify STP to ensure that S1 becomes the root bridge.
    - Document operation.
- **Test 3: VLAN routing test**
    - Demonstrate routing of traffic between separate VLANs, unrestricted.
    - Demonstrate routing of traffic between separate VLANs, with restrictions.
    - Document operation.

Part 1: Perform Test 1—Basic Connectivity Test

Task 1: Build the Prototype Network

Step 1.   Select the necessary equipment and cables as specified in the Equipment section of the LAN Design Test Plan. See your instructor for assistance in identifying the appropriate equipment.

Note: If the PCs used in this lab are also connected to your Academy LAN or to the Internet, ensure that you record the cable connections and TCP/IP settings so that these can be restored at the conclusion of the lab.

Step 2.   Using the topology diagram and IP address plan contained in the Design and Topology Diagram section of the test plan in Lab 7-2, connect and configure the prototype network.

Note: Before configuring the devices apply the "Erasing and Reloading the Router and Erasing and Reloading the Switch" instructions in Appendix C of Part II of this Learning Guide to all routers and switches before continuing.

Step 3.   Following the procedures in the Test 1: Procedures section of the LAN Design Test Plan, console into one of the devices and verify that you can ping all the other device addresses. If you are unsuccessful, verify each device configuration. Repeat the connectivity testing.

Step 4.   Copy and paste the initial device configurations into a document using Notepad or a word processing program. Save or print the document to include with the completed test plan.

Task 2: Verify the Functionality of the Prototype Network

Step 1. Following the procedures in the Test 1: Procedures section, enter the various commands and record the results of the testing.

Step 2. Copy and paste the output of the various commands into a document using Notepad or a word processing program. Save or print the document to include with the completed test plan.

Task 3: Record the Test Results in the Results and Conclusions Section of the Test Plan

Step 1. Compare the results that you observed during the testing with the expected results listed in the Test 1: Expected Results and Success Criteria section.

Step 2. Determine whether the testing indicates that the network meets the success criteria. If it does, indicate that the test is successful.

Part 2: Perform Test 2—VLAN Configuration Test

Task 1: Configure the Prototype Network

Step 1. Follow the steps you created in the Test 2: Procedures section of the test plan to configure the VLANs on the prototype network.

Step 2. Using the VLAN plan specified in the Design and Topology Diagram section of the test plan, configure the switches with the appropriate VLANs.

Step 3. Configure the links between the switches as trunk links and permit all VLANs across the trunks.

Step 4. Configure one switch to be the root bridge.

Step 5. Configure port security on the ports attached to the two PCs to only accept one MAC address.

Step 6. Copy and paste the initial device configurations into a document using Notepad or a word processing program. Save or print the document to include with the completed test plan.

Task 2: Verify the VLAN Configuration Design

Step 1. Configure the port that connects to PC1 to be in one VLAN, and the port that connects to PC2 to be in a different VLAN.

Step 2. Following the procedures in the Test 2: Procedures section, configure each PC with an IP address that is correct for the VLAN they are assigned, using the IP addresses from the IP Address Plan in the Design and Topology Diagram section of the test plan.

Step 3. Execute the various **show** commands to verify that the VLANs and STP are operating as expected. Copy and paste the results of the commands into a document using Notepad or a word processing program. Save or print the document to include with the completed test plan.

Step 4. Attempt a ping from PC1 to PC2 to verify that the VLANs are successfully isolating traffic between the two PCs.

Step 5. Record the results in the Test 2: Results and Conclusions section of the test plan.

Task 3: Record the Test Results in the Results and Conclusions Section of the Test Plan

Step 1.   Compare the results that you observed during the testing with the expected results listed in the Test 2: Expected Results and Success Criteria section.

Step 2.   Determine whether the testing indicates that the network meets the success criteria. If it does, indicate that the test is successful.

Part 3: Perform Test 3—VLAN Routing Test

Task 1: Configure the Prototype Network

Step 1.   Follow the steps you created in the Test 3: Procedures section of the test plan to configure the router to route between VLANs.

Step 2.   Using the topology diagram shown in the Design and Topology Diagram section of the LAN Test Plan, configure the appropriate router to route between the VLANs created in Task 2.

Step 3.   Following the steps you listed in the Test 3: Procedures section, console into the switch that is directly connected to the router. Configure the link between the switch and the router as an 802.1Q trunk link and permit all VLANs across the trunk.

Step 4.   Console into the router and configure the router interface directly connected to the switch for 802.1Q encapsulation.

Step 5.   Configure the router with the appropriate IP addresses for the various VLANs. Verify that the routes appear correctly in the routing table.

Step 6.   Copy and paste the initial device configurations into a document using Notepad or a word processing program. Save or print the document to include with the completed test plan.

Task 2: Verify the VLAN Routing Design

Step 1.   Verify that the PCs are configured to be in different VLANs and that the IP address configuration on the PCs is correct. Configure the IP addresses assigned to the router, in Step 5 of Task 1, as the default gateway addresses for the PCs. Verify that the default gateway addresses are on the same networks as the addresses assigned to the PCs.

Step 2.   Following the procedures in the Test 3: Procedures section, ping from PC1 to PC2. Copy and paste the results into a document using Notepad or a word processing program. Save or print the document to include with the completed test plan.

Step 3.   Execute the various **show** commands to verify that the routing is correct.

Step 4.   Record the results in the Test 3: Results and Conclusions section of the test plan.

Task 3: Record the Test Results in the Results and Conclusions Section of the Test Plan

Step 1.   Compare the results that you observed during the testing with the expected results listed in the Test 3: Expected Results and Success Criteria section.

Step 2.   Determine whether the testing indicates that the network meets the success criteria. If it does, indicate that the test is successful.

Reflection

Was the prototype testing of the FilmCompany LAN design successful? Did having a test plan to work from help you organize your testing?

_____

_____

_____

_____

_____

_____

_____

Lab 7-4: Analyzing Results of Prototype Tests (7.2.6)

Upon completion of this lab, you will be able to analyze a network design and the results of a prototype test to determine whether weaknesses exist in the proposed design.

This lab contains skills that relate to the following 640-802 CCNA exam objectives:

- Interpret network diagrams.

- Identify and correct common network problems at Layers 1, 2, 3, and 7 using a layered model approach.

Expected Results and Success Criteria

Before starting this lab, read through the tasks that you are expected to perform. What do you expect the result of performing these tasks will be?

_____

_____

_____

Why do you think it is important to identify any weaknesses or risks contained in a proposed network design?

_____

_____

_____

Background/Preparation

Network designs often have weaknesses or areas of risk because the designer must work within constraints applied by the customer. These weaknesses can include obvious risks, such as no firewall or security filtering, or can be more difficult to identify. Using the results and conclusions of the LAN Design Test Plan you finished in Lab 7-3, determine whether there are areas where risk exists in your proposed design.

Task 1: Identify Any Design Weaknesses

Is the design able to scale to meet the growth, or do budget constraints limit the types of hardware and infrastructure that can be included?

_____

_____

_____

_____

_____

Do the IP addressing and VLAN configurations allow for the proposed growth?

_____

_____

_____

_____

_____

_____

_____

Can the selected hardware be upgraded easily without a major reconfiguration of the network?

_____

_____

_____

_____

_____

Can new access layer modules be integrated into the network without disrupting services to existing users?

_____

_____

Does the design provide for the smallest possible failure domains?

_____

_____

Are there multiple paths and redundant devices to protect against losing connectivity to important services?

_____

_____

_____

_____

_____

Task 2: Determine Risks of Identified Weaknesses

If, in Step 1, you identify weaknesses in the proposed design, what risks do these weaknesses present to FilmCompany?

_____

_____

_____

Task 3: Suggest Design Improvements to Reduce Risks

In what ways could the proposed design be improved to reduce the areas of risk?

_____

_____

_____

_____

_____

Task 4: Document Weaknesses and Risks

In the Results and Conclusions section of the LAN Design Test Plan, record any weaknesses, risks, and suggested improvements.

Ensure the completed LAN Design Test Plan is included in your lab portfolio.

Reflection

Why do you think it is important to identify weaknesses and risks in the proposed design before presenting it to the customer? What are some reasons that weaknesses cannot be corrected?

_____

_____

_____

_____

Lab 7-5: Creating a Server Farm Test Plan (7.3.2)

Upon completion of this lab, you will be able to create a test plan designed to test the functionality of the server farm. The plan should include the following:

- The subject and scope of the proposed test
- The methods and tools for testing
- Data to record
- The potential results

This lab contains skills that relate to the following 640-802 CCNA exam objectives:

- Interpret network diagrams.
- Determine the path between two hosts across a network.
- Select the components required to meet a network specification.
- Select the appropriate media, cables, ports, and connectors to connect switches to other network devices and hosts.
- Perform and verify initial switch configuration tasks, including remote-access management.
- Verify network status and switch operation using basic utilities (including ping, traceroute, Telnet, SSH, arp, ipconfig) and **show** and **debug** commands.
- Describe enhanced switching technologies (including VTP, RSTP, VLAN, PVSTP, 802.1Q).
- Describe how VLANs create logically separate networks and the need for routing between them.
- Configure, verify, and troubleshoot VLANs.
- Configure, verify, and troubleshoot trunking on Cisco switches.
- Configure, verify, and troubleshoot inter-VLAN routing.
- Implement static and dynamic addressing services for hosts in a LAN environment.
- Select the appropriate media, cables, ports, and connectors to connect routers to other network devices and hosts.
- Access and use the router to set basic parameters, including CLI/SDM.
- Connect, configure, and verify operation status of a device interface.
- Verify device configuration and network connectivity using ping, traceroute, Telnet, SSH, or other utilities.

Expected Results and Success Criteria

Before starting this lab, read through the tasks that you are expected to perform. What do you expect the result of performing these tasks will be?

_____

_____

_____

What considerations will influence your decisions about equipment to use for the test?

_____

_____

_____

What are the uptime requirements for a server farm?

_____

_____

_____

Background/Preparation

In this lab, you develop a test plan to support the business goal of improving server availability and security. You determine the nature of the tests to be performed, the methods and tools to be used, and the expected results.

The Server Farm Design Test Plan you use is provided on the CD-ROM as file Server_Farm_Design_Test_Plan.pdf. If possible, print out this file so that it is more convenient to refer to while doing this lab. This test plan is used as a basis for subsequent Labs 7-7 and 7-8, to test the simulated server farm prototype.

The Prototype Network Installation Checklist provided on the CD-ROM in file Prototype_Network_Installation_Checklist.pdf is followed when conducting the tests. If possible, print out this file so that it is more convenient to refer to while doing this lab.

Task 1: Review the Supporting Documentation

Step 1.   Before completing the Server Farm Design Test Plan, review the following material:

- The Server Farm Design Test Plan prototype network topology diagram.

- The IP address and the VLAN plans for the prototype topology shown in the IP Address Plan and VLAN Plan tables in the Server Farm Design Test Plan.

- The Prototype Network Installation Checklist created by the network designer.

- The partially completed Server Farm Design Test Plan.

Step 2.   Describe the functions of the network that the designer wants to test with this prototype.

_____

_____

_____

_____

Step 3.   Referring to the Server Farm Design Prototype Topology diagram in the test plan, create a
list of the equipment necessary to complete the prototype tests.

List any cables needed to connect the devices as shown in the Prototype Topology diagram. Use the information from this list to fill out the chart in the Equipment section of
the test plan document.

_____

_____

_____

_____

Task 2: Determine the Testing Procedures

Using the information contained on the Prototype Network Installation Checklist and the partially
completed Server Farm Design Test Plan document, determine what procedures should be followed to
perform each test listed on the plan. Using Test 1 as an example, fill out the Procedures sections for
Tests 2, 3, and 4 in the test plan.

Think about which commands and tools (such as ping, traceroute, and **show** commands) you can use
to verify that the prototype network is functioning as designed. Decide which outputs to save to prove
the results of your tests.

Task 3: Document the Expected Results and Success Criteria

Carefully identify what you expect the results of each test to show. What results would indicate that
the tests were a success?

Test 2: VLAN Configuration Test

_____

_____

_____

_____

Test 3: VLAN Routing Test

_____

_____

_____

_____

Test 4: ACL Filtering Test

_____

_____

_____

_____

Step 1.   Fill in the Expected Results and Success Criteria section for each test, using the information collected from the preceding tests.

Step 2.   Save the completed Server Farm Design Test Plan in your project portfolio. It is used in subsequent labs.

Reflection

Why is it important to think about and document the expected results and success criteria for each of the individual tests?

_____

_____

_____

_____

Lab 7-6: Configuring and Testing the Rapid Spanning Tree Prototype (7.3.3)

Upon completion of this lab, you will be able to

- Configure trunking on trunk ports to provide access to a router on the network.

- Configure separate VLANs for separate logical networks for production users and the server farm.

- Verify inter-VLAN connectivity.

- Enable RSTP and configure the root switch and backup root switch.

- Verify that the network can converge after inducing link and switch failures.

This lab contains skills that relate to the following 640-802 CCNA exam objectives:

- Describe enhanced switching technologies, including VTP, RSTP, VLAN, PVSTP, 802.1Q.

- Verify network status and switch operation using basic utilities (including ping, traceroute, Telnet, SSH, arp, ipconfig) and **show** and **debug** commands.

- Configure, verify, and troubleshoot RSTP operation.

Expected Results and Success Criteria

Before starting this lab, read through the tasks that you are expected to perform. What do you expect the result of performing these tasks will be?

_____

_____

_____

How will the tests performed in the lab illustrate the purpose of the Rapid Spanning Tree Protocol?

_____

_____

_____

Background/Preparation

The network designer has developed a test plan for the proposed FilmCompany server farm. The tests depend on the ability of the technicians to configure the switches to use STP, because the server farm test topology implements redundant switched links. In this lab, you review the basic functionality of Cisco Rapid Per VLAN Spanning Tree (PVST).

This lab uses the network topology shown in Figure 7-2, and the hostnames, addresses, and subnet masks given in Table 7-4.

Note: If the PCs used in this lab are also connected to your Academy LAN or to the Internet, ensure that you record the cable connections and TCP/IP settings so that these can be restored at the conclusion of the lab.

Figure 7-2   Lab 7-6 Network Topology

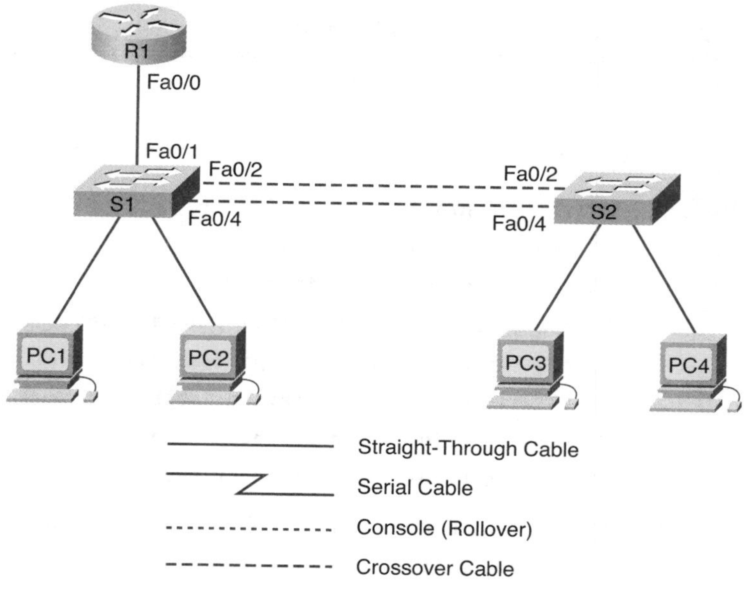

Table 7-4   Addressing Table for Lab 7-6

Device Designation	Device Name	IP Address	Subnet Mask	Default Gateway
R1	BR4	Fa0/0.110.0.0.1	255.255.255.0	
		Fa0/0.1010.10.10.254	255.255.255.0	
		Fa0/0.2010.10.20.254	255.255.255.0	
S1	FC-ASW-1	VLAN1: 10.0.0.2	255.255.255.0	10.0.0.1
S2	ProductionSW	VLAN1: 10.0.0.3	255.255.255.0	10.0.0.1
PC1	H1	10.10.10.10	255.255.255.0	10.10.10.254
PC2	H2	10.10.20.10	255.255.255.0	10.10.20.254
PC3	H3	10.10.10.11	255.255.255.0	10.10.10.254
PC4	H4	10.10.20.11	255.255.255.0	10.10.20.254

Task 1: Configure Switch S1 and S2

Step 1.   Confirm that the switch is ready for lab configuration by ensuring that all existing VLAN and general configurations are removed. Refer to the section "Erasing and Reloading the Switch" in Appendix C of Part II of this Learning Guide for these instructions.

Step 2.   Configure the hostname, access, and command mode passwords on the switch.

Step 3.   Configure FC-ASW-1 interface VLAN 1 with the VLAN1 IP address given in the addressing table.

Step 4.   Configure the switch default gateway.

Step 5.   Configure FC-ASW-1 for server and end-user VLANs in accordance with Table 7-5.

Table 7-5   Switch FC-ASW-1 VLANs

VLAN Number	VLAN Name
10	Servers
20	Users

Step 6.   Assign ports to VLANs on FC-ASW-1:

```
FC-ASW-1# configure terminal
FC-ASW-1(config)# interface Fa0/5
FC-ASW-1(config-if)# switchport mode access
FC-ASW-1(config-if)# switchport access VLAN10
FC-ASW-1(config-if)# interface Fa0/6
FC-ASW-1(config-if)# switchport mode access
FC-ASW-1(config-if)# switchport access VLAN20
```

Step 7.   Configure trunk ports on FC-ASW-1 to the router and ProductionSW:

```
FC-ASW-1(config)# interface Fa0/1
FC-ASW-1(config-if)# switchport mode trunk
FC-ASW-1(config-if)# interface Fa0/2
FC-ASW-1(config-if)# switchport mode trunk
FC-ASW-1(config-if)# interface Fa0/4
FC-ASW-1(config-if)# switchport mode trunk
```

Step 8.   Configure FC-ASW-1 as the VTP server:

```
FC-ASW-1# vlan database
FC-ASW-1(vlan)# vtp server
```

Step 9.   Configure Per VLAN Rapid Spanning Tree Protocol:

```
FC-ASW-1(config)# spanning-tree mode rapid-pvst
```

Task 2: Configure Switch S2

Step 1.   Confirm that the switch is ready for lab configuration by ensuring that all existing VLAN and general configurations are removed. Refer to the section "Erasing and Reloading the Switch" in Appendix C of Part II of this Learning Guide for these instructions.

Step 2.   Configure the hostname, access, and command mode passwords on each switch.

Step 3.   Configure ProductionSW interface VLAN 1 with the VLAN1 IP address given in the addressing table.

Step 4.   Configure the switch default gateway.

Step 5.   Configure ProductionSW for server and end-user VLANs in accordance with Table 7-6.

Table 7-6   Switch ProductionSW VLANs

VLAN Number	VLAN Name
10	Servers
20	Users

Step 6.   Assign ports to VLANs on ProductionSW:

```
ProductionSW# configure terminal
ProductionSW(config)# interface Fa0/5
ProductionSW(config-if)# switchport mode access
ProductionSW(config-if)# switchport access VLAN10
ProductionSW(config-if)# interface Fa0/6
ProductionSW(config-if)# switchport mode access
ProductionSW(config-if)# switchport access VLAN20
```

Step 7.   Configure trunk ports on ProductionSW to FC-ASW-1:

```
ProductionSW(config)# interface Fa0/2
ProductionSW(config-if)# switchport mode trunk
ProductionSW(config-if)# interface Fa0/4
ProductionSW(config-if)# switchport mode trunk
```

Step 8.   Configure ProductionSW to be a VTP client:

```
ProductionSW# vlan database
ProductionSW(vlan)# vtp client
ProductionSW(vlan)# vtp domain ServerFarm
```

Step 9.   Configure Per VLAN Rapid Spanning Tree Protocol:

```
ProductionSW(config)# spanning-tree mode rapid-pvst
```

Task 3: Configure Router R1

Step 1.   Confirm that the router is ready for lab configuration by ensuring that all existing configurations are removed. Refer to the section "Erasing and Reloading the Router" in Appendix C of Part II of this Learning Guide for these instructions.

Step 2.   Configure hostname, passwords, and line access on R1.

Step 3.   Configure subinterfaces on interface Fa0/0:

```
BR4# configure terminal
BR4(config)# interface Fa0/0
BR4(config-if)# no shut
BR4(config-if)# interface Fa0/0.1
BR4(config-subif)# description VLAN1
BR4(config-subif)# encapsulation dot1q 1
BR4(config-subif)# ip address 10.0.0.1 255.255.255.0
BR4(config-subif)# interface Fa0/0.10
BR4(config-subif)# description VLAN10
BR4(config-subif)# encapsulation dot1q 10.
BR4(config-subif)# ip address 10.10.10.254 255.255.255.0
BR4(config-subif)# interface Fa0/0.20
BR4(config-subif)# description VLAN20
BR4(config-subif)# encapsulation dot1q20
BR4(config-subif)# ip address 10.10.20.254 255.255.255.0
BR4(config-subif)# end
BR4#
```

Task 4: Configure the Hosts

Step 1.   Configure H1 and H3 to have IP addresses in the Servers VLAN, each with a default gateway of 10.10.10.254.

Step 2.   Configure H2 and H4 to have IP addresses in the Users VLAN, each with a default gateway of 10.10.20.254.

Task 5: Perform Basic Connectivity Tests

Step 1.   Test intra-VLAN connectivity for the Servers VLAN.

Ping from H1 to H3.

Was the ping successful? _____

If the ping fails, troubleshoot the configuration on the hosts and the VLAN configuration on the switches.

Step 2.   Test intra-VLAN connectivity for the Users VLAN.

Ping from H2 to H4.

Was the ping successful? _____

If the ping fails, troubleshoot the configuration on the hosts and the VLAN configuration on the switches.

Step 3.   Test inter-VLAN connectivity.

Ping from a host on the Servers VLAN to a host on the Users VLAN.

Was the ping successful? _____

If the ping fails, troubleshoot the router and switch configurations.

Task 6: Observe Results of Introduced Link and Device Failures

Step 1.   Issue the **show spanning-tree** command to determine the port status of the spanning tree on the server switch, FC-SW-1:

```
FC-ASW-1# show spanning-tree
VLAN0010
  Spanning tree enabled protocol ieee
  Root ID    Priority    32778
             Address     0030.F2C9.90A0
             Hello Time   2 sec  Max Age 20 sec  Forward Delay 15 sec
  Bridge ID  Priority    32778   (priority 32768 sys-id-ext 10)
             Address     0090.21AC.0C10
             Aging Time 300

Interface        Role Sts Cost       Prio.Nbr Type
---------------- ---- --- ---------- -------- ------------------------
Fa0/1            Desg FWD 19         128.3    Shr
Fa0/2            Root FWD 19         128.3    Shr
Fa0/4            Altn BLK 19         128.3    Shr
```

```
Fa0/5                Desg FWD 19        128.3   Shr
VLAN0020
  Spanning tree enabled protocol ieee
  Root ID    Priority    32788
             Address     0030.F2C9.90A0
             Hello Time   2 sec  Max Age 20 sec  Forward Delay 15 sec
  Bridge ID  Priority    32788  (priority 32768 sys-id-ext 20)
             Address     0090.21AC.0C10
             Aging Time 300


Interface         Role Sts Cost      Prio.Nbr Type
----------------  ---- --- --------- -------- ------------------------

Fa0/1             Desg FWD 19        128.3    Shr
Fa0/2             Root FWD 19        128.3    Shr
Fa0/4             Altn BLK 19        128.3    Shr
Fa0/6             Desg FWD 19        128.3    Shr
```

Which port is not currently participating in forwarding data?

Step 2. Induce a link failure on the server switch.

Remove the cable from one of the forwarding ports on FC-ASW-1.

Step 3. View the adjustment to the spanning tree.

Reissue the **show span** command.

How long did it take the switches to determine and use a backup link?

Step 4. Induce a device failure on the network.

Turn off the ProductionSW switch.

Ping from H1 to H2.

Was the ping successful? _____

Why was the ping was successful or unsuccessful?

Task 7: Clean Up

Erase the configurations and reload the routers and switches. Disconnect and store the cabling. For PC hosts that are normally connected to other networks (such as the school LAN or to the Internet), reconnect the appropriate cabling and restore the TCP/IP settings.

Reflection

In a network with multiple branch offices, why is the use of Rapid Spanning Tree Protocol important?

_____

_____

_____

Why is RSTP important when implementing a server farm?

_____

_____

Lab 7-7: Testing a Prototype Network (7.3.5)

Upon completion of this lab, you will be able to

- Connect and configure the devices for the prototype FilmCompany server farm.

- Verify successful implementation of RSTP, VLAN trunking, and VTP.

- Configure routing between VLANs.

- Create and apply appropriate ACLs to filter undesirable traffic.

- Evaluate network performance based on previously determined checklist criteria.

This lab contains skills that relate to the following 640-802 CCNA exam objectives:

- Interpret network diagrams.

- Determine the path between two hosts across a network.

- Select the components required to meet a network specification.

- Select the appropriate media, cables, ports, and connectors to connect switches to other network devices and hosts.

- Perform and verify initial switch configuration tasks, including remote-access management.

- Verify network status and switch operation using basic utilities (including ping, traceroute, Telnet, SSH, arp, ipconfig) and **show** and **debug** commands.

- Describe enhanced switching technologies (including VTP, RSTP, VLAN, PVSTP, 802.1Q).

- Describe how VLANs create logically separate networks and the need for routing between them.

- Configure, verify, and troubleshoot VLANs.

- Configure, verify, and troubleshoot trunking on Cisco switches.

- Configure, verify, and troubleshoot inter-VLAN routing.

- Select the appropriate media, cables, ports, and connectors to connect routers to other network devices and hosts.

- Access and use the router to set basic parameters, including CLI/SDM.

- Connect, configure, and verify operation status of a device interface.

- Verify device configuration and network connectivity using ping, traceroute, Telnet, SSH, or other utilities.

Expected Results and Success Criteria

Before starting this lab, read through the tasks that you are expected to perform. What do you expect the result of performing these tasks will be?

_____

_____

_____

Why is connectivity testing performed before configuring and applying ACLs, and after?

_____

_____

_____

Background/Preparation

In this lab, you construct the FilmCompany server farm prototype network and perform the tests described in the Server Farm Design Test Plan. You analyze the network performance after applying all the configurations, and complete the Results and Conclusions sections of the test plan.

Task 1: Assemble and Connect Network Devices

Step 1.   Review the Design and Topology Diagram and the Equipment sections of the Server Farm Design Test Plan.

Determine which equipment or suitable substitutes are required to meet the objectives of the lab.

Modify the topology diagram as necessary to fit available equipment.

Step 2.   Review the Prototype Network Installation Checklist used in Lab 7-5.

Accommodate any equipment limitations with the use of loopback addresses.

Task 2: Perform Test 1—Basic Connectivity Test

Step 1.   Using the Prototype Network Installation Checklist, perform the steps to connect and configure the prototype network to perform Test 1. Initial and date the Completed column as each step of the checklist is completed.

Step 2.   Perform the Test 1 procedures according to the Server Farm Design Test Plan and record the results in the Results and Conclusions section.

Determine whether the test was successful. If not, discuss your results with your instructor and the other students in your class. Perform the test again if necessary.

Task 3: Perform Test 2—VLAN Configuration Test

Step 1.   Using the Prototype Network Installation Checklist, perform the steps to connect and configure the prototype network to perform Test 2. Initial and date the Completed column as each step of the checklist is completed.

Step 2.   Perform the Test 2 procedures according to the Server Farm Design Test Plan and record the results in the Results and Conclusions section.

Determine whether the test was successful. If not, discuss your results with your instructor and the other students in your class. Perform the test again if necessary.

Task 4: Perform Test 3—VLAN Routing Test

Step 1. Using the Prototype Network Installation Checklist, perform the steps to connect and configure the prototype network to perform Test 3. Initial and date the Completed column as each step of the checklist is completed.

Step 2. Perform the Test 3 procedures according to the Server Farm Design Test Plan and record the results in the Results and Conclusions section.

Determine whether the test was successful. If not, discuss your results with your instructor and the other students in your class. Perform the test again if necessary.

Task 5: Perform Test 4—ACL Filtering Test

Step 1. Review security goals for the FilmCompany network developed when the network upgrade technical requirements were established and filed in your portfolio in Lab 2-5.

Examine the test plan, checklist, and other documentation to determine how ACLs can support the security goals.

Step 2. Examine results of connectivity tests to determine targets for the ACLs.

Decide which devices should be permitted, which protocols should be used, and where ACLs should be placed.

Step 3. Create ACLs.

Complete Table 7-7 to record the structure and syntax of the proposed ACLs.

Table 7-7   Proposed Access Control Lists

Firewall Rule	ACL Statements

Step 4. Using the Prototype Network Installation Checklist, perform the steps to connect and configure the prototype network to perform Test 4. Initial and date the Completed column as each step of the checklist is completed.

Step 5. Perform the Test 4 procedures according to the Server Farm Design Test Plan and record the results in the Results and Conclusions section.

Determine whether the test was successful. If not, discuss your results with your instructor and the other students in your class. Perform the test again if necessary.

Reflection

Examine the test results and conclusions. How would this network be affected if

- The number of servers was doubled?

  _____

  _____

- The S2 switch had a system failure?

  _____

- A new branch office with 25 new hosts was added?

  _____

  _____

Now that you have followed the process of prototyping from creating the plan through testing and recording results and conclusions, what are the advantages and disadvantages of using a simulation program, such as Packet Tracer, compared to building the prototype with physical devices?

_____

_____

_____

_____

_____

Lab 7-8: Identifying Risks and Weaknesses in the Design (7.3.6)

Upon completion of this lab, you will be able to

- Identify areas of risk and weakness in the server farm design implementation.

- Recommend solutions that will support eventual growth of the data center while maintaining desired network performance.

This lab contains skills that relate to the following 640-802 CCNA exam objectives:

- Interpret network diagrams.

- Identify and correct common network problems at Layers 1, 2, 3, and 7 using a layered model approach.

Expected Results and Success Criteria

Before starting this lab, read through the tasks that you are expected to perform. What do you expect the result of performing these tasks will be?

_____

_____

_____

What documentation should you gather to help you with the tasks you will perform in this lab?

_____

_____

_____

Background/Preparation

At the conclusion of the server farm prototype testing, the network designer is satisfied that the network performs as expected. However, several areas of concern exist that should be addressed. Future growth in the network could magnify these areas of risk and weakness, resulting in suboptimal network performance. Some design changes should be considered at this stage to prevent this from happening. In this lab, you identify possible areas of risk and weakness, and suggest possible changes to eliminate or minimize them.

Task 1: Identify Areas of Risk and Weakness in the Server Farm Implementation

Step 1.   Analyze the physical topology.

Examine the server farm topology as one entity and as a part of the entire FilmCompany topology. Consider each of the risks and weaknesses listed in Table 7-8. In the Description of Location and Devices column, describe the devices, connections, and issues that you find. Record **None found** if the design appears to avoid risks in that area.

Table 7-8   Server Farm Weaknesses and Risks

Weakness	Risk	Description of Location and Devices
Single point of failure	If a device fails, a portion of the network will be inoperable.	
Large failure domain	If a device or link fails, a large portion of the network will be affected.	
Possible bottlenecks	If the traffic volume increases, there is a potential for response time to degrade.	
Limited scalability	If the network grows more rapidly than expected, a costly upgrade will be needed.	
Overly complex design	If the design is too complex, the current staff will not be able to support it properly.	
Other possible weaknesses (specify):		

Step 2.   Analyze the results and conclusions of the testing.

Basic router and switch configurations were modified to support the following protocols and functions. Evaluate the results and conclusions that were drawn from the testing. Identify any areas where modifications to the configuration would provide better results, both now and in the future. Indicate the action required in Table 7-9.

Table 7-9   Server Farm Network Modification Checklist

	No Change Needed	Modifications Possible
VLAN port assignments		
VTP client/server assignments		
Root bridge designations		
Switch security		
Traffic filtering through ACLs		
Other (specify):		

Task 2: Suggest Design Modifications to Address Identified Risks and Weaknesses

From the analysis performed in Task 1, list each risk or weakness and suggest possible changes to the design to minimize or eliminate it in Table 7-10.

Table 7-10   Server Farm Network Suggested Modifications

Risk or Weakness Identified	Modification Suggested

Reflection

This lab focused on the weaknesses and associated risks of the proposed server farm network. Discuss why weaknesses and risks were analyzed rather than the strengths of the network design.

Prototyping the WAN: Labs

The lab exercises included in this chapter cover all the Chapter 8 online curriculum labs to ensure that you have mastered the practical, hands-on skills needed to plan, prototype, and test WAN and secure remote network connections, including Frame Relay and VPNs. As you work through these labs, use Chapter 8 in Part I of this book or use the corresponding Chapter 8 in the Discovery Designing and Supporting Computer Networks online curriculum for assistance.

Lab 8-1: Simulating WAN Connectivity (8.1.3)

Upon completion of this lab, you will be able to describe ways to simulate WAN connectivity in a prototype lab.

This lab contains skills that relate to the following 640-802 CCNA exam objectives:

- Configure and verify a basic WAN serial connection.
- Troubleshoot WAN implementation issues.
- Configure and verify a PPP connection between Cisco routers.

Expected Results and Success Criteria

Before starting this lab, read through the tasks that you are expected to perform. What do you expect the result of performing these tasks will be?

_____

_____

_____

What different issues do you need to consider when configuring a WAN connection compared to a LAN connection?

_____

_____

_____

Background/Preparation

In this lab, you will review the configuration of WAN links.

Any router or combination of routers that meets the interface requirements in the diagram (shown in Figure 8-1), such as 1600, 1700, 1800, 2500, or 2600 routers, can be used. Refer to the "Router Interface Summary" section in Appendix C, "Lab Equipment Interfaces and Initial Configuration Restoration" of Part II of this Learning Guide to correctly identify the interface identifiers to be used based on the equipment in the lab. Depending on the model of router, your output may vary from the output shown in this lab.

This lab will use the network topology shown in Figure 8-1, and the hostnames, addresses, and subnet masks given in Table 8-1.

Note: If the PCs used in this lab are also connected to your Academy LAN or to the Internet, ensure that you record the cable connections and TCP/IP settings so that these can be restored at the conclusion of the lab.

Figure 8-1   Lab 8-1 Network Topology

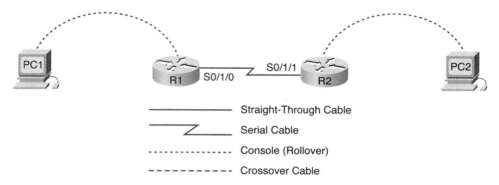

Straight-Through Cable

Serial Cable

Console (Rollover)

Crossover Cable

Table 8-1   Addressing Table for Lab 8-1

Device Designation	Device Name	Address	Subnet Mask
R1	Router1	S0/1/0 192.168.1.1	255.255.255.0
R2	Router2	S0/1/1 192.168.1.2	255.255.255.0

Task 1: Cable the Network

Step 1.   Cable and connect the devices as shown in Figure 8-1.

Step 2.   Apply power to all PCs and routers and establish a console session to each router using a terminal emulation program.

Step 3.   Confirm that each router is ready for lab configuration by ensuring that all existing configurations are removed. Refer to the section "Erasing and Reloading the Router" in Appendix C of Part II of this Learning Guide.

Task 2: Configure the Serial Interface on R1

Within the global configuration mode of R1, issue the following commands:

```
Router(config)# hostname Router1
Router1(config)# interface serial 0/1/0
Router1(config-if)# ip address 192.168.1.1 255.255.255.0
Router1(config-if)# no shutdown
Router1(config-if)# end
Router1#
```

Task 3: Configure the Serial Interface on R2

Within the global configuration mode of R2, enter the following commands:

```
Router(config)# hostname Router2
Router2(config)# interface serial 0/1/1
Router2(config-if)# ip address 192.168.1.2 255.255.255.0
Router2(config-if)# clock rate 56000
Router2(config-if)# no shutdown
Router2(config-if)# end
Router2#
```

Task 4: View the show interface Output

Step 1.   On Router1, issue the **show interface serial 0/1/0** command from the privileged EXEC mode to view the encapsulation type:

```
Router1# show interface serial 0/1/0
Serial0/1/0 is up, line protocol is up
  Hardware is GT96K Serial
  Internet address is 192.168.1.1/24
  MTU 1500 bytes, BW 128 Kbit, DLY 20000 usec,
     reliability 255/255, txload 1/255, rxload 1/255
  Encapsulation HDLC, loopback not set
  Keepalive set (10 sec)
  Last input 00:00:09, output 00:00:08, output hang never
  Last clearing of "show interface" counters 00:19:54
  Input queue: 0/75/0/0 (size/max/drops/flushes); Total output drops: 0
  Queueing strategy: fifo
  Output queue: 0/40 (size/max)
  5 minute input rate 0 bits/sec, 0 packets/sec
  5 minute output rate 0 bits/sec, 0 packets/sec
     14 packets input, 980 bytes, 0 no buffer
     Received 9 broadcasts, 0 runts, 0 giants, 0 throttles
     0 input errors, 0 CRC, 0 frame, 0 overrun, 0 ignored, 0 abort
     14 packets output, 1026 bytes, 0 underruns
     0 output errors, 0 collisions, 8 interface resets
     0 output buffer failures, 0 output buffers swapped out
     0 carrier transitions
     DCD=up  DSR=down  DTR=up  RTS=up  CTS=up
```

What is the encapsulation type?

Step 2.   On Router2, issue the **show interface serial 0/1/1** command from the privileged EXEC mode to view the encapsulation type:

```
Router2# show interface serial 0/1/1
Serial0/1/1 is up, line protocol is up
  Hardware is HD64570
  Internet address is 192.168.1.2/24
  MTU 1500 bytes, BW 1544 Kbit, DLY 20000 usec, rely 255/255, load 1/255
  Encapsulation HDLC, loopback not set, keepalive set (10 sec)
  Last input 00:00:05, output 00:00:06, output hang never
  Last clearing of "show interface" counters never
  Queueing strategy: fifo
  Output queue 0/40, 0 drops; input queue 0/75, 0 drops
  5 minute input rate 0 bits/sec, 0 packets/sec
  5 minute output rate 0 bits/sec, 0 packets/sec
     9 packets input, 616 bytes, 0 no buffer
     Received 4 broadcasts, 0 runts, 0 giants, 0 throttles
     2673 input errors, 2673 CRC, 0 frame, 0 overrun, 0 ignored, 1 abort
     101 packets output, 4001 bytes, 0 underruns
     0 output errors, 0 collisions, 43 interface resets
     0 output buffer failures, 0 output buffers swapped out
     5 carrier transitions
     DCD=up  DSR=up  DTR=up  RTS=up  CTS=up
```

What is the encapsulation type?

Task 5: Test Router Connectivity

From Router2, ping Router1 to test connectivity:

```
Router2# ping 192.168.1.1
Type escape sequence to abort.
Sending 5, 100-byte ICMP Echos to 192.168.1.1, timeout is 2 seconds:
!!!!!
Success rate is 100 percent (5/5), round-trip min/avg/max = 32/32/36 ms
```

If the ping is unsuccessful, troubleshoot the routers until connectivity is attained.

Task 6: Change the Encapsulation Type to PPP

Step 1.   From the privileged EXEC mode of Router1, issue the following commands to change the encapsulation type on the connecting serial interface to PPP:

```
Router1# config terminal
Router1(config)# interface serial 0/1/0
Router1(config-if)# encapsulation ppp
Router1(config-if)# end
Router1#
```

Step 2.   From the privileged EXEC mode of Router2, issue the following commands to change the encapsulation type on the connecting serial interface to PPP:

```
Router2# config terminal
Router2(config)# interface serial 0/1/1
Router2(config-if)# encapsulation ppp
Router2(config-if)# end
Router2#
```

Task 7: View the show interface Output

Step 1.   On Router1, issue the **show interface serial 0/1/0** command from the privileged EXEC mode to view the encapsulation type:

```
Router1# show interface serial 0/1/0
Serial0/1/0 is up, line protocol is up
  Hardware is GT96K Serial
  Internet address is 192.168.1.1/24
  MTU 1500 bytes, BW 128 Kbit, DLY 20000 usec,
     reliability 255/255, txload 1/255, rxload 1/255
  Encapsulation PPP, LCP Open
  Open: IPCP, CDPCP, loopback not set
  Keepalive set (10 sec)
  Last input 00:00:18, output 00:00:03, output hang never
  Last clearing of "show interface" counters 00:01:49
  Input queue: 0/75/0/0 (size/max/drops/flushes); Total output drops: 0
  Queueing strategy: fifo
  Output queue: 0/40 (size/max)
  5 minute input rate 0 bits/sec, 0 packets/sec
  5 minute output rate 0 bits/sec, 0 packets/sec
     31 packets input, 1837 bytes, 0 no buffer
     Received 0 broadcasts, 0 runts, 0 giants, 0 throttles
     0 input errors, 0 CRC, 0 frame, 0 overrun, 0 ignored, 0 abort
     40 packets output, 2960 bytes, 0 underruns
     0 output errors, 0 collisions, 2 interface resets
     0 output buffer failures, 0 output buffers swapped out
     8 carrier transitions
     DCD=up  DSR=down  DTR=up  RTS=up  CTS=up
```

Step 2.   On Router2, issue the **show interface serial 0/1/1** command from privileged EXEC mode to view the encapsulation type:

```
Router2# show interface serial 0/1/1
Serial0/1/1 is up, line protocol is up
  Hardware is HD64570
  Internet address is 192.168.1.2/24
  MTU 1500 bytes, BW 1544 Kbit, DLY 20000 usec, rely 255/255, load 1/255
  Encapsulation PPP, loopback not set, keepalive set (10 sec)
```

```
LCP Open
Open: IPCP, CDPCP
Last input 00:00:01, output 00:00:01, output hang never
Last clearing of "show interface" counters never
Queueing strategy: fifo
Output queue 0/40, 0 drops; input queue 0/75, 0 drops
5 minute input rate 0 bits/sec, 0 packets/sec
5 minute output rate 0 bits/sec, 0 packets/sec
   54 packets input, 4042 bytes, 0 no buffer
   Received 28 broadcasts, 0 runts, 0 giants, 0 throttles
   2673 input errors, 2673 CRC, 0 frame, 0 overrun, 0 ignored, 1 abort
   137 packets output, 6252 bytes, 0 underruns
   0 output errors, 0 collisions, 47 interface resets
   0 output buffer failures, 0 output buffers swapped out
   5 carrier transitions
   DCD=up  DSR=up  DTR=up  RTS=up  CTS=up
```

Can the serial interface on Router2 be pinged from Router1?

Can the serial interface on Router1 be pinged from Router2?

If the answer is **no** for either question, troubleshoot the router configurations to find the error.

Then reissue the pings until the answer to both questions is **yes**.

Task 8: Configure PPP Authentication with CHAP

Step 1. Configure the CHAP username and password on the R1 router. The username must be identical to the hostname of the other router. Both the password and usernames are case sensitive. Define the username and password to expect from the remote router. On Cisco routers, the secret password must be the same for both routers:

```
Router1(config)# username Router2 password cisco
Router1(config)# interface serial 0/1/0
Router1(config-if)# ppp authentication chap
Router1(config-if)# end
Router1#
```

Step 2. Configure the CHAP username and password on the R2 router. The passwords must be the same on both routers. The username must be identical to the hostname on the other router. Both the password and user names are case sensitive. Define the username and password to expect from the remote router:

```
Router2(config)# username Router1 password cisco
Router2(config)# interface serial 0/1/1
Router2(config-if)# ppp authentication chap
Router2(config-if)# end
Router2#
```

Task 9: Verify That the Serial Connection Is Functioning

Verify that the serial connection is functioning by pinging the serial interface of R1.

Was the ping successful?

_____

If the ping was unsuccessful, troubleshoot the router configurations to find the error. Reissue the pings until successful.

Why or why not?

_____

_____

Task 10: Clean Up

Erase any configurations and reload the router. Disconnect and store the cabling. For PC hosts that are normally connected to other networks (such as the school LAN or to the Internet), reconnect the appropriate cabling and restore the TCP/IP settings.

Challenge

Determine why it is necessary to set the encapsulation types when configuring a network.

_____

_____

_____

_____

Lab 8-2: Creating a WAN Connectivity Test Plan (8.2.2)

Upon completion of this lab, you will be able to do the following:

- Create a WAN connectivity test plan with multiple tests to determine the following:
    - Simulated Frame Relay connectivity
    - Backup Simulated VPN link functionality
- Describe the necessary information for each test to include the following:
    - Description of the test
    - Procedures
    - Anticipated results and success criteria

This lab contains skills that relate to the following 640-802 CCNA exam objectives:

- Interpret network diagrams.
- Determine the path between two hosts across a network.
- Select the components required to meet a network specification.
- Select the appropriate media, cables, ports, and connectors to connect switches to other network devices and hosts.
- Access and use the router to set basic parameters, including CLI/SDM.
- Connect, configure, and verify operation status of a device interface.
- Verify device configuration and network connectivity using ping, traceroute, Telnet, SSH, or other utilities.
- Perform and verify routing configuration tasks for a static or default route given specific routing requirements.
- Configure, verify, and troubleshoot EIGRP.
- Troubleshoot routing issues.
- Verify router hardware and software operation using **show** and **debug** commands.
- Implement basic router security.
- Describe different methods for connecting to a WAN.
- Configure and verify a basic WAN serial connection.
- Configure and verify Frame Relay on Cisco routers.
- Troubleshoot WAN implementation issues.

Expected Results and Success Criteria

Before starting this lab, read through the tasks that you are expected to perform. What do you expect the result of performing these tasks will be?

_____

_____

_____

How does creating a test plan help you organize your thoughts and plan for the actual network prototyping?

_____

_____

_____

Why do you think a pilot test, in addition to the prototype test, may be necessary to validate the WAN design?

_____

_____

_____

Background/Preparation

In this lab, you will demonstrate the ability to develop a test plan to support the business goal of improving network availability. This is accomplished by configuring backup connections so that connectivity is not lost for major applications if the Frame Relay link fails. These requirements include testing a Frame Relay WAN simulation with backup links. You will determine the nature of the tests to be performed, the methods and tools to be used, and the expected results. This test plan will be used as a basis for subsequent labs 8-3 and 8-4, to test simulated Frame Relay WAN prototypes.

Task 1: Review the Supporting Documentation

Step 1.   Review the contents of the test plan document.

Review the WAN Design Test Plan provided on the book's CD-ROM. If possible, print out this file so that it is more convenient to refer to while doing this lab.

What is the purpose of this WAN design test? Which elements of the design will be tested using this plan?

_____

_____

_____

_____

_____

Step 2.   Document the purpose of the test in the Introduction section of the WAN Design Test Plan.

Step 3.   Review the tests that will be run to validate the prototype.

Test 1 Title/Purpose:

_____

_____

Test 2 Title/Purpose:

_____

_____

_____

Task 2: Review the Test Equipment

Review the list of all equipment needed to build the prototype and to perform the tests. Be sure to include cables, optional connectors or components, and software. If the recommended equipment is not available in your lab, discuss possible substitutes with your instructor and classmates, based on interface requirements of the topology.

Step 1.   If substitute equipment must be used, list the devices here:

_____

_____

_____

Step 2.   Determine the amount of each type of cabling necessary to create the prototype test topology. Record the information on the Equipment chart in the WAN Design Test Plan.

Step 3.   Document any special configuration or cabling issues that might arise if substitute equipment is used.

_____

_____

_____

Task 3: Document Test 1 Information

Test 1. Description:

_____

Step 1.   Determine the goals of Test 1. Record them on the WAN Design Test Plan in the appropriate section.

Goals of Test:

The goals of this test are as follows:

_____

_____

_____

_____

Step 2.   Read through the Test 1 Procedures section in the test plan.

Add any additional procedures that you think are necessary to document the operation of the Frame Relay link and the EIGRP routing between Edge2 and BR3.

_____

_____

_____

_____

_____

Step 3.   Review the Expected Results and Success Criteria for Test 1.

Add any additional results you expect as an outcome of performing the procedures outlined for Test1.

_____

_____

_____

_____

_____

Task 4: Document Test 2 Information

Test 2. Description:

_____

_____

Complete the sections in the WAN Design Test Plan document for Test 2.

Step 1.   Fill in the Test 2 Description, Procedures, and Expected Results and Success Criteria sections.

Step 2.   Save the test plan in your portfolio. The WAN Design Test Plan is the basis for the next two labs in this course.

Reflection/Challenge

Why is Frame Relay a good choice as a primary WAN technology?

_____

_____

_____

_____

_____

When is it most important to have a backup link? How does a backup link compare to a redundant link?

_____

_____

_____

_____

Lab 8-3: Configuring and Verifying WAN Backup Links (8.2.5)

Upon completion of this lab, you will be able to do the following:

- Use a test plan to test the functionality of a Frame Relay WAN.

- Verify that the backup route is installed and connectivity is restored if the primary Frame Relay link goes down.

This lab covers skills that relate to the following 640-802 CCNA exam objectives:

- Interpret network diagrams.

- Determine the path between two hosts across a network.

- Select the components required to meet a network specification.

- Select the appropriate media, cables, ports, and connectors to connect switches to other network devices and hosts.

- Access and use the router to set basic parameters, including CLI/SDM.

- Connect, configure, and verify operation status of a device interface.

- Verify device configuration and network connectivity using ping, traceroute, Telnet, SSH, or other utilities.

- Perform and verify routing configuration tasks for a static or default route given specific routing requirements.

- Configure, verify, and troubleshoot EIGRP.

- Troubleshoot routing issues.

- Verify router hardware and software operation using **show** and **debug** commands.

- Implement basic router security.

- Describe different methods for connecting to a WAN.

- Configure and verify a basic WAN serial connection.

- Configure and verify Frame Relay on Cisco routers.

- Troubleshoot WAN implementation issues.

Expected Results and Success Criteria

Before starting this lab, read through the tasks that you are expected to perform. What do you expect the result of performing these tasks will be?

_____

_____

_____

How is an understanding of WAN technologies and Frame Relay important in network design?

_____

_____

_____

What methods can be used to provide backup communications links?

_____

_____

_____

Background/Preparation

This lab simulates the use of a Frame Relay circuit to interconnect the stadium site to the FilmCompany site. The focus of the lab is the simulation of a backup VPN link to be used if the primary link goes down. Use the WAN Design Test Plan provided on the book's CD-ROM (and reviewed in Lab 8-2) to determine the testing to be performed, the methods and tools to be used, and the potential results.

The configuration output used in this lab matches that of 1841 series and 2600 series router. The same or similar commands can be used with other Cisco routers but may produce slightly different output. Any router that meets the interface requirements displayed on the topology diagram may be used. Refer to the WAN Test Plan equipment notes made in Lab 8-2.

Perform Test 1: Frame Relay Configuration Test

The first test confirms the operation of Frame Relay in the WAN.

Task 1: Build the Network

Step 1.   Select the necessary equipment and cables as specified in the Equipment section of the WAN Design Test Plan. If necessary, see your instructor for assistance in identifying the appropriate equipment.

Note: If the PCs used in this lab are also connected to your Academy LAN or to the Internet, ensure that you record the cable connections and TCP/IP settings so that these can be restored at the conclusion of the lab.

Step 2.   Using the topology diagram and IP address plan contained in the Design and Topology Diagram section of the WAN Design Test Plan, connect and configure the prototype network.

Note: Before configuring the devices, apply the instructions in the section "Erasing and Reloading the Router" of Appendix C of Part II of this Learning Guide to all routers.

Step 3.   Ensure that the router functioning as the Frame Relay switch, FR1, is configured. If this router has not been preconfigured, your instructor will provide you with the necessary configuration commands.

Task 2: Configure Router ISPX as a Backup

Step 1.   Perform basic configuration of the ISPX router.

Configure the router with hostname, passwords, message-of-the–day, and **no ip domain lookup**.

```
Router(config)# hostname ISPX
ISPX(config)# line console 0
ISPX(config-line)# password cisco
ISPX(config-line)# login
ISPX(config-line)# exit
ISPX(config)# line vty 0 4
ISPX(config-line)# password cisco
ISPX(config-line)# login
ISPX(config-line)# exit
ISPX(config)# enable password cisco
ISPX(config)# enable secret class
ISPX(config)# no ip domain-lookup
ISPX(config)# banner motd #Unauthorized use prohibited#
ISPX(config)# end
```

Step 2. Configure ISPX router FastEthernet interfaces for the backup links to the Edge2 and BR3 routers.

Configure a description and the IP address, and activate each interface.

Step 3. Configure a static route on the ISPX router to the FilmCompany local network.

On the ISPX router, configure a normal static route to the BR3 network 172.18.225.0/25 via the Fa0/0 interface on BR3.

Step 4. Configure a static route on the ISPX router to the stadium local network.

On the ISPX router, configure a normal static route to the Edge2 network 172.18.3.0/24 via the Fa0/1 interface on Edge2.

Task 3: Configure the Stadium Edge2 Router

Step 1. Perform basic configuration of the router.

Configure the router with a hostname, passwords, message-of-the–day, and **no ip domain lookup**.

Step 2. Configure stadium router Edge2 serial interface.

Configure the Serial 0/1/1 interface with Frame Relay encapsulation.

Configure a point-to-point subinterface for DLCI 110.

```
Edge2(config)# interface serial0/1/1
Edge2(config-if)# description primary link to BR3
Edge2(config-if)# encapsulation frame-relay
Edge2(config-if)# no shutdown
Edge2(config-if)# interface serial0/1/1.110 point-to-point
Edge2(config-subif)# ip address 172.18.0.9 255.255.255.252
Edge2(config-subif)# frame-relay interface-dlci 110
Edge2(config-fr-dlci)# end
```

Step 3.   Configure stadium router Edge2 FastEthernet interfaces.

Configure FastEthernet 0/0 interface for the stadium LAN network with the address 172.18.3.0/24 and appropriate description.

Configure FastEthernet 0/1 interface for the backup link to the ISPX router in accordance the topology diagram.

Step 4.   Configure a dynamic routing protocol on stadium router Edge2.

On Edge2, configure the EIGRP routing protocol to advertise the 172.18.3.0/24 network and the 172.18.0.8/30 network. Use EIGRP process ID 10. Disable autosummary.

Configure EIGRP MD5 authentication to accept updates from the FilmCompany router BR3 on the Frame Relay subinterface.

The commands to configure EIGRP authentication are as follows:

```
Edge2# configure terminal
Edge2(config)# key chain MYCHAIN
Edge2(config-keychain)# key 1
Edge2(config-keychain-key)# key-string securetraffic
Edge2(config-keychain-key)# exit
Edge2(config)# interface serial 0/1/1.110
Edge2(config-subif)# ip authentication mode eigrp 10 md5
Edge2(config-subif)# ip authentication key-chain eigrp 10 MYCHAIN
Edge2(config-subif)# end
Edge2#
```

Note: Until EIGRP and MD5 configuration are complete on router BR3, no EIGRP updates will be received. The **debug eigrp packet** command can be used to view the EIGRP exchange as it is occurring between the routers.

Task 4: Configure the FilmCompany BR3 Router

Step 1.   Perform basic configuration of the router.

Configure the router with a hostname, passwords, message-of-the–day, and **no ip domain lookup**.

Step 2.   Configure router BR3 serial interface.

Configure Serial 0/1/0 interface with Frame Relay encapsulation. Configure a point-to-point subinterface for DLCI 100.

```
BR3(config)# interface serial0/1/0
BR3(config-if)# description primary link to Edge2
BR3(config-if)# encapsulation frame-relay
BR3(config-if)# no shutdown
BR3(config-if)# interface serial0/1/0.100 point-to-point
BR3(config-subif)# ip address 172.18.0.10 255.255.255.252
BR3(config-subif)# frame-relay interface-dlci 100
BR3(config-fr-dlci)# end
```

Step 3.   Configure router BR3 serial interface.

Configure FastEthernet 0/1 interface for the FilmCompany LAN network with the address 172.18.225.0/25 and appropriate description.

Configure FastEthernet 0/0 interface for the backup link to the ISPX router per the topology diagram.

Step 4.   Configure the dynamic routing protocol on router BR3.

On BR3, configure the EIGRP routing protocol to advertise the 172.18.225.0/25 network and the 172.18.0.8/30 network. Use EIGRP process ID 10. Disable autosummary.

Configure EIGRP MD5 authentication to accept routing updates from the Edge2 router on interface serial0/1/0.100.

The commands to configure EIGRP authentication are as follows:

```
BR3# configure terminal
BR3(config)# key chain MYCHAIN
BR3(config-keychain)# key 1
BR3(config-keychain-key)# key-string securetraffic
BR3(config-keychain-key)# exit
BR3(config)# interface serial 0/1/0.100
BR3(config-subif)# ip authentication mode eigrp 10 md5
BR3(config-subif)# ip authentication key-chain eigrp 10 MYCHAIN
BR3(config-subif)# end
```

Step 5.   When authentication is configured, both Edge2 and BR3 should begin accepting EIGRP updates. Use the **show ip route command** to verify that the routes to the LAN devices have been learned.

Until EIGRP and MD5 configuration are complete on router BR3, no EIGRP updates will be received successfully. The command **debug eigrp packet** shows when EIGRP authentication is successful. The following shows output of the **debug eigrp packet** command after BR3 has been correctly configured:

```
BR3# debug eigrp packet
00:47:04: EIGRP: received packet with MD5 authentication, key id = 1
00:47:04: EIGRP: Received HELLO on Serial0/1/0.100 nbr 172.18.0.9
```

Task 5: Conduct Primary Frame Relay Link Testing Based on the Test Plan

Execute the procedures outlined in WAN Test Plan Test 1 to test the simulated Frame relay network. Record the results of the tests in the Test 1: Results and Conclusions section.

Step 1.   Console into routers Edge2 and BR3 and verify the basic configuration, IP addressing, Frame Relay.

Issue the **show running-config** command for each of the routers to verify passwords, IP addressing, and Frame Relay configuration.

Step 2.   Verify the Frame Relay configuration on Edge2, BR3, and FR1.

Use **show frame-relay** commands to verify the Frame Relay configurations.

- **show frame-relay map:** Status of point-to-point links

- **show frame-relay pvc:** Permanent Virtual Circuit (PVC) status and statistics

- **show frame-relay lmi**: Local Management Interface (LMI) statistics

- **show frame-relay route**: DLCI/interface routing (FR1 switch only)

Step 3.   Verify routing table contents on router Edge2.

Display the routing table for Edge2 using the **show ip route** command.

```
Edge2# show ip route
Codes: C - connected, S - static, R - RIP, M - mobile, B - BGP
       D - EIGRP, EX - EIGRP external, O - OSPF, IA - OSPF inter area
       N1 - OSPF NSSA external type 1, N2 - OSPF NSSA external type 2
       E1 - OSPF external type 1, E2 - OSPF external type 2
       i - IS-IS, su - IS-IS summary, L1 - IS-IS level-1, L2 - IS-IS level-2
       ia - IS-IS inter area, * - candidate default, U - per-user static
route
       o - ODR, P - periodic downloaded static route


Gateway of last resort is not set


     172.18.0.0/16 is variably subnetted, 4 subnets, 3 masks
C       172.18.0.248/30 is directly connected, FastEthernet0/1
D       172.18.225.0/25
           [90/2172416] via 172.18.0.10, 00:09:33, Serial0/0/1.110
C       172.18.0.8/30 is directly connected, Serial0/0/1.110
C       172.18.3.0/24 is directly connected, FastEthernet0/0
```

Locate the EIGRP route to the FilmCompany LAN 172.18.225.0/25.

What is the AD of this route?

_____

What is the next hop IP address to get to this network?

_____

Does the primary route take the Frame Relay link?

_____

Step 4.   Verify routing table contents on router BR3.

Display the routing table for BR3 using the **show ip route** command.

```
BR3# show ip route
Codes: C - connected, S - static, R - RIP, M - mobile, B - BGP
       D - EIGRP, EX - EIGRP external, O - OSPF, IA - OSPF inter area
       N1 - OSPF NSSA external type 1, N2 - OSPF NSSA external type 2
       E1 - OSPF external type 1, E2 - OSPF external type 2
       i - IS-IS, su - IS-IS summary, L1 - IS-IS level-1, L2 - IS-IS level-2
       ia - IS-IS inter area, * - candidate default, U - per-user static
route
       o - ODR, P - periodic downloaded static route
```

```
Gateway of last resort is not set


     172.18.0.0/16 is variably subnetted, 4 subnets, 3 masks
C        172.18.225.0/25 is directly connected, FastEthernet0/1
C        172.18.225.248/30 is directly connected, FastEthernet0/0
C        172.18.0.8/30 is directly connected, Serial0/0/0.100
D        172.18.3.0/24 [90/2172416] via 172.18.0.9, 00:11:59, Serial0/0/0.100
```

Locate the EIGRP route to the Edge2 network 172.18.3.1/24.

What is the AD of this route?

Step 5.   Verify routing table contents on router ISPX.

Display the routing table for ISPX using the **show ip route** command.

```
ISPX# show ip route
Codes: C - connected, S - static, R - RIP, M - mobile, B - BGP
       D - EIGRP, EX - EIGRP external, O - OSPF, IA - OSPF inter area
       N1 - OSPF NSSA external type 1, N2 - OSPF NSSA external type 2
       E1 - OSPF external type 1, E2 - OSPF external type 2
       i - IS-IS, su - IS-IS summary, L1 - IS-IS level-1, L2 - IS-IS level-2
       ia - IS-IS inter area, * - candidate default, U - per-user static
route
       o - ODR, P - periodic downloaded static route


Gateway of last resort is not set


     172.18.0.0/16 is variably subnetted, 4 subnets, 3 masks
C        172.18.0.248/30 is directly connected, FastEthernet0/1
S        172.18.225.0/25 [1/0] via 172.18.225.249
C        172.18.225.248/30 is directly connected, FastEthernet0/0
S        172.18.3.0/24 [1/0] via 172.18.0.249
```

Are there any EIGRP routes?

Why or why not?

List any static routes shown.

What is the purpose of these static routes?

_____

_____

Test IP connectivity between routers Edge2 and BR3 via the primary Frame Relay link.

Step 1. Ping from Edge2 to the IP address of host PC2.

Was the ping successful?

_____

If not, troubleshoot until successful.

Step 2. Ping from BR3 to the IP address of host PC1.

Was the ping successful?

_____

If not, troubleshoot until successful.

Step 3. Verify that traffic is taking the correct path by using the **traceroute** command.

Step 4. Turn off all debugging using the **undebug all** command.

Step 5. Record all results in the WAN Design Test Plan document in the Test 1: Results and Conclusions section.

Perform Test 2: Backup Link Configuration Test

This test checks the operation of the WAN backup link.

Task 1: Configure Floating Static Routes

Configure a floating static route on Edge2 and BR3 via the backup Frame Relay link.

Note: Recall, as presented in CCNA Discovery: Introducing Routing and Switching in the Enterprise, Chapter 5, by default, a static route has a lower administrative distance than the route learned from a dynamic routing protocol. A floating static route has a higher administrative distance than the route learned from a dynamic routing protocol. For that reason, a floating static route does not display in the routing table. The floating static route entry appears in the routing table only if the dynamic information is lost.

Step 1. On Edge2, configure a static route to the FilmCompany LAN (172.18.225.0/25) using the next hop address of the interface Fa0/1 on router ISPX. Configure the administrative distance on the floating static routes to be 130, greater than the administrative distance of the EIGRP learned route.

Step 2. On BR3, configure a static route to the stadium LAN (172.18.3.0/24) using the next hop address of the interface Fa0/0 on router ISPX. Configure the administrative distance on the floating static route to be 130, greater than the administrative distance of the EIGRP learned route.

Task 2: Conduct Backup Link Test

Step 1.   Test the backup link though the ISPX router by taking down the primary Frame Relay link.

Cause the Frame Relay link from Edge2 to FR1 to fail by shutting down the Serial 0/1/1 interface.

Step 2.   Verify routing table contents on router Edge2.

Display the routing table for Edge2 using the **show ip route** command.

```
Edge2# show ip route
Codes: C - connected, S - static, R - RIP, M - mobile, B - BGP
       D - EIGRP, EX - EIGRP external, O - OSPF, IA - OSPF inter area
       N1 - OSPF NSSA external type 1, N2 - OSPF NSSA external type 2
       E1 - OSPF external type 1, E2 - OSPF external type 2
       i - IS-IS, su - IS-IS summary, L1 - IS-IS level-1, L2 - IS-IS level-2
       ia - IS-IS inter area, * - candidate default, U - per-user static
route
       o - ODR, P - periodic downloaded static route

Gateway of last resort is not set

     172.18.0.0/16 is variably subnetted, 3 subnets, 3 masks
C       172.18.0.248/30 is directly connected, FastEthernet0/1
S       172.18.225.0/25 [130/0] via 172.18.0.250
C       172.18.3.0/24 is directly connected, FastEthernet0/0
```

Is there an EIGRP route to the FilmCompany network 172.18.225.0/25 now?

_____

Is the floating static backup route to the FilmCompany network 172.18.225.0/25 that you defined earlier now present?

_____

What is the AD of this route?

_____

What is the next hop IP address to get to the 172.18.225.0/25 network?

_____

Does the backup route take the ISPX link?

_____

Step 3.   Verify routing table contents on router BR3.

Display the routing table for BR3 using the **show ip route** command.

```
BR3# show ip route
Codes: C - connected, S - static, R - RIP, M - mobile, B - BGP
       D - EIGRP, EX - EIGRP external, O - OSPF, IA - OSPF inter area
       N1 - OSPF NSSA external type 1, N2 - OSPF NSSA external type 2
```

```
          E1 - OSPF external type 1, E2 - OSPF external type 2
          i - IS-IS, su - IS-IS summary, L1 - IS-IS level-1, L2 - IS-IS level-2
          ia - IS-IS inter area, * - candidate default, U - per-user static
route
          o - ODR, P - periodic downloaded static route


Gateway of last resort is not set


      172.18.0.0/16 is variably subnetted, 3 subnets, 3 masks
C        172.18.225.0/25 is directly connected, FastEthernet0/1
C        172.18.225.248/30 is directly connected, FastEthernet0/0
S        172.18.3.0/24 [130/0] via 172.18.225.250
```

Note: It will take BR3 some time to declare that the EIGRP route to the Edge2 172.18.3.1 network via the Frame Relay link is down. The link from BR3 to the Frame Relay switch appears to be good from the BR3 side. BR3 will have to wait until the timers expire after receiving no EIGRP updates from Edge2.

Continue to issue the **show ip route** command until the EIGRP route is gone and the floating static route is installed; otherwise, ping responses (echo reply) cannot be sent back to Edge2.

Is there an EIGRP route to the Edge2 network 172.18.3.0/24?

Is there a floating static route?

What is the AD of this route?

What is the next hop IP address to get to the 172.18.3.0/24 network?

Step 4.   Test IP connectivity between routers Edge2 and BR3 via the backup Ethernet link.

Ping from PC1 on Edge2 to the IP address of host PC2.

Was the ping successful?

If not successful, troubleshoot until successful.

Note: While the backup link route is active, pings from router Edge2 to the IP address of host PC2 will not be successful. The source of the ping will be the IP address of the Fa0/1 interface (172.18.0.249) instead of the PC1 IP address, and router BR3 does not have a route back to that network when static routing is in effect.

Step 5.   Verify that traffic is taking the backup link by using the **tracert** command from PC1 to PC2. Record the results in the WAN Design Test Plan section Test 2: Results and Conclusions.

Step 6.   Turn off any debugging using the **undebug all** command.

Task 3: Clean Up

Erase the configurations and reload the routers. Disconnect and store the cabling. For PC hosts that are normally connected to other networks (such as the school LAN or to the Internet), reconnect the appropriate cabling and restore the TCP/IP settings.

Reflection/Challenge

When is it most important to have a backup link? How does a backup link compare to a redundant link?

_____

_____

_____

_____

This lab uses the RIP dynamic routing protocol and floating static routes to demonstrate primary and backup routes. Would it be possible to use all static routes and no dynamic routing protocol?

_____

_____

_____

_____

Lab 8-4: Evaluating the Prototype WAN Test (8.2.6)

Upon completion of this lab, you will be able to do the following:

- Analyze the results of the WAN Connectivity prototype test.

- Document the results and identify potential risks or weaknesses in the prototype and planned design.

- Complete the Results and Conclusions section of the test plan.

This lab contains skills that relate to the following 640-802 CCNA exam objectives:

- Interpret network diagrams.

- Identify and correct common network problems at Layers 1, 2, 3, and 7 using a layered model approach.

Expected Results and Success Criteria

Before starting this lab, read through the tasks that you are expected to perform. What do you expect the result of performing these tasks will be?

_____

_____

_____

Why do you think it is important to identify any weaknesses or risks contained in a proposed WAN network design?

_____

_____

_____

Background/Preparation

Network designs often have weaknesses or areas of risk because the designer must work within constraints applied by the customer. These weaknesses can include obvious risks, such as no firewall or security filtering, or can be harder to identify. Using the results and conclusions of the WAN Design Test Plan you finished in Lab 8-3, determine whether there are areas where risk exists in your proposed design.

Task 1: Identify Any Weaknesses in the Design

Step 1.   Is the Frame Relay WAN design able to scale to meet the expected growth?

_____

_____

Step 2. Do the results of the prototype test indicate that the Frame Relay configuration will work as expected?

_____

_____

_____

_____

_____

Step 3. Are there any weaknesses associated with using the VPN connections as backup to the Frame Relay WAN?

_____

_____

_____

_____

_____

_____

_____

_____

Step 4. Will a failure of the primary link cause the FilmCompany to lose connectivity to the Stadium LAN?

_____

_____

Step 5. Does the EIGRP authentication provide for a secure transmission of the routing updates?

_____

_____

_____

Task 2: Determine the Risks If Weaknesses Are Not Corrected

If you identified weaknesses in the proposed design in Task 1, what risks do these weaknesses present to FilmCompany?

_____

_____

_____

_____

Task 3: Suggest How Design Improvements Can Reduce Risk

In what ways could the proposed design be improved to reduce the areas of risk?

_____

_____

_____

_____

_____

_____

_____

Task 4: Document the Weaknesses and Risks on the Test Plan

In the Results and Conclusions section of the WAN Test Plan, record any weaknesses, risks, and suggested improvements.

Reflection

Why do you think it is important to identify weaknesses and risks in the proposed design before presenting it to the customer? What are some reasons that weaknesses cannot be corrected?

_____

_____

_____

_____

_____

Lab 8-5: Creating a VPN Connectivity Test Plan (8.3.2)

Upon completion of this lab, you will be able to:

- Create a VPN connectivity test plan with multiple tests to determine the following:

    - How to set up a VPN server on an edge router

    - How to simulate VPN client connectivity

- Describe the necessary information for the overall Test Plan to include the following:

    - Introduction

    - Equipment

    - Design and topology diagram

- Describe the necessary information for each test to include the following:

    - Description of the test

    - Procedures

    - Anticipated results and success criteria

    - Conclusions

This lab contains skills that relate to the following 640-802 CCNA exam objectives:

- Interpret network diagrams.

- Determine the path between two hosts across a network.

- Select the components required to meet a network specification.

- Select the appropriate media, cables, ports, and connectors to connect switches to other network devices and hosts.

- Access and use the router to set basic parameters, including CLI/SDM.

- Connect, configure, and verify operation status of a device interface.

- Verify device configuration and network connectivity using ping, traceroute, Telnet, SSH, or other utilities.

- Describe VPN technology (including the importance, benefits, role, impact, and components).

Expected Results and Success Criteria

Before starting this lab, read through the tasks that you are expected to perform. What do you expect the result of performing these tasks will be?

_____

_____

_____

What functions of a VPN do you think can be tested in a prototype environment?

_____

_____

_____

Why is using a VPN critical to supporting remote workers?

_____

_____

_____

Background/Preparation

An important business goal for both the stadium and the FilmCompany is the ability to support remote workers. An important technical requirement includes providing secure VPN connectivity via the Internet with ease of manageability. This can be accomplished using Cisco EasyVPN Server to configure and manage a VPN server and installing Cisco VPN on clients.

This lab demonstrates the ability to develop a test plan to support the network VPN prototype. The prototype includes the configuration and testing of a VPN client, to simulate a remote worker, and a VPN server, to simulate the server, to be installed on the network.

The Cisco SDM GUI on the 1841 is used to configure the EasyVPN Server for the remote clients. In this lab, you will determine the nature of the tests to be performed, the methods and tools to be used, and the expected results. This test plan will be used as a basis for subsequent Labs 8-6 and 8-7.

Task 1: Review the VPN Design Test Plan

Review the VPN Design Test Plan provided on the accompanying CD-ROM as file VPN_Design_Test_Plan.pdf. Note the tests that the designer indicates are necessary to perform using the prototype network.

Test 1: Description and purpose:

_____

Test 2: Description and purpose:

_____

Task 2: Review the Equipment Section

Which device will be used as the VPN server in the prototype network?

_____

What IOS software version is necessary to configure the EasyVPN server?

_____

Is equipment available in your lab with the correct IOS to build the prototype network configuration?

_____

Task 3: Review the Design and Topology Section

The network topology given in the VPN Test Plan is to be used for testing the VPN part of the network design. Figure 8-2 shows the actual production VPN network topology that has been designed. Compare and note the differences between both topologies.

Remote workers usually connect to the Internet and then use client software to create the VPN tunnel to the server. In the prototype environment, the connection between the VPN client and the VPN server is a much more direct connection.

What is the risk of testing the VPN operation in a prototype environment?

_____

_____

_____

The VPN server will assign a logical address to the remote host H1 that is valid on the internal network. This address will be assigned dynamically, when the VPN tunnel is created.

Figure 8-2   VPN Production Network Topology

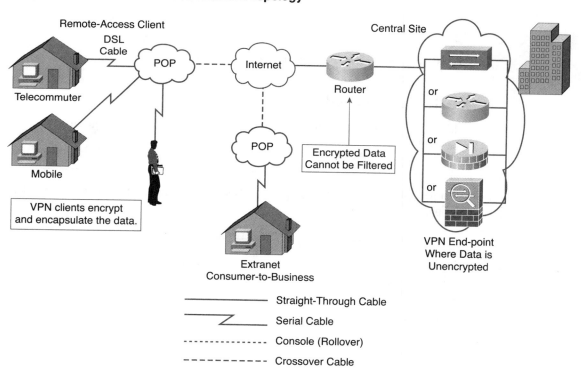

Task 4: Review the Test 1 Description, Procedures, and Expected Results

The designer needs to verify that the EasyVPN server can be configured and managed by the existing personnel. It is important to document how the Cisco SDM software can be used to configure and manage the VPN server.

Task 5: Review the Test 2 Description, Procedures, and Expected Results

Read through the Test 2 information in the test plan. Determine an appropriate goal for Test 2 and fill in the table in the VPN Design Test Plan.

After reading the Procedures section, what do you think would be a successful outcome of completing the Test 2 procedures?

_____

_____

_____

_____

Record your answers in the Expected Results and Success Criteria section for Test 2.

Reflection/Challenge

Why do you think it is important to test the VPN operation in a pilot installation, as well as a prototype test?

_____

What are the benefits of managing the VPN server with internal personnel, rather than using the ISP to manage it?

_____

_____

_____

_____

Lab 8-6: Creating a Cisco EasyVPN Server (Optional Lab) (8.3.4.3)

Upon completion of this lab, you will be able to do the following:

- Configure basic router global settings using IOS for SDM access.

- Configure EasyVPN Server using SDM on a Cisco router.

This lab contains skills that relate to the following 640-802 CCNA exam objectives:

- Describe VPN technology (including the importance, benefits, role, impact, and components).

Expected Results and Success Criteria

Before starting this lab, read through the tasks that you are expected to perform. What do you expect the result of performing these tasks will be?

_____

_____

_____

How is the ability to create a VPN server important in network design and prototyping?

_____

_____

_____

Background/Preparation

In this lab you will configure a Cisco 1841 (or equivalent) router as a VPN server using the SDM graphical user interface and the EasyVPN Server Wizard. This router will simulate the VPN server in the Stadium network prototype for remote worker access. The router will provide the endpoint for an IPsec VPN tunnel for VPN clients. You will test the VPN configuration using the built-in test options according to the VPN Design Test Plan reviewed in Lab 8-5.

Note: If the equipment is not available to actually perform this lab, read it and work through it on paper to develop a better understanding of how VPNs function.

The following resources are required:

- Cisco 1841 router with IOS 12.4 Advanced IP Services IOS image, a Virtual Private Network (VPN) Module, and SDM version 2.4 installed (or equivalent configured router)

- Windows XP computer with Internet Explorer 5.5 or higher and SUN Java Runtime Environment (JRE) version 1.4.2_05 or later (or Java Virtual Machine [JVM] 5.0.0.3810)

- Access to PC network TCP/IP configuration and command prompt

- Console cable with DB-9 to RJ-45 adapter

- Cabling as shown in the network topology diagram in Figure 8-3

Task 1: Connect the Network and Configure the Devices for SDM Access

Step 1.   Select the necessary equipment and cables as specified in the Equipment section of the VPN Design Test Plan, provided on the book's accompanying CD-ROM. If necessary, see your instructor for assistance in identifying the appropriate equipment.

Note: If the PCs used in this lab are also connected to your Academy LAN or to the Internet, ensure that you record the cable connections and TCP/IP settings so that these can be restored at the conclusion of the lab.

Step 2.   Connect the devices in accordance with the lab network topology shown in Figure 8-3.

Figure 8-3   Lab 8-6 Network Topology

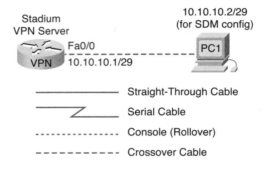

Note: Before configuring the routers, apply the instructions in the section, "Erasing and Reloading the Router" of Appendix C of Part II of this Learning Guide to all routers.

Step 3.   Configure basic router settings to prepare the router for access using SDM.

```
Router(config)# hostname VPN
VPN(config)# line console 0
VPN(config-line)# password cisco
VPN(config-line)# login
VPN(config-line)# line vty 0 4
VPN(config-line)# password cisco
VPN(config-line)# login
VPN(config-line)# enable password cisco
VPN(config)# enable secret class
VPN(config)# no ip domain-lookup
VPN(config)#
VPN(config)# interface Fa0/0
VPN(config-if)# ip address 10.10.10.1 255.255.255.248
VPN(config-if)# no shutdown
VPN(config-if)#
VPN(config-if)# ip http server
VPN(config)# ip http authentication local
VPN(config)# username admin privilege 15 password 0 cisco123
VPN(config)# end
```

Step 4.   Copy the **running-config** to the **startup-config**.

Task 2: Configure the PC to Connect to the Router and Launch Cisco SDM

Step 1.   Disable any popup blocker programs on PC H1. Popup blockers prevent SDM windows from displaying.

Step 2.   Connect the PC NIC to the FastEthernet 0/0 port on the Cisco 1841 ISR router with an Ethernet crossover cable. This in-band connection will be used to configure VPN using the PCs browser and the SDM graphical user interface.

Note: An SDM router other than the 1841 may require connection to a different interface to access SDM.

Step 3.   Configure the IP address of the PC as 10.10.10.2 with a subnet mask of 255.255.255.248.

Step 4.   SDM does not load automatically on the router. You must open the web browser to reach the SDM. Open the web browser on the PC and connect to the following URL: http://10.10.10.1.

Step 5.   In the **Connect to** dialog box, shown in Figure 8-4, enter **admin** for the username and **cisco123** for the password. Click **OK**. The main SDM web application will start and you will be prompted to use HTTPS. Click **Cancel**. In the Security Warning window, click **Yes** to trust the Cisco application.

Figure 8-4   Cisco SDM Login Window

Step 6.   Verify that you are using the latest version of SDM. The initial SDM window that displays immediately after the login shows the current version number. It is also displayed on the main SDM window shown in Figure 8-5, along with the IOS software version.

Figure 8-5   Cisco SDM Main Window

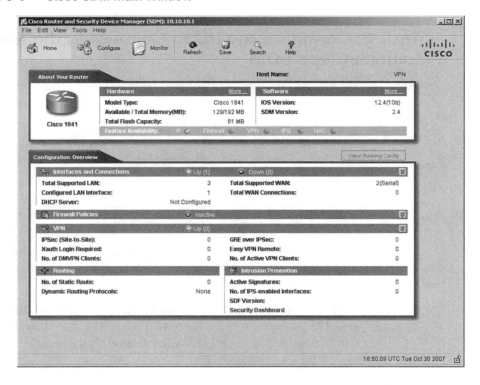

Note: If the current SDM version is not 2.4 or higher, notify your instructor before continuing with this lab.

Note: The Windows PC you are using must have Internet Explorer 5.5 or higher and SUN Java Runtime Environment (JRE) version 1.4.2_05 or later (or Java Virtual Machine [JVM] 5.0.0.3810). If it does not, SDM will not start. JRE will have to be downloaded from http://java.com/en/download/windows_automatic.jsp and installed on the PC before continuing with the lab.

Step 7.   Configure SDM to show Cisco IOS CLI commands.

From the **Edit** menu in the main SDM window, select **Preferences**.

Select the **Preview commands before delivering to router** checkbox. With this option checked, you can see the Cisco IOS CLI commands that will carry out the configuration function on the router before these commands are sent to the router.

This is a useful way to learn about Cisco IOS CLI commands required for VPN configuration.

Task 3: Use EasyVPN to Configure the Router as a VPN Server

Step 1.   Launch the EasyVPN Server Wizard from SDM.

From the **Configure** menu, click the **VPN** button to view the VPN configuration page. Select **Easy VPN Server** from the main VPN window, and then click **Launch Easy VPN Server Wizard** as shown in Figure 8-6.

Figure 8-6   Launch the Easy VPN Server Wizard

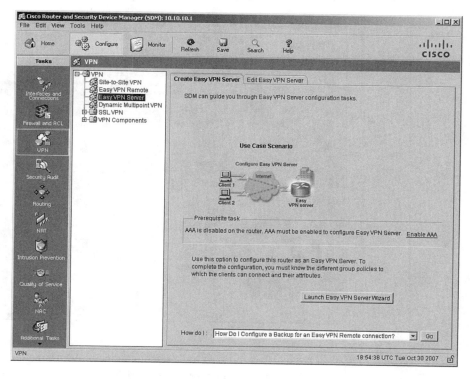

Step 2.   The Enable AAA window will display as shown in Figure 8-7. AAA must be enabled on the router before the Easy VPN Server configuration starts. Click **Yes** to continue with the configuration. Click the **Deliver** button to deliver the AAA configuration to the router. The AAA has been successfully enabled on the router's message displays on the window.

Figure 8-7   Easy VPN Authentication and Authorization

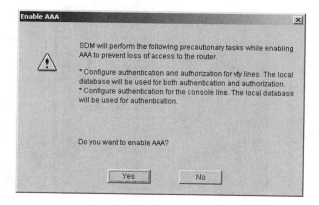

Step 3.   Click **OK** to continue to the VPN Wizard Welcome window. Then as shown in Figure 8-8, click **Next** to start the **Easy VPN Server Wizard**.

Figure 8-8   Easy VPN Wizard Welcome Window

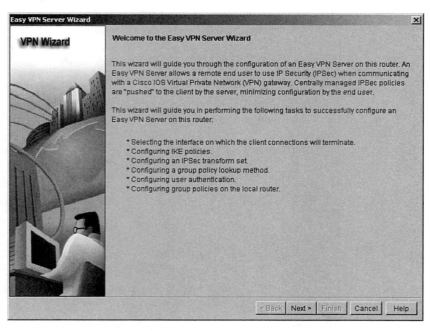

Step 4.   Select the interface on which the client connections terminate. This connection terminates on Fa0/0 and preshared keys will be used. The Easy VPN Interface and Authentication window is shown in Figure 8-9.

Figure 8-9   Easy VPN Wizard Interface and Authentication Window

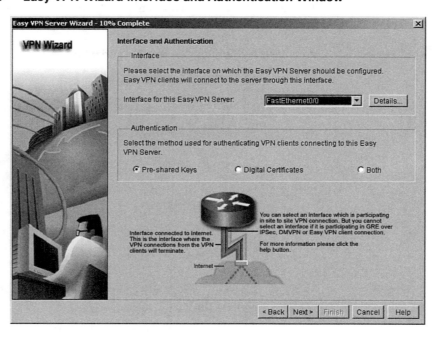

Step 5.   To select the Authentication method, click **Next** to configure the Internet Key Exchange (IKE) policies.

The IKE Proposals window is shown in Figure 8-10. Use the **Add** button to create the new policy. Configurations on both sides of the tunnel must match exactly. However, the Cisco VPN Client automatically selects the proper configuration for itself. Therefore, no IKE configuration is necessary on the client PC.

Press **Next** to continue to the Transform Set window.

Figure 8-10   Easy VPN IKE Configuration Window

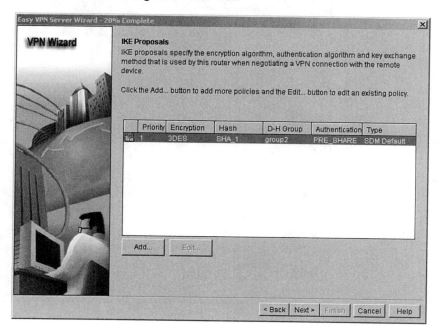

Step 6.   Specify the Transform Set by clicking **Next** in the Transform Set window (see Figure 8-11) to accept the default Transform Set for data encryption and authentication algorithms.

Figure 8-11   Easy VPN Transform Set Selection Window

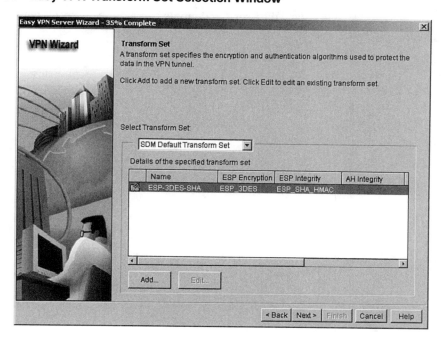

Step 7.   Specify Group Authorization and Group Policy Lookup.

Accept the default of **Local** for policy lookup (see Figure 8-12). Click **Next** to create a new Authentication, Authorization, and Accounting (AAA) authorization network method list for group policy lookup.

Figure 8-12   Easy VPN Group Authorization and Policy Lookup Window

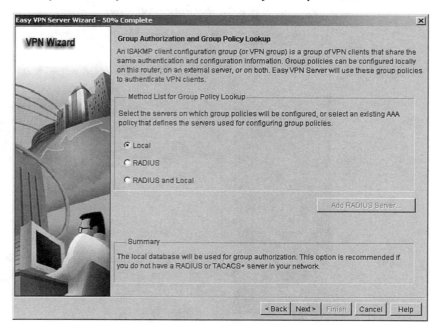

Step 8.   Configure User Authentication (XAuth).

Refer to Figure 8-13. User authentication details can be stored on an external server, such as a RADIUS server or a local database or on both. Select the **Enable User Authentication** checkbox and accept the default of **Local Only**.

Click the **Add User Credentials** button to see users currently defined or to add users.

Figure 8-13   Easy VPN User Authentication Window

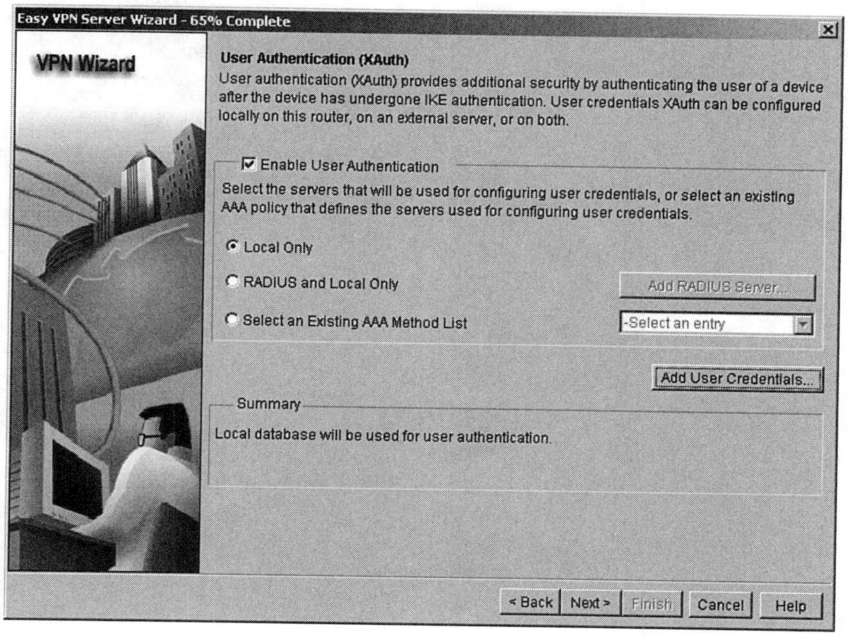

What is the name of the user currently defined, and what is the user privilege level?

_____

How was this user defined?

_____

Step 9.   Configure the Group Policy.

Click **Next** to go to the Group Authorization and User Group Policies window as shown in Figure 8-14. You must create at least one group policy for the VPN server.

Figure 8-14   Easy VPN Group Authorization and User Group Policies Window

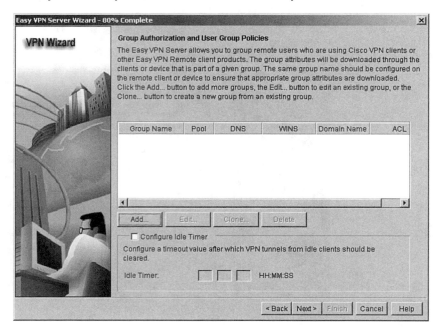

Click **Add** to create a policy. In the Add Group Policy window (see Figure 8-15), enter **VPN** as the Tunnel Group Name. Enter a new preshared key of **cisco** and then re-enter it.

Figure 8-15   Easy VPN Add Group Policy Window

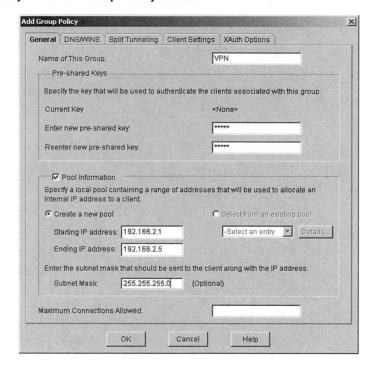

Ensure that the Pool Information box is checked and enter the following data:

- Starting IP Address: **192.168.2.1**
- Ending IP address: **192.168.2.5**
- Subnet Mask: **255.255.255.0**

Click **OK** to accept the entries. When you return to the Group Authorization window, click **Next**.

Step 10. Review the Summary of the VPN Configuration you created.

Figure 8-16 shows the Summary of the Configuration window, which summarizes the actions that you have taken. Click **Finish** if you are satisfied with your configuration.

Figure 8-16   Easy VPN Configuration Summary

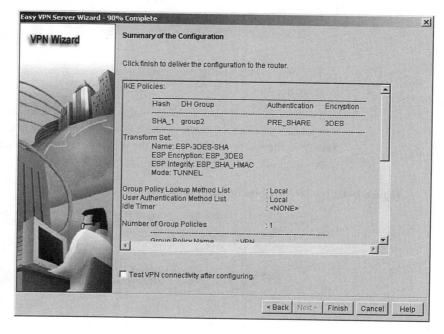

Step 11. Deliver the configuration to the router.

The window shown in Figure 8-17 displays the IOS commands that will be delivered to the router as a result of selections and entries you have made. Select the checkbox **Save running-config. to router's startup config**. Click **Deliver** to complete the transfer of commands to the router.

Figure 8-17   Easy VPN Deliver Configuration to Router Window

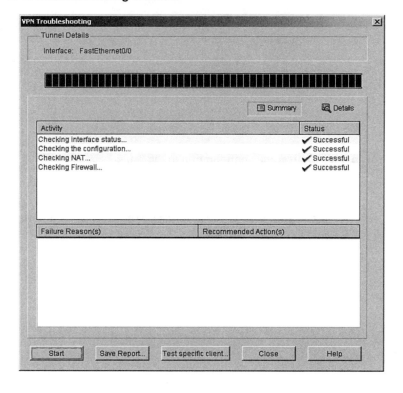

Step 12.   Test the basic VPN config on the router in accordance with Test 1 in the VPN Design Test Plan created in Lab 8-5.

After the commands have been delivered, you will be returned to the main VPN configuration window. Select the name of the VPN configuration you created and click **Test VPN Server** in the lower-right corner of the window. After clicking **Start**, you should get a response similar to that shown in Figure 8-18.

Figure 8-18   VPN Troubleshooting Window

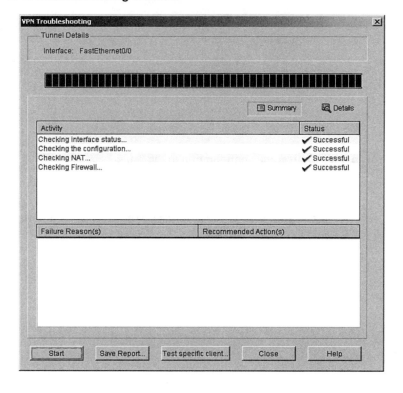

Close the Easy VPN window when the test has concluded successfully and exit SDM.

Task 4: Record Test Plan Results

Record the results of this test and the conclusions that can be drawn from the results in the Test 1: Results and Conclusions section of the VPN Test Plan.

Compare these actual results with the Test 1: Expected Results and Conclusions considered when the test plan was created in Lab 8-5.

Task 5: Clean Up

You may now go immediately to Lab 8-7 (Configuring and Testing the VPN Client).

If you are not proceeding to Lab 8-7 at this time, erase any configurations and reload the router. Disconnect and store the cabling. For PC hosts that are normally connected to other networks (such as the school LAN or to the Internet), reconnect the appropriate cabling and restore the TCP/IP settings.

Reflection

Why would you configure VPN using the SDM EasyVPN Server Wizard instead of using the command line?

_____

_____

_____

Summarize the steps that are configured by the SDM EasyVPN Server Wizard.

_____

_____

_____

_____

_____

_____

_____

Lab 8-7: Configuring and Testing the VPN Client (Optional Lab) (8.3.4.4)

Upon completion of this lab, you will be able to do the following:

- Configure basic router settings using IOS.
- Configure a VPN client for remote access.
- Configure the internal network.
- Verify VPN tunnel establishment between client and server.
- Verify VPN client access to internal network resources.

This lab contains skills that relate to the following 640-802 CCNA exam objectives:

- Describe VPN technology (including the importance, benefits, role, impact, and components).

Expected Results and Success Criteria

Before starting this lab, read through the tasks that you are expected to perform. What do you expect the result of performing these tasks will be?

_____

_____

_____

How is the ability to implement VPN technology important in network design and prototyping?

_____

_____

_____

Background/Preparation

In this lab you will configure a VPN client to simulate remote access to the Stadium network internal LAN resources through a VPN server.

Note: This lab requires that Cisco VPN Client software be installed on one PC. Please see your instructor if this software is not available.

Prior to starting this lab, you must complete Lab 8-6 to configure the 1841 VPN server using the SDM graphical user interface and the EasyVPN Server Wizard. You will test the remote VPN client access in accordance with the VPN Design Test Plan created in Lab 8-5.

Note: If the equipment and software are not available to actually perform this lab, read it and work through it on paper to develop a better understanding of how VPNs function.

The following resources are required:

- Cisco 1841 router with IOS 12.4 Advanced IP Services IOS image, a Virtual Private Network (VPN) Module, and SDM version 2.4 installed (or equivalent configured router)

- Switch (or hub) or 4-port switch add-in module for Cisco 1841 router

- Windows XP computer for use with SDM EasyVPN configuration and to act as VPN client with the following:

    - Internet Explorer 5.5 or higher

    - SUN Java Runtime Environment (JRE) version 1.4.2_05 or later (or Java Virtual Machine [JVM] 5.0.0.3810)

    - Cisco VPN Client installed (see preceding note)

- Windows XP computer or other computer to act as internal host (Discovery CD Server can be used in this role, but addressing for the internal network will need to match the 172.16.1.1/16 address of the server)

- Console cable with DB-9 to RJ-45 adapter

- Access to PC network TCP/IP configuration and command prompt

- Cabling as shown in the topology and described in the test plan for Lab 8-5

Task 1: Connect the Network and Configure the Devices for SDM Access

In this lab the devices will be connected as shown in Figure 8-19 and the hostnames, addresses, and subnet masks given in Table 8-2.

Figure 8-19   Lab 8-7 Network Topology

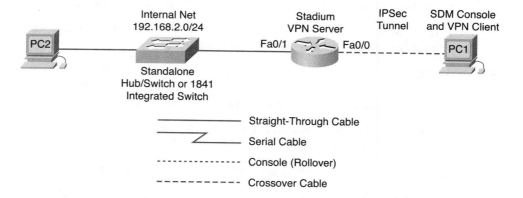

Table 8-2   Lab 8-2 Addressing Table

Device	Host Name	FastEthernet 0/0 or NIC IP Address	FastEthernet 0/1 IP Address	Default Gateway	Enable Secret Password	Enable, vty, and Console Password
Router 1	VPN	10.10.10.1 /29	192.168.2.99 /24		class	cisco
Switch 1	S1					
Host 1	PC1	10.10.10.2 /29		10.10.10.1		
Host 2	PC2	192.168.2.6 /24		192.168.2.99		

Note: If the PCs used in this lab are also connected to your Academy LAN or to the Internet, ensure that you record the cable connections and TCP/IP settings so that these can be restored at the conclusion of the lab.

Step 1.   Connect the PCs and devices as shown in the topology diagram in Figure 8-19 (and the VPN Design Test Plan).

Step 2.   Configure Host 1 with the name and IP addresses and mask as given in Table 8-2.

Step 3.   The internal VPN router interface Fa0/1 may be connected to the integrated 1841 Ethernet switch, if one is installed; or it may be attached to a standalone hub or switch.

It is not necessary to configure the switch. Confirm that the switch is ready for lab configuration by ensuring that all existing VLAN and general configurations are removed. Refer to the section "Erasing and Reloading the Switch" in Appendix C for these instructions.

Connect host PC2 to the same switch (1841 integrated or standalone hub/switch) as the router Fa0/1 interface. Configure the IP address as shown in Table 8-2.

Task 2: Configure the Router as a VPN Server

If you have just completed Lab 8-6 and the router is still configured as a VPN Server, then proceed directly to Step 3 and then to Step 5 of this task.

Step 1.   Confirm that the router is ready for lab configuration by ensuring that all configurations are removed. Refer to the section "Erasing and Reloading the Switch" in Appendix C of Part II of this Learning Guide for these instructions.

Step 2.   Host PC1 connects to the router console port for basic IOS configuration and connects via the router Fa0/0 port for SDM EasyVPN configuration.

Perform the basic configuration of the router as shown in Step 3 of Task 1 in Lab 8-5.

Step 3.   Confirm basic connectivity between PC1 and the VPN router. Open a command-prompt window and verify the VPN connection. Click **Start > Run**, type **cmd** and press **Enter**. Use the **ipconfig /all** command to see the network connections currently in use.

Output similar to the following will be displayed.

```
C:\>ipconfig /all

Windows IP Configuration
```

```
Host Name . . . . . . . . . . . . : PC1
Primary Dns Suffix  . . . . . . . :
Node Type . . . . . . . . . . . : Hybrid
IP Routing Enabled. . . . . . . . : No
WINS Proxy Enabled. . . . . . . . : No


Ethernet adapter Local Area Connection 1:


        Connection-specific DNS Suffix  . :
        Description . . . . . . . . . . . : Intel(R) PRO/100 VE Network
   Connection
        Physical Address. . . . . . . . . : 00-07-E9-63-CE-53
        Dhcp Enabled. . . . . . . . . . . : No
        IP Address. . . . . . . . . . . . : 10.10.10.2
        Subnet Mask . . . . . . . . . . . : 255.255.255.248
        Default Gateway . . . . . . . . . : 10.10.10.1
```

Record:

Host IP address _____

Host Subnet Mask _____

Default Gateway _____

Step 4. Refer to Lab 8-6 for PC setup to access the router SDM GUI and for instructions on configuring the 1841 as a VPN server using IOS commands and SDM. After configuring the router as a VPN server, host PC1 acts as the VPN client.

Step 5. Assign an IP internal LAN address to the VPN server Fa0/1 interface to act as the gateway for internal hosts:

```
VPN(config)# interface FastEthernet0/1
VPN(config-if)# ip address 192.168.2.99 255.255.255.0
VPN(config-if)# no shutdown
```

Task 3: Configure the VPN Client

Step 1. Install the Cisco VPN client software, if not already installed, on host PC1. If you do not have the Cisco VPN Client software or are unsure of the process, see your instructor.

Step 2. To configure the PC as a VPN client to access the VPN server, first start the **Cisco VPN Client** and in the opening window, shown in Figure 8-20, select **Connection Entries > New**.

Figure 8-20   VPN Client Opening Window

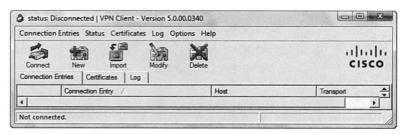

Step 3.   Enter the following information to define the new connection entry as shown in Figure 8-21:

- Connection Entry: **VPN**

- Description: **Connection to Stadium network**

- Host: **10.10.10.1**

- Group Authentication Name: **VPN** (Configured in Lab 8-6)

- Password: **cisco** (Configured in Lab 8-6)

- Confirm Password: **cisco**

    Click **Save** when you are finished.

Note: Name and password are case sensitive and must match the ones created on the VPN server.

Figure 8-21   VPN Client Connection Properties

Step 4.   Select the newly created connection on the main window shown in Figure 8-22 and click **Connect**.

Figure 8-22   VPN Client: Select Connection

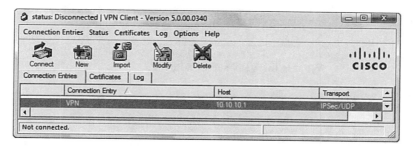

Step 5.   In the window shown in Figure 8-23, enter the user name **admin** created previously on the VPN router and enter the password of **cisco123**. Click **OK** to continue. The VPN Client window will minimize to an icon in the tools tray of the taskbar.

Figure 8-23   VPN Client User Authentication

Task 4: Verify VPN Tunnel Between Client, Server, and the Internal Network

Perform testing as outlined in Lab 8-5, Test 2 of the VPN Connectivity Test Plan and described in the following steps.

Step 1.   Check the tunnel statistics.

Open the VPN Client icon and click the **Status** menu and then the **Statistics** option to display the Tunnel Details tab as shown in Figure 8-24.

Figure 8-24   VPN Client Statistics

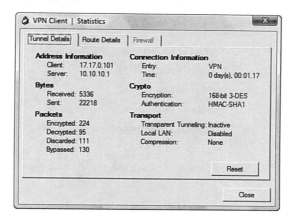

What is the Client IP address obtained from the VPN server?

_____

_____

What is the VPN server address?

_____

How many packets have been encrypted?

_____

What is the encryption method being used?

_____

What is the authentication being used?

_____

Step 2.   From the command-prompt window, issue the **ipconfig /all** command to verify the VPN connection.

Output similar to the following will be displayed:

```
C:\>ipconfig /all

Windows IP Configuration

        Host Name . . . . . . . . . . . : PC1
        Primary Dns Suffix  . . . . . . . :
        Node Type . . . . . . . . . . . : Hybrid
        IP Routing Enabled. . . . . . . : No
        WINS Proxy Enabled. . . . . . . : No

Ethernet adapter Local Area Connection 1:

        Connection-specific DNS Suffix  . :
        Description . . . . . . . . . . : Intel(R) PRO/100 VE Network
Connection
        Physical Address. . . . . . . . : 00-07-E9-63-CE-53
        Dhcp Enabled. . . . . . . . . . : No
        IP Address. . . . . . . . . . . : 10.10.10.2
        Subnet Mask . . . . . . . . . . : 255.255.255.248
        Default Gateway . . . . . . . . :

Ethernet adapter Local Area Connection 2:

        Connection-specific DNS Suffix  . :
        Description . . . . . . . . . . : Cisco Systems VPN Adapter
        Physical Address. . . . . . . . : 00-05-9A-3C-78-00
```

```
Dhcp Enabled. . . . . . . . . . . : No
IP Address. . . . . . . . . . . . : 192.168.2.3
Subnet Mask . . . . . . . . . . . : 255.255.255.0
Default Gateway . . . . . . . . . : 192.168.2.4
```

What is the IP configuration for the first Local Area Connection?

IP Address: _____

Subnet Mask: _____

Default Gateway: _____

Description: _____

What is the IP configuration for the second Local Area Connection?

IP Address: _____

Subnet Mask_____

Default Gateway: _____

Description: _____

What is the significance of the default gateway information?

_____

_____

Step 3.   Test connectivity between the remote VPN client and the internal stadium network.

Ping from the external (remote) host PC1 to host PC2 (IP address 192.168.2.6) on the internal stadium network to simulate access to internal resources.

Were the pings successful?

_____

If the pings were not successful, troubleshoot until they are.

```
C:\>ping 192.168.2.6

Pinging 192.168.2.6 with 32 bytes of data:

Reply from 192.168.2.6: bytes=32 time=1ms TTL=64
Reply from 192.168.2.6: bytes=32 time<1ms TTL=64
Reply from 192.168.2.6: bytes=32 time<1ms TTL=64
Reply from 192.168.2.6: bytes=32 time<1ms TTL=64

Ping statistics for 192.168.2.6:
    Packets: Sent = 4, Received = 4, Lost = 0 (0% loss),
Approximate round trip times in milli-seconds:
    Minimum = 0ms, Maximum = 1ms, Average = 0ms
```

Task 5: Verify VPN Access to an Internal Network Server (Alternate Configuration)

This optional task uses Discovery Server as the internal network host. By simulating the accessing of network services over a VPN, this test reflects more realistically the use a remote worker would make of a VPN connection.

Step 1.   Configure the VPN router interface Fa 0/1 to have an IP address of 172.17.0.1/16 so that the internal network matches the 172.16.1.1/16 address of Discovery Server.

Step 2.   Replace host H2 with Discovery Server.

Step 3.   The VPN Pool addresses have to be changed to be within the Discovery Server network.

If the router is **not** currently configured as a VPN Server, then perform the SDM VPN configuration as described in Lab 8-6. However, in Task 3, Step 9, of Lab 8-6, use **172.17.0.100** and **172.170.200** as the starting and ending IP addresses respectively of the VPN Pool in place of 192.168.2.1 and 192.168.2.5.

If the router is currently configured as a VPN Server, then issue the following commands from the global configuration mode of the CLI:

```
VPN(config)# no ip local pool SDM_POOL_1 192.168.2.1 192.168.2.5
VPN(config)# ip local pool SDM_POOL_1 17.17.0.100 17.17.0.200
VPN(config)# end
```

Step 4.   Establish a VPN connection from PC1 as described in Task 3 of this lab.

Step 5.   Verify the tunnel connection from PC1 to Discovery Server using the steps described in Task 4 of this lab.

Record the result of issuing the **ipconfig /all** command from PC1 and note the differences between these results and those of Task 4, Step 2.

IP configuration of Local Area Connection 1

IP Address: _____

Subnet Mask: _____

Default Gateway: _____

Description: _____

IP configuration for Local Area Connection 2

IP Address: _____

Subnet Mask: _____

Default Gateway: _____

Description: _____

What is the significance of the default gateway information?

_____

_____

Step 6.   Launch a web browser on PC1 and enter the URL **http://172.17.1.1** at the address bar to access the Discovery Server web page remotely over the VPN.

Step 7.   Test remote VPN access from PC1 to other Discovery Server services such as DNS, FTP, and Streaming Video.

Task 6: Record Test Plan Results

Record the results of this test and the conclusions that can be drawn from the results in the Test 2: Results and Conclusions section of the VPN Design Test Plan.

Compare these actual results with the Test 2: Expected Results and Conclusions considered when the test plan was created in Lab 8-5.

Task 7: Clean Up

Erase any configurations and reload the router. Disconnect and store the cabling. For PC hosts that are normally connected to other networks (such as the school LAN or to the Internet), reconnect the appropriate cabling and restore the TCP/IP settings.

Reflection

Why is VPN a good option for remote users?

_____

_____

_____

_____

_____

_____

What would happen if the VPN client tunneling protocol or encryption did not match that of the VPN server?

_____

_____

_____

Presenting and Implementing the Network Design: Labs

The lab exercises included in this chapter cover all the Chapter 9 online curriculum labs to ensure that you have mastered the practical, hands-on skills to organize the complete network design information into a formal presentation. As you work through these labs, use Chapter 9 in Part I of this book or use the corresponding Chapter 9 in the Discovery Designing and Supporting Computer Networks online curriculum for assistance.

Lab 9-1: Editing and Organizing the Existing Information (9.1.2)

Upon completion of this lab, you will be able to collect and organize information into a network proposal.

Expected Results and Success Criteria

Before starting this lab, read through the tasks that you are expected to perform. What do you expect the result of performing these tasks will be?

_____

_____

_____

What are the benefits of the systematic and thorough recording and collecting of information in the preparation of a Project Proposal?

_____

_____

_____

Background/Preparation

Having tested the proposed network design using a prototype, you now collect information from the Request For Proposal (RFP) in Chapter 2, "Gathering Network Requirements," and previous Prepare, Plan, Design, Implement, Operate, Optimize (PPDIOO) labs to create a network proposal. In this lab, you prepare an outline for the FilmCompany network upgrade proposal. You do this by assembling portions of the proposal from the information that you compiled from earlier labs and saved in your portfolio.

Task 1: Collate and Organize the Information

Step 1.   Gather and read through all the project documents that you created in previous labs.

Step 2.   Ensure that multipage documents are together and that the pages are in the correct sequence.

Task 2: Review Existing Information

Ensure that the documents are complete and contain the information specified. Any incomplete documents, or missing information that was not recorded at the time of that lab, now need to be checked and included at this stage.

Task 3: Organize the Information

A Project Proposal typically contains the sections shown in Table 9-1.

Table 9-1   Project Proposal Sections

Section	Description
Executive Summary	Discusses the project goals and project scope at a high level. This section demonstrates that the network vendor understands the extent of the project and the role of the network in meeting the business goals. The goal of the summary is to convince the decision makers of the business benefits of the design. This section is typically one to two pages long.
Network Requirements	Reviews the business goals and network requirements, including users and applications that need to be supported. This section often lists the business goals, in order of priority, with critical goals marked. This section includes the topologies, protocols, hardware, software, and training required to meet the business goals.
Current Network Environment	Documents the state of the existing network. This section includes physical and logical diagrams and the IP addressing scheme. The section summarizes the results of the network characterization, including strengths and weaknesses of the existing network. It also documents the user community and applications currently in use, based on the network characterization.
Proposed Physical Design	Describes the physical layout of the proposed design. This section documents trade-offs made to accommodate business goals and technical requirements. The section describes the features and recommended uses for the technologies and devices proposed for the new network design. This section documents the new WAN service and new network equipment. The section also includes proposed network diagrams.
Proposed Logical Design	Describes the logical topology of the proposed network. This section documents any proposed addressing and naming conventions. It describes the routing and switching protocols recommended for the planned network. This section includes recommended security mechanisms and products that support the security policy of the business. The section may include information on recommended network management procedures and applications.

Section	Description
Implementation Plan	Provides a detailed list of the tasks that must be performed to install and implement the new network. This section includes tasks, steps, time required, and proposed schedules.
Cost Proposal	Provides cost proposal for equipment, software, installation, and ongoing support.

Important notes about the Executive Summary:

■ The Executive Summary is presented first because it provides the reader with an overview of the complete proposal. The proposal will be read by people with different roles and requirements. These may include managers, network engineers and technicians, marketing and sales consultants, and finance and accounting personnel. By reviewing the Executive Summary first, readers can then decide whether to read through the complete document or read only those sections that apply to their role.

■ Although presented first, the Executive Summary cannot be written until the rest of the proposal document has been compiled. This section is therefore the final section to be written.

Organize the information into the sequence given in Table 9-1.

Task 4: Edit and Finalize the Information

Step 1. Review all the material to ensure that it is complete. It is important that the FilmCompany management and technical staff are able to easily find and understand the material contained in the proposal. A disorganized or incomplete proposal can cause the customer to choose another contractor to complete the project.

Step 2. Ensure that all the information has a consistent format and style. If necessary, edit or rewrite sections so that the proposal has the appearance of a single document and not a set of separate documents.

Step 3. Complete diagrams and other graphics and finalize what is to be included in the proposal.

Step 4. Clearly note those sections of the proposal that have to be completed; these sections will be compiled in the following labs.

Step 5. Save the word processing documents and file the hard-copy information in your portfolio.

Lab 9-2: Creating an Implementation Plan (9.2.1)

Upon completion of this lab, you will be able to

- Create an Implementation Plan.

- Recognize the importance of customer approval.

Expected Results and Success Criteria

Before starting this lab, read through the tasks that you are expected to perform. What do you expect the result of performing these tasks will be?

_____

_____

_____

What potential issues could arise if the project proceeds without the customer approving the Implementation Plan?

_____

_____

_____

Background/Preparation

In the PPDIOO process, the next step after completing the network design is to develop the Implementation Plan. It is important to include as much detail as possible. The network engineers and technicians use the Implementation Plan documentation to perform the network upgrade.

This lab is the first of four that leads you through the creation of an Implementation Plan for the FilmCompany network upgrade. In this lab, you establish the format of the Implementation Plan using the results of earlier design and testing labs.

In the next three labs, you compile and finalize the details for three sections of the Implementation Plan: the Installation Method, the Timeline and Resource Estimates, and the Maintenance and Downtime Planning.

Task 1: Determine the Tasks to Implement the Network Design

Implementing a network design requires the completion of a set of tasks, such as installing hardware, configuring systems, testing the network, and launching the network into production. Each task consists of several steps.

Each task requires the following documentation:

- A description of the task

- References to design documents

- Detailed implementation guidelines

- Detailed rollback guidelines in case of failure
- The estimated time required for implementation
- Completion sign-off

Analyze the FilmCompany network design documentation that you have compiled in previous labs. Determine and list the three main sets of tasks required to be performed to implement the network upgrade. These sets of tasks will be referred to as phases.

Phase 1

_____

_____

_____

_____

_____

_____

Phase 2

_____

_____

_____

_____

_____

Phase 3

_____

_____

_____

_____

Task 2: Note Identified Success and Failure Criteria

When implementing a design, the possibility of a failure must be considered—even after a successful pilot or prototype network test. Each step of the implementation may require additional testing to ensure that the network operates as designed.

In the "Reflection" section of Lab 2-4, "Prioritizing Business Goals," in Chapter 2, "Gathering Network Requirements: Labs," you considered success criteria when determining the objectives of the FilmCompany network upgrade. List two or three success or failure criteria for each phase of the project.

Phase 1

_____

_____

_____

Phase 2

_____

_____

_____

Phase 3

_____

_____

_____

Task 3: Include Provision for Customer Approval

The Implementation Plan details the work required to accomplish the project goals. The plan includes the customer expectations and the success criteria for customer approval and project sign-off.

As soon as customer approval of the Implementation Plan is obtained, the installation can begin.

The customer is given a detailed list of all devices required and the work to be completed. This list forms part of the Implementation Plan. A signed copy of this list is kept by the network designer and account manager.

Upon completion of each task, the customer is required to sign off that the work was completed and that the results are as expected.

Step 1.   Include in the documentation a signature page for an authorized FilmCompany representative to sign and approve the Implementation Plan.

Step 2.   Include in the documentation a signature page at the end of each task for an authorized FilmCompany representative to sign and accept the completion of each task.

Task 4: Document Phase 1

Create a table for Phase 1 with the headings as shown.

Task/Step	Date	Description	Implementation Details	Complete

Save this table in your portfolio. You enter details into the table over the next three labs.

Task 5: Document Phase 2

Create a table for Phase 2 with the headings as shown.

Task/Step	Date	Description	Implementation Details	Complete

Save this table in your portfolio. You enter details into the table over the next three labs.

Task 6: Document Phase 3

Create a table for Phase 3 with the headings as shown.

Task/Step	Date	Description	Implementation Details	Complete

Save this table in your portfolio. You enter details into the table over the next three labs.

Lab 9-3: Creating a Phased Installation Plan (9.2.2)

Upon completion of this lab, you will be able to determine the best installation method.

Expected Results and Success Criteria

Before starting this lab, read through the tasks that you are expected to perform. What do you expect the result of performing these tasks will be?

_____

_____

_____

What are some of the issues that might have to be discussed and negotiated with the customer regarding their expectations of what impact the installation process might have on their current network operations?

_____

_____

_____

Background/Preparation

In this lab, you compile and finalize the details of the Implementation Plan related to the planned installation method of the FilmCompany network upgrade.

An Installation Plan may be subject to a number of factors, including the following:

- Budget constraints that can affect the project by limiting the money available to purchase the equipment needed

- Time constraints based on business factors, such as the inability to handle downtime for transaction processing and major events happening in a short period of time

- Lack of trained personnel or the need for training, which could prevent a new installation from being fully implemented at one time

Task 1: Compare the Installation Methods

There are three possible installation methods:

- **New installation**, sometimes referred to as a _green field installation_

- **Phased installation** into an existing, functioning network

- **Complete replacement**, sometimes referred to as a _forklift upgrade_

Consider and list the advantages and disadvantages of the three installation methods.

New Installation

Advantages:

_____

_____

_____

_____

Disadvantages:

_____

_____

_____

_____

Phased Installation into Existing Network

Advantages:

_____

_____

_____

Disadvantages:

_____

_____

_____

Complete Network Replacement

Advantages:

_____

_____

_____

_____

Disadvantages:

_____

_____

_____

_____

_____

Task 2: Select the Installation Method

Two of the FilmCompany requirements are as follows:

- The company network services must be available during the upgrade.

- Existing equipment must be used in the new network design.

Select the appropriate installation approach for the FilmCompany network upgrade.

_____

Task 3: Complete Details for Each Installation Phase

Using the charts created in Lab 9-2, fill out the information for each of the installation phases.

Step 1.   On the table created in Lab 9-2 for Phase 1, fill in the Task/Step, Description, and Implementation Details information:

- Install distribution and core layer equipment.

- Configure new IP addressing and VLAN scheme.

- Configure routing.

Step 2.   On the table for Phase 2, fill in the Task/Step, Description, and Implementation Details information:

- Upgrade the WAN connectivity.

- Extend the network to the remote site.

- Configure ACLs and security.

Step 3.   On the table for Phase 3, fill in the Task/Step, Description, and Implementation Details information:

- Install and configure the wireless and associated mobility network equipment.

Step 4. Add the details of your Phased Installation Plan to your project portfolio.

Lab 9-4: Creating a Timeline (9.2.3)

Upon completion of this lab, you will be able to estimate timelines and resources.

Expected Results and Success Criteria

Before starting this lab, read through the tasks that you are expected to perform. What do you expect the result of performing these tasks will be?

_____

_____

_____

What do you expect to be the result of one phase or task of a project being delayed? Under what circumstances would the entire project be adversely affected?

_____

_____

_____

Background/Preparation

In this lab, you create a timeline for the FilmCompany network upgrade project. The timeline should include the start and end dates for the phased installation method.

The project duration is part of the contractual agreement. To meet the deadlines of the customer, the network designer creates a project timeline. The availability of materials, the schedule of the contractor, and the schedule of the customer are all considerations in determining the start date and the completion date.

Developing an Implementation Plan and effectively managing the project time and resources is a highly regarded skill in the networking and communications industry. Developing an understanding of these project management issues is therefore an important outcome of this lab.

Task 1: List and Prioritize Factors Affecting the Timeline

Note issues such as equipment and material availability, skilled personnel, and customer requirements that should be considered for the following factors when developing a project timeline. Consider the possibility that the project might not begin on the proposed start date.

Equipment order and delivery

_____

_____

Service installation, such as WAN links

_____

_____

Customer schedule, including available maintenance and downtime windows

_____

_____

Availability of appropriate technical personnel

_____

_____

Task 2: Complete Time Details for Each Installation Phase

The FilmCompany network upgrade is linked to the StadiumCompany network redevelopment. It would be efficient to align the FilmCompany stadium remote site work with that project. The StadiumCompany RFP states that the project must be completed during the off-season for the two teams. This requirement gives the project a timeline of four months, which can be also applied to the FilmCompany upgrade.

Step 1.   On the table created in Lab 9-2 for Phase 1, fill in the Date information:

- Install distribution and core layer equipment.

- Configure new IP addressing and VLAN scheme.

- Configure routing.

Step 2.   On the table for Phase 2, fill in the Date information:

- Upgrade the WAN connectivity.

- Extend the network to the remote site.

- Configure ACLs and security.

Step 3.   On the table for Phase 3, fill in the Date information:

- Install and configure the wireless and associated mobility network equipment.

Task 3: Consider Customer-Caused Delays

Customers may make changes to the requirements during the installation of a project. When changes occur, the timeline is used to make adjustments to personnel and other available resources. The timeline documentation can also be used to show the customer how delays affect the project completion date.

Based on the timeline, write a Project Variation statement showing the possible delay in the project completion date if the FilmCompany were to decide at this stage to relocate an additional three production staff and their workstations to the stadium.

Task 4: Using Project Management Software (Optional)

Project management tools such as Microsoft Project can be used to create a project timeline. This software can be useful for

- Tracking the progress of the project

- Keeping the project on schedule

- Identifying milestones

- Tracking labor assignments and costs

- Alerting the designer if the project is falling behind schedule

If this software is available, enter the resources and timeline for one phase of the Implementation Plan and examine the output.

Note: Ensure that all your Network Design Timeline details are added to your project portfolio.

Lab 9-5: Creating an Installation Schedule (9.2.4)

Upon completion of this lab, you will be able to create an installation schedule based on maintenance windows and downtime allowances.

Expected Results and Success Criteria

Before starting this lab, read through the tasks that you are expected to perform. What do you expect the result of performing these tasks will be?

_____

_____

_____

Why is ensuring that the customer and users are informed of network and services downtime an important part of the project implementation?

_____

_____

_____

Background/Preparation

Maintenance windows and planned downtime need to be included in the installation timeline. If only a few hours a day are available to make network changes, the project timeline must reflect this constraint. Otherwise, the time estimates are not accurate, and the project may be late. Scheduling downtime for the network needs to be carefully planned to prevent a major disruption for the customer.

In this lab, you create a maintenance schedule that includes the equipment involved, the time required, and suggestions for scheduling the maintenance that will cause the least impact on FilmCompany daily operations. Note that the maintenance windows allow for maintenance downtime to occur only from 2 a.m. to 6 a.m. (0200 to 0600), Monday through Friday.

Task 1: List and Prioritize Tasks Requiring Current Network Downtime

List the tasks that require network downtime.

_____

_____

_____

_____

_____

_____

_____

_____

Task 2: Document Required Downtime on Project Timeline

Sometimes it is not possible to complete all the required tasks during an approved maintenance window. If an installation task requires the network, or part of the network, to be down during normal business hours, it is important to obtain permission from the customer. As soon as the time frame is determined and approved, all the people involved need to be notified accordingly.

Step 1.   List those tasks that can be completed during a scheduled maintenance window.

_____

_____

_____

_____

Step 2.   List those tasks that require the network to be down during normal business hours.

_____

_____

_____

_____

Task 3: Document Customer Approved Downtime

Step 1.   Indicate on the Installation Plan Timeline when the network downtime will occur.

_____

_____

_____

_____

Step 2.   Include a provision for customer approval to be recorded for this downtime.

Step 3.   Include a task that requires that the users who will be affected are notified with adequate advance notice of the network downtime. Ensure that the users are also notified when the network or service returns to full operation.

Step 4.   Include your schedule document in your project portfolio.

Lab 9-6: Creating the Bill of Materials (9.3.4)

Upon completion of this lab, you will be able to

- Create a bill of materials (BOM).

- Add equipment costs to the proposal.

- Add service and maintenance support costs to the proposal.

Expected Results and Success Criteria

Before starting this lab, read through the tasks that you are expected to perform. What do you expect the result of performing these tasks will be?

_____

_____

_____

What are the potential issues that an inaccurate or incomplete BOM could have on the project implementation?

_____

_____

_____

Background/Preparation

In this lab, you create the BOM and enter the appropriate information into the Costs section of the FilmCompany proposal.

A bill of materials is a document that details all the required hardware and components necessary to implement the proposed upgrade. It consists of an itemized list of hardware, software, and other items that must be ordered and installed. The network designer uses this list to obtain quotations and to create the equipment orders. The BOM is then used to order new equipment and replacement parts for existing equipment. Therefore, every required item must be included in this list. Items left off the order will delay installation of that device.

To develop the BOM, each section of the FilmCompany network is examined to determine the networking equipment required and the capabilities needed in each device.

New equipment decisions are constrained by the project budget. As the network designer, you would normally collaborate with your company account manager assigned to the FilmCompany account to ensure that the equipment models selected are within the budget constraints and meet current and future business goals.

Use the design information and results of previous labs to compile the BOM for the FilmCompany network upgrade. Include the equipment required, software, and support costs.

Task 1: List the Items Required

Step 1.   Use the table that follows, or create a similar one, to list all the items and equipment that need to be purchased for the FilmCompany network upgrade project.

Part Number	Item Description	Quantity	Cost	Maintenance Cost	Total Cost	Vendor	Notes

Step 2.   Search the Internet or use information provided by your instructor to add possible suppliers or vendors to the BOM table.

Step 3.   Add costs to the BOM. Where possible, obtain costs from local vendors and suppliers. If this information is not readily available, your instructor will provide estimated costs for you to use.

Task 2: Determine the Software Requirements

Step 1.   During the early stages of the network Design phase, existing applications were identified. Add new applications required by the network upgrade to the BOM. Categorize these as either Network or Specialist applications.

Step 2.   Add the new applications, installation costs, and required training to the BOM with the identified hardware. Also, indicate whether the network upgrade requires additional licenses to be purchased for existing software applications.

Task 3: Add Maintenance Contracts

Step 1.   Investigate the maintenance support service contracts available for both the new and existing equipment.

Step 2.   Add the details and costs to the BOM.

Task 4: Create the BOM

Step 1.   Create the BOM using word processing or spreadsheet software. Using a spreadsheet will facilitate the calculation of total costs and enable easy updating of the document if costs or quantities are amended.

Step 2.   Save this file and include it in the proposal document. Add a hard copy of the file to your project portfolio.

Lab 9-7: Compiling the Documentation (9.4.1)

Upon completion of this lab, you will be able to

- Complete the proposal.

- Develop a proposal presentation.

Expected Results and Success Criteria

Before starting this lab, read through the tasks that you are expected to perform. What do you expect the result of performing these tasks will be?

_____

_____

_____

What preparation could facilitate the compilation of the proposal?

_____

_____

_____

Background/Preparation

In this lab, you compile the implementation and costing information created for the FilmCompany network upgrade and integrate this in the Project Proposal documentation.

You then develop a presentation of this proposal in a form that could be presented to the FilmCompany for their acceptance.

Part 1: Compile the Project Proposal

Task 1: Finalize the Documentation Requirements

Step 1.   Finalize the documentation created in the previous labs and in your project portfolio.

Step 2.   Insert and compile the information under the following headings:

- Executive Summary

- Network Requirements

- Current Network Environment
- Proposed Physical Design
- Proposed Logical Design
- Implementation Plan
- Cost Proposal

Task 2: Prepare the Cover Page

Include a cover page at the beginning of the proposal. The cover page describes the proposal, including the RFP or solicitation number and date, the customer contact information, and the vendor name and contact information.

Task 3: Prepare the Table of Contents

Develop a table of contents for the proposal document.

Note: The Executive Summary must be the first document in the table of contents.

Task 4: Create the Proposal

Complete the proposal document. The proposal layout should be highly readable and should aid the reader in locating information.

- Use graphics to enhance the readability of a proposal and convey information where appropriate.
- Text should be legible, typically a serif typeface such as Times Roman, at 10-point to 12-point type.
- Page margins should be at least 0.5 inches (125 mm).
- Page numbers should be included at the top or bottom of each page.

Task 5: Update the Executive Summary

Use information from the completed implementation and costing sections to update the Executive Summary.

Task 6: Organize the Proposal Binder

Arrange the proposal components in a binder, based on the order cited in the table of contents.

Task 7: Prepare Terms and Signatures Page

Step 1.   Prepare the terms of agreement and an acceptance page for customer signatures to be included at the end of the proposal. The terms and conditions describe all relevant legal terms and contracts that will be required. These terms and conditions support the supply of goods and services related to network improvements and installations.

Important clauses in the terms and conditions usually include the following:

- Details about the proposal expiration date

- Obligations of the customer to obtain permission or other consents within their organization

- Obligations of the vendor to provide services and equipment with care and skill

- Dates when completed milestone deliverables are payable

- Interest chargeable on outstanding payments

- The amount of notice the customer must give to cancel their equipment and service orders

- Details about guarantees (if any) provided by the vendor

- Details about escalating and resolving complaints or issues

If the customer accepts the proposal, an appropriate customer representative signs the Terms and Signatures page.

Your instructor will advise you of the standard terms and conditions that will apply to all proposals.

Step 2.   Save this file and include in the Project Proposal document.

Part 2: Prepare the Presentation

Task 1: Plan the Presentation

After compiling a proposal, network designers review the entire proposal with their management organization by means of a formal presentation. During this stage of the design proposal, the designer must first sell the concept to the internal management and then to the customer.

For your presentation, list the important points to include that illustrate the proposal. A proposal presentation includes slides or other visual aids to graphically represent the proposal. The presentation, along with the proposal document, is vital to ensuring a successful meeting and increasing the probability of a customer sign-off.

Task 2: Create the Presentation

This step assumes that the presentation will use Microsoft PowerPoint or equivalent presentation software. Your instructor will advise you of the presentation requirements and resources available.

Step 1.   The content and presentation format are important in a business environment. Create a presentation that considers the following points:

- Every slide should have a heading that summarizes the information presented on the slide.

- Computer presentations should not contain full paragraphs of text. Use a bulleted list or outline format and elaborate on the points during the delivery.

- All type should be legible. Use large fonts; small fonts are often hard to read.

- Use contrasting colors, either a dark background with light text or a light background with dark text.

- Keep the format and style consistent throughout the presentation. Do not change text font, text color, background color, or theme except for an occasional special emphasis.

- Avoid backgrounds that make the text hard to read. Keep the background simple.

- Do not use ALL CAPS! Their use is unprofessional, and they are more difficult to read.

- Include a combination of words, pictures, and graphics. Variety keeps the presentation interesting.

Step 2.   Save the presentation file and any other presentation aids that you created, and add everything to your project portfolio.

Lab 9-8: Presenting the Project Proposal (9.4.2)

Upon completion of this lab, you will be able to

- Present network design proposal.
- Achieve project sign-off.

Expected Results and Success Criteria

Before starting this lab, read through the tasks that you are expected to perform. What do you expect the result of performing these tasks will be?

_____

_____

_____

_____

What could be the outcome if the Project Proposal is prepared or presented poorly?

_____

_____

_____

_____

Background/Preparation

In this lab, you present your FilmCompany network upgrade Project Proposal to the instructor and the class.

Part 1: Prepare for the Presentation

Task 1: Review the Content

Step 1.   Ensure that your presentation is complete.

Step 2.   Review the content to ensure that there are no technical errors.

Step 3.   Rehearse the presentation to become familiar with the flow of the content and develop a sense of the timing required.

Task 2: Prepare for Questions

Your presentation might seem complete and clear to you, but to others there may be points that need clarification or that contain too much information.

Read through your presentation as if seeing it for the first time, Note the points that you would ask questions about. Remind yourself that you cannot prepare for every possible question.

Task 3: Prepare Yourself

Your instructor will advise you on the details (time, location, audience) of the presentation class. On the day of the presentation, try to observe the following guidelines:

- If possible, and appropriate, wear professional attire.
- Try not to be too nervous. The other students in your class are probably feeling the same as you are.
- If other students are presenting before or after you, give them your attention and participate in the class. Do not think too much about your presentation; instead, focus on what is happening in the class.

Part 2: Deliver the Presentation

Task 1: Submit Your Portfolio and Proposal

Submit your portfolio and proposal to your instructor before delivering the presentation.

Task 2: Begin the Presentation

Step 1.   Introduce yourself.

Step 2.   Deliver the presentation, using your portfolio and a slide presentation such as PowerPoint.

- Speak slowly and clearly.
- Stay with your slide sequence. A common mistake is to introduce material and then continue to talk about it in detail without advancing from the general overview slide for that topic to the detailed slides that follow.

Step 3.   Demonstrate that you know the content of the proposal and sell it as the one that the customer should adopt.

Step 4.   Be prepared to respond to questions from the instructors and students.

Task 3: Conclude the Presentation

Step 1.   Invite any final questions from the audience.

Step 2.   Finish your presentation by assuring the audience that your proposal meets their requirements and thank them for the opportunity to present it.

Part 3: Participate in the Class Debrief

Discuss and reflect on your presentation with other students. Note those aspects of your presentation that were considered successful. Review those aspects of your presentation that might not have been as successful as you expected.

Putting It All Together: Lab

The lab exercise included in this chapter covers the Chapter 10 online curriculum lab to ensure that you are prepared and capable of applying for an IT networking position. As you work through this lab, use Chapter 10 in Part I of this book or use the corresponding Chapter 10 in the Discovery Designing and Supporting Computer Networks online curriculum for assistance.

 ## Lab 10-1: Finding the Right Networking Job (10.0.2)

Upon completion of this lab, you will be able to:

- Research networking jobs that match skill strengths and interests.
- Create a résumé with a cover letter for a networking job or internship.

Expected Results and Success Criteria

Before starting this lab, read through the tasks that you are expected to perform. What do you expect the result of performing these tasks will be?

_____

_____

_____

What benefits are gained from creating a résumé and cover letter for a networking job that interests you?

_____

_____

_____

What resources are available to help evaluate your résumé and cover letter?

_____

_____

_____

Background/Preparation

In this lab, you will research an IT position that interests you and then create a résumé and cover letter to apply for the position.

There are many resources available today to provide job seekers with a better idea of their attitudes and interests in terms of career choices. The resources available vary widely—from free self-assessment tools to resources that require a fee. Some sites may have an age requirement as well as a fee.

Some of the resources available can be found on websites, in books, or through memberships with companies that specialize in helping people identify and make career choices. One method is not necessarily better than the other.

Over time, you may find that your career choices change as your skill set, experience, and knowledge-base broadens. Career choices may also change as you discover other areas of interest related to your chosen career path. As you perform your job search, remember that the areas of strength and interest identified by the assessment tools are areas that can always be improved upon.

Task 1: Perform a Skills Strength and Interest Assessment

Several career paths are available for individuals interested in an IT career. If you have not already participated in a strength and interest assessment, or if you have not yet determined which career path is of interest to you, research some of the tools available. They can help provide a starting point for an IT career selection. There are many resources available—the list below is only a small sampling.

Resources available:

Secondary school guidance departments and local college career departments can provide helpful information.

Public libraries or websites, such as amazon.com, offer books on researching career choices and skill strength assessments such as:

- *Information Technology Jobs in America* [2007] Corporate & Government Career Guide (Paperback) by Info Tech Employment (Editor)
- *Discover What You're Best At* by Linda Gale
- *The IT Career Builder's Toolkit* by Matthew Moran (sample provided on the CD-ROM)

Company websites offering a mix of free and fee related services, such as:

- **Promoting IT Careers: Virtual Field Trips**:
  http://www.cisco.com/web/learning/netacad/career_connection/promoteIT/VFT/index.html
- **Cisco Networking Academy Career Connection**: http://cc.netacad.net/home.do#
- **CompTIA TechCareer Compass**: http://tcc.comptia.org/default.aspx
- **CyberCareers for the Net Generation**: http://www.cybercareers.org/students/itcareercenter/
- **Quintcareers**: http://www.quintcareers.com/student.html

During your search, remember that many IT careers are not limited to IT Companies, but may be associated with the Education, Healthcare, Finance, Manufacturing, Farming, Mining or Transport industries.

Step 1. Use one of the resources above or similar resources to research possible career choices in the networking field.

For example, in addition to identifying skill strengths, the CompTIA TechCareer Compass site has a page via the **Explore Job Roles** link (http://tcc.comptia.org/job_roles.aspx) that allows you to search for a job based on a job title or job criteria. If you are not sure of a job title, the **Search Using Job Concentrations** section of that page lists job roles that are divided into three areas: Administration, Development, and Integration. Clicking one of the three areas displays a list of job titles. You can then click any title to see a description of critical job functions, compare your skill strengths with the position requirements, and identify the certifications required for the job.

Step 2.   Select one of the job titles that is of interest to you as a possible career path.

Task 2: Search a Job Website for Possible IT Position

After identifying a possible career position, search one of the many job sites available. If you are interested in experiencing other cultures or are willing to travel, consider employment opportunities outside your state and country. Internship offerings may also be available.

Some possible job sites to use to search include:

- http://www.cisco.apply2jobs.com/index.cfm

- www.monster.com

- www.jobing.com

- www.careerbuilders.com

Task 3: Create a Résumé and Cover Letter

Step 1.   When a potential job has been found, create a cover letter and résumé that you can use to apply for the position.

Print the job description and use it as your guide for creating a customized résumé and cover letter.

If the selected job description requests a particular form of résumé, be sure to create your résumé in that format. For example, some jobs require that résumés be submitted via a website only, while others require a paper copy submission. There are many free resources available to assist with the creation of the résumé and cover letter. The websites listed below offer tutorials or information related to writing a résumé and cover letter.

- http://www.cisco.com/web/learning/netacad/career_connection/promoteIT/VFT

- http://content.monster.com/resume/industry/12/home.aspx

- http://www.quintcareers.com/tutorials.html

Step 2.   After your cover letter and résumé are complete, submit them and the job description to your instructor.

Reflection

What other areas related to applying for a job are not covered in this particular lab?

_____

_____

_____

StadiumCompany Story

The Discovery "Designing and Supporting Computer Networks" course uses the fictional StadiumCompany network upgrade story in the main text and media presentation and in Packet Tracer activities. StadiumCompany is a stadium management company that manages a large sports facility, as illustrated in Figure A-1.

Figure A-1   StadiumCompany Facility

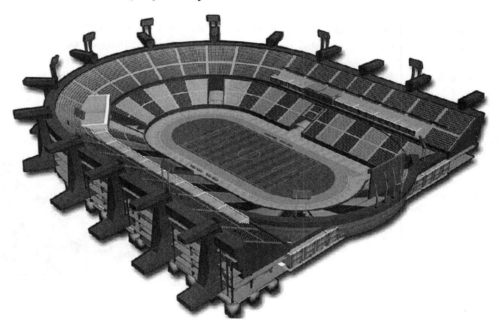

When the sports facility was built, the network that supported its business offices and security services provided state-of-the-art communications capabilities. Over the years, the company added new equipment and increased the number of connections without considering the overall business goals and long-term infrastructure design. Some projects went ahead without an understanding of the bandwidth, traffic prioritization, and other requirements needed to support this advanced and business-critical network. Now the StadiumCompany management wants to improve the customer experience by adding high-tech features and support for concerts, but the underlying network cannot support these additions.

The StadiumCompany management understands that they do not have sufficient network expertise to support the network upgrade. The StadiumCompany decides to hire network consultants to provide design, project management, and implementation support. The project will be implemented in three phases:

- The first phase is to plan the project and prepare the high-level network design.

- The second phase is to develop the detailed network design.

- The third phase is to implement the design.

After a few meetings, StadiumCompany hires the NetworkingCompany, a local network design and consulting firm, to support the phase one, high-level design. NetworkingCompany is a Cisco Premier Partner employing 20 network engineers who have various CCNA, CCDA, CCNP, CCDP, and CCIE certifications and significant industry experience.

To create the high-level design, the NetworkingCompany first interviewed the staff at the stadium and developed a profile of the organization and the facility.

StadiumCompany Organization

The StadiumCompany provides the network infrastructure and facilities at the stadium. The StadiumCompany has 170 full-time people:

- 35 managers and executives

- 135 salaried personnel

Approximately 80 additional hourly workers are hired as needed to support events in the facility and security departments. Figure A-2 illustrates the Stadium Management offices.

Figure A-2   Stadium Management Offices

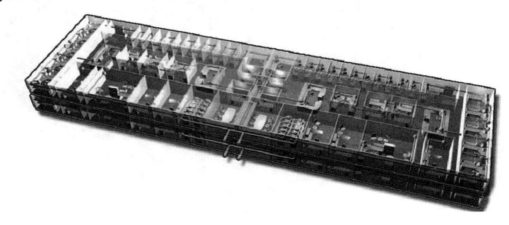

StadiumCompany Phones and PCs

All the managers and executives at the StadiumCompany use PCs and phones connected to a digital voice PBX. With the exception of the full-time groundskeepers and the janitors, all the salaried personnel also use PCs and phones.

Fifty shared phones for the security staff are distributed throughout the stadium. There are also 12 analog phones, some that support faxes and others that provide direct access to the police and fire stations. The security group also has 30 security cameras implemented on a separate network.

Existing Facilities and Support

The StadiumCompany provides facilities and network support for two sports teams (Team A and Team B), a visiting team, a restaurant, and a concession vendor, as illustrated in Figure A-3.

Figure A-3   StadiumCompany Facilities

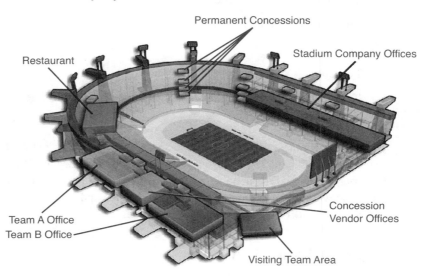

The stadium is approximately 725 feet wide by 900 feet long (approximately 220 meters wide by 375 meters long). There are two levels. Because of the size of the facility, multiple wiring closets connected with fiber-optic cabling are distributed throughout the stadium.

The Team A and Team B locker rooms and player lounges are on the first level of the south side of the stadium. The team offices are on the second level and measure 50 feet by 200 feet (approximately 15 meters wide by 60 meters long).

The office and locker room of the visiting team are also located on the first level.

StadiumCompany offices are on the north side of the stadium on both levels. The office space on the first level measures 200 feet by 60 feet (approximately 60 meters wide by 18 meters long), and measures 200 feet by 50 feet (approximately 60 meters wide by 15 meters long) on the second level.

Team A and Team B are in different sports leagues with different seasons. They both contract with the StadiumCompany for offices and services at the stadium.

Team A Organization

Team A has 90 people in the organization:

- 4 executives

- 12 coaches

- 14 support staff (including doctors, masseuse, secretary, assistants, finance and accounting)

- 60 players

Team A has 15 offices in the stadium to support their nonplayer staff. Five of these offices are shared. There are 24 PCs and 28 phones installed in the offices.

Team A also has a player locker room and a large player lounge and workout room. The nonplayer staff use the facility year round. Players have access to the locker room and workout equipment both during the season and the off-season. There are 5 phones in the locker room, and 15 phones in the player lounge. There are rumors that Team A recently installed a wireless hub in the player lounge.

Team B Organization

Team B has 64 people in the organization:

- 4 executives

- 8 coaches

- 12 support staff (including doctors, masseuse, secretary, assistants, finance and accounting)

- 40 players

Team B has 12 offices in the stadium to support their nonplayer staff. Three of the offices are shared. There are 19 PCs and 22 phones installed in the offices. They also have a player locker room and a large player lounge. The nonplayer staff use the facility year round. Players have access to the locker room and workout equipment both during the season and the off-season. There are 5 phones in the locker room, and 15 phones in the player lounge.

Visiting Team Support

The visiting team locker room and lounge has ten phones. Each visiting team requires temporary support on the game day and for a few days before the game. The visiting teams also contract with the StadiumCompany for office support and services at the stadium.

Concession Vendor

A concession vendor manages the concessions provided at games and events. There are five full-time employees. They use two private and two shared offices with five PCs and seven phones. These offices are located on the south side of the stadium between the Team A and Team B office space. Two part-time employees take orders from the luxury boxes during events. The concession vendor uses seasonal hourly workers to support 32 permanent concession stands and other services distributed throughout the stadium. At this time, there are no phones or PCs in the concession areas.

Luxury Restaurant Organization

The stadium has one luxury restaurant, which is open year round. In addition to the customer and kitchen areas, the restaurant contracts for office space from the StadiumCompany. The four managers have private offices. The two salaried financial and accounting staff share an office. Six PCs and phones are supported. Two additional phones are used for reservations in the customer area. Figure A-4 illustrates the placement of the luxury restaurant and skyboxes.

Figure A-4   Luxury Restaurant and Skyboxes

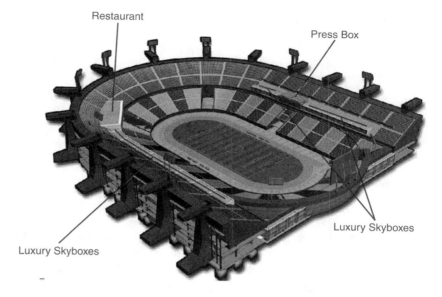

Luxury Skybox Support

There are 20 luxury skyboxes. The StadiumCompany provides a phone in each skybox that supports local calls and calls to the luxury restaurant and the concession vendor.

Press Area Support

The StadiumCompany provides a press box with three shared areas:

- The press print area typically houses 40 to 50 reporters during a game. There are ten analog phones available in this shared area, and two shared data ports. It is known that one newspaper intern brings in a small wireless access point for games that she covers.

- The press radio area supports 15 to 20 radio announcers and has 10 analog phone lines.

- The press TV area typically supports ten people. Five phones are available here.

Remote Site Support

The StadiumCompany currently has two remote locations: a ticketing office located in the downtown area, and a souvenir shop in a local shopping mall. The remote locations are connected using digital subscriber line (DSL) service to a local Internet service provider (ISP), as shown in Figure A-5.

Figure A-5   Remote Site Connectivity

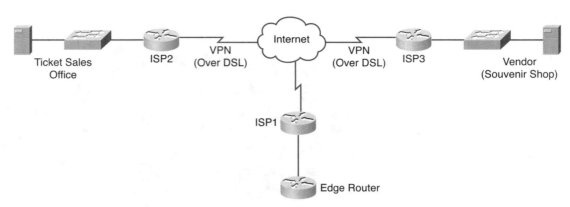

The stadium is connected to the local ISP using ISP1, a managed services router owned by the ISP. The two remote sites have a connection to the same ISP supported by the ISP2 and ISP3 routers provisioned and managed by the ISP. This connection provides the remote sites access to the databases located on servers in the StadiumCompany management offices. The StadiumCompany also has a perimeter router named Edge Router that connects to the ISP1 router at the stadium.

StadiumCompany Plans

The StadiumCompany wants to add new services, such as video, to their network. They are also thinking about replacing the existing digital voice PBX. They would like better access to their existing security camera network. Two new remote sites are planned in the near future:

- A film production company that has been hired to provide video during and after the sporting events and concerts needs to connect to the stadium network to exchange files.

- Team A is expanding to a remote office location. They are requesting access to the same network resources that they use on the stadium LAN.

FilmCompany Story

FilmCompany recently purchased AnyCompany, a smaller video firm with production expertise in sports videos. FilmCompany needed the additional staff and facilities to support a new contract with the StadiumCompany. The two branches of the FilmCompany are located in the same office park. A LAN interconnects the networks. Most of the production personnel have been consolidated in the original FilmCompany branch office, located in Building F as illustrated in Figure B-1. The web team is also located in this building. The majority of the administration, sales, and management functions are supported in the original AnyCompany office, located in Building A. When adjacent office space becomes available, these groups will be consolidated.

Figure B-1   FilmCompany Overview

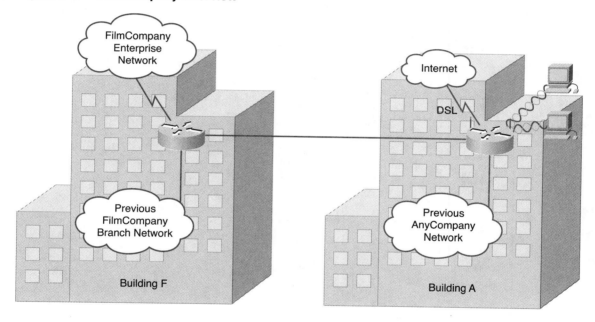

> **Note**
>
> The scope of this case study is the network design for the original FilmCompany branch office. This branch is referred to as the FilmCompany in this case study. The network for the entire FilmCompany is referred to as the FilmCompany enterprise network.

The two groups of the FilmCompany are initially in separate buildings, the floor plans for which are illustrated in Figure B-2. When office space is available, these groups will be consolidated.

Figure B-2   FilmCompany Floor Plans

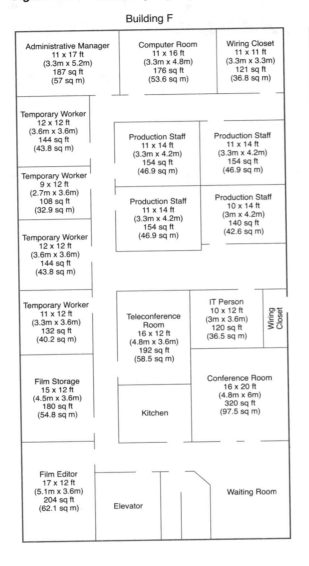

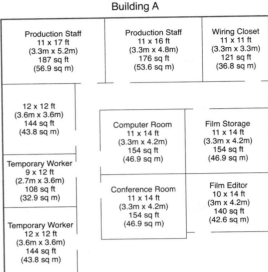

FilmCompany Background

FilmCompany has just been awarded a substantial video support contract by the StadiumCompany, resulting in a business growth of around 70 percent.

FilmCompany will film events and provide video services to the stadium customers. The video services include live feeds and prerecorded videos available from a web server. When the next sports season starts, five to eight FilmCompany people will be at the stadium for each event.

FilmCompany will manage all of the video services and provide immediate support when problems occur. StadiumCompany management expects FilmCompany to manage the video stored on the StadiumCompany server. Video needs to be available as both live and recorded feeds from the StadiumCompany website. StadiumCompany also wants FilmCompany to manage all the video services and to provide immediate support when there are problems. Timely support is essential because if the video services are not available during a sporting event or concert, the stadium can lose revenue and customer confidence.

FilmCompany is concerned about the ability of the existing Internet link to the stadium to provide reliable communications of media content back to the production suites in Building A. The FilmCompany IT staff is also concerned about whether its internal network is able to support high-volume, real-time video delivery or the types of services that the stadium requires. FilmCompany believes that it may need to upgrade its network.

FilmCompany thinks that the preferred way to support the stadium may be to connect directly to the stadium network to transfer files, monitor video performance, and manage the video in real time. StadiumCompany indicates to FilmCompany that the stadium network is going through a redesign process to update it and to improve and increase customer service. FilmCompany meets with NetworkingCompany, the company who is developing the new network design for StadiumCompany, and decides to work with them for their network redesign.

As a member of the network design team for NetworkingCompany, you will investigate the existing network of FilmCompany. You will plan, design, and prototype the upgrades necessary to enable the branch to support this growth in business.

Interview with FilmCompany on Current and Future Organization

The following transcript is from your interview with the FilmCompany branch manager, Kevin Lim.

Kevin Lim: I am the branch manager of FilmCompany. I am very glad that we have hired you to help us plan and design our network upgrade. Our recent contract with the sports stadium requires a significant upgrade to our capabilities. I understand that you have already been supplied with a list of our current staff and information about the network.

You: It is nice to meet you, Kevin. We are looking forward to working on this project. Yes, I have information about your current staff and network. We will be reviewing the current network to define a baseline of its performance as a metric on which to design the upgrade. There are some details we should discuss to clarify your requirements for the new contract. First, what are the business goals you want this network upgrade to support? This information will help us to understand the scale of this project.

Kevin Lim: When this stadium contract is up and in full production, it will increase our business by 70 percent.

You: Where specifically do you see this growth?

Kevin Lim: Financially, we hope to achieve positive cash flow from the stadium contract within six months, and increase our gross revenue by 75 percent within 18 months. My technical staff projects that the data traffic across our network will increase by 80 percent as we provide video services to the StadiumCompany. The increased revenue is a result of the new contract. We hope that the network upgrade reduces unit production costs by 15 percent over six months, and 20 percent over 12 months.

You: How will you know if your business expectations are being achieved?

Kevin Lim: We have given that some thought and are considering surveying the customer monthly. Our goal is to achieve a satisfaction measure of at least four on a scale of five within four months after upgrade. We have also set targets of responding to 90 percent of customer non-live media production requests within 12 hours, and 100 percent within 18 hours. We want to be able to meet customer live media production targets 97.5 percent of the time.

You: Do you see a significant increase in staff and any changes in how they carry out their work in achieving these targets?

Kevin Lim: We are looking to hire up to six temporary and part-time production staff and at least one IT and communications technician. The network is a critical component of the way we do business, and it will need looking after.

You: Where do you see these staff members being located?

Kevin Lim: We currently have the majority of our staff in two buildings in this office park. We plan to consolidate our staff and facilities into Building F. I expect that initially we will have one or two production people located at the stadium, with an additional six to eight staff members at the stadium when there is an event we are supporting. A fast reliable network link to the stadium is very important. All pre- and postproduction work will occur on our premises using the communications link from the stadium. Staff working at both locations will probably use a wireless connection here in the office.

You: Thanks for that information. It is important to know those details. What targets do you see the network upgrade project meeting?

Kevin Lim: We do have a very tight budget. We need to reuse at least 75 percent of the existing network components, and we would like to reuse all of it. Our time to production is very important, too. We see a successful project as one where the network is in full production meeting the deadlines of the StadiumCompany. And of course, the network has to perform!

You: We have examined your current network equipment and cabling. It seems to be capable of being scaled to support the new requirements. During the design phase, we will prototype the network load and adjust the design, if necessary.

Kevin Lim: What about reliability?

You: After you consolidate your personnel in one building, you can use redundant links and technology to ensure high availability to the appropriate resources. We will look at that in more detail during the network design. We can also look at mean time to failure under specified load conditions for all network components. There will be network monitoring so that your network personnel can identify and resolve issues. Are there any specific network security issues that you feel need attention?

Kevin Lim: The media content is very valuable. We cannot have the network go down because of a virus or something. What do you recommend?

You: We can include in the network design the means for all unauthorized network intrusions to be intercepted, prevented, logged, and reported. Your network technician will have a role here.

Kevin Lim: Is there anything else I can tell you at this time?

You: I would like to recap the business goals for the FilmCompany. Based on our conversation today, and my discussions with your staff, I understand that your prioritized business goals are as follows:

1. Upgrade the network to support 80% more traffic
2. Provide a fast reliable link between FilmCompany facilities and the StadiumCompany network
3. Implement a highly available network
4. Continue to support wireless access at FilmCompany facilities
5. Implement QoS to support the video applications
6. Implement network monitoring and security

Is this list correct?

Kevin Lim: Yes, that list summarizes our goals. At this time, I would like you to concentrate on the top four goals.

You: I will make that our focus. I do not have any more questions at this time. Thank you for taking the time to meet with me.

FilmCompany Network and Topology

The FilmCompany branch network has grown without much planning. The LAN cabling in both offices is CAT5e Ethernet. The office complex provides an Ethernet link between the two buildings. Because of the recent acquisition of AnyCompany, the addressing and naming are inconsistent. The combined network infrastructure has not been optimized or redesigned. It is basically a flat network design with minimal redundancy. A small wireless LAN is currently only used occasionally by a few project managers with laptops and by guests at Building F. FilmCompany believes that the WLAN may be used more regularly when the StadiumCompany contract work starts because the additional mobile and contract workers will require network access. In addition, FilmCompany plans to consolidate all its staff and resources in one building.

Remote access into the FilmCompany network is provided through an ADSL Internet link terminating in Building A. Currently two FilmCompany staff members are onsite at the stadium. The StadiumCompany provides them with office space in the stadium management offices. Figure B-3 illustrates the branch layout.

Figure B-3   FilmCompany Branch Layout

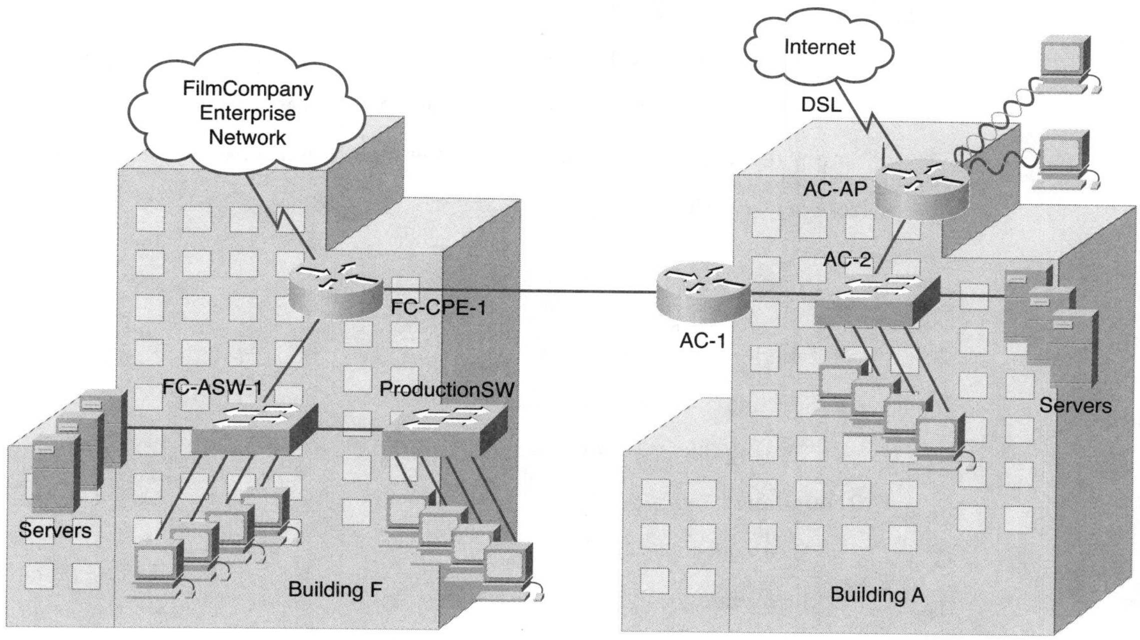

The current network equipment includes the following:

- Two 1841 routers (FC-CPE-1, AC-1)
- Three 2960 switches (FC-ASW-1, FC-ASW-2, ProductionSW)
- One network and business server

- One Linksys WRT300N wireless router (AC-AP)

- One ADSL modem (Internet access)

The current network has two VLANs.

The General VLAN serves the general office and managers, including reception, accounts, and administration. It consists of 12 PCs and two printers. The General VLAN uses this addressing:

- Network 10.0.0.0/24

- Gateway 10.0.0.1

- Hosts (dynamic) 10.0.0.200–10.0.0.254

- Hosts (static) 10.0.0.10–10.0.0.20

The Production VLAN serves the production suites and provides networking for the media development and storage. It consists of nine high-performance workstations, five office PCs, and two printers. The Production VLAN uses this addressing:

- Network 10.10.0.0/24

- Gateway 10.10.0.254

- Hosts (dynamic) 10.10.0.100–10.10.0.200

- Hosts (static) 10.10.0.1–10.10.0.99

Design Considerations

Here are some design considerations to consider for the FilmCompany expansion.

- **Capacity/scalability**: Addressing and naming to be easily scaled

- **Future technologies**: Possibility of greater mobile and converged network services

- **Network security**:
    - DMZ
    - NAT
    - Filtering
    - Separate management VLAN
    - Network device passwords and access

- **Redundancy**:
    - Access switches and links
    - Server farm design

- **QoS**:
    - Required for video streaming
    - Future implementation of voice over data network system

Lab Equipment Interfaces and Initial Configuration Restoration

This appendix provides a reference for router interface designations and instructions for restoring routers and switches to their default configurations. This appendix includes the following instruction sections:

- Router Interface Summary
- Erasing and Reloading the Router
- Erasing and Reloading the Switch
- SDM Router Basic IOS Configuration

Router Interface Summary

To find out exactly how the router is configured, look at the interfaces. This will identify the type of router as well as how many interfaces the router has. There is no way to effectively list all the combinations of configurations for each router class. The interface chart shown in Table C-1 provides the identifiers for the possible combinations of Ethernet and Serial interfaces applicable to CCNA Discovery. This interface chart does not include any other type of interface a specific router may contain; for example, ISDN BRI interfaces are not shown. The string in parentheses is the legal abbreviation that can be used in a Cisco IOS command to represent the interface.

Table C-1 **Router Interface Summary**

Router Model	Ethernet Interface #1	Ethernet Interface #2	Serial Interface #1	Serial Interface #2
800 (806)	Ethernet 0 (E0)	Ethernet 1 (E1)	–	–
1600	Ethernet 0 (E0)	Ethernet 1 (E1)	Serial 0 (S0)	Serial 1 (S1)
1700	Fast Ethernet 0 (FA0)	Fast Ethernet 1 (FA1)	Serial 0 (S0)	Serial 1 (S1)
1800	Fast Ethernet 0/0 (FA0/0)	Fast Ethernet 0/1 (FA0/1)	Serial 0/0/0 (S0/0/0)	Serial 0/0/1 (S0/0/1)
2500	Ethernet 0 (E0)	Ethernet 1 (E1)	Serial 0 (S0)	Serial 1 (S1)
2600	Fast Ethernet 0/0 (FA0/0)	Fast Ethernet 0/1 (FA0/1)	Serial 0/0 (S0/0)	Serial 0/1 (S0/1)

Erasing and Reloading the Router

For the majority of the labs in *CCNA Discovery*, it is necessary to start with an unconfigured router. Using a router with an existing configuration may produce unpredictable results. The following instructions prepare the router before you perform the lab so that previous configuration options do not interfere. These instructions apply to most Cisco routers.

Step 1.   Enter privileged EXEC mode by entering **enable**:

```
Router> enable
```

Step 2.   In privileged EXEC mode, enter the **erase startup-config** command:

```
Router# erase startup-config
```

Step 3.   Press **Enter** to confirm.

The response is

```
Erase of nvram: complete
```

Step 4.   In privileged EXEC mode, enter the **reload** command:

```
Router(config)# reload
```

The responding line prompt is

```
System configuration has been modified. Save? [yes/no]:
```

Step 5.   Enter **n** and press **Enter**.

The responding line prompt is

```
Proceed with reload? [confirm]
```

Step 6.   Press **Enter** to confirm.

The first line of the response is

```
Reload requested by console.
```

After the router has reloaded, the line prompt is

```
Would you like to enter the initial configuration dialog? [yes/no]:
```

Step 7.   Enter **n** and press **Enter**.

The responding line prompt is

```
Press RETURN to get started!
```

Step 8.   Press **Enter**.

The router is ready for the assigned lab to be performed.

Erasing and Reloading the Switch

For the majority of the labs in *CCNA Discovery*, it is necessary to start with an unconfigured switch. Using a switch with an existing configuration may produce unpredictable results. The following instructions prepare the switch before you perform the lab so that previous configuration options do not interfere. Instructions are provided for the 29xx series of switches.

Step 1. Enter privileged EXEC mode by entering **enable**. If you're prompted for a password, enter **class**. (If that doesn't work, ask the instructor.)

```
Switch> enable
```

Step 2. Remove the VLAN database information file:

```
Switch# delete flash:vlan.dat
```

```
Delete filename [vlan.dat]?[Enter]
Delete flash:vlan.dat? [confirm] [Enter]
```

If there was no VLAN file, you see this message:

```
%Error deleting flash:vlan.dat (No such file or directory)
```

Step 3. Remove the switch startup configuration file from NVRAM:

```
Switch# erase startup-config
```

The responding line prompt is

```
Erasing the nvram filesystem will remove all files! Continue? [confirm]
```

Press **Enter** to confirm.

The response should be

```
Erase of nvram: complete
```

Step 4. Check that the VLAN information was deleted.

Verify that the VLAN configuration was deleted in Step 2 using the **show vlan** command. If previous VLAN configuration information (other than the default management VLAN 1) is still present, you must power-cycle the switch (hardware restart) instead of issuing the **reload** command. To power-cycle the switch, remove the power cord from the back of the switch or unplug it, and then plug it back in. If the VLAN information was successfully deleted in Step 2, go to Step 5 and restart the switch using the **reload** command.

Step 5. Restart the software using the **reload** command.

Note

This step is not necessary if the switch was restarted using the power-cycle method.

    a. In privileged EXEC mode, enter the reload command:

```
Switch(config)# reload
```

       The responding line prompt is

```
System configuration has been modified. Save? [yes/no]:
```

    b. Enter n and press Enter.

       The responding line prompt is

```
Proceed with reload? [confirm] [Enter]
```

       The first line of the response is

```
Reload requested by console.
```

    c. After the switch has reloaded, the line prompt is

```
Would you like to enter the initial configuration dialog? [yes/no]:
```

       Enter n and press Enter.

       The responding line prompt is

```
Press RETURN to get started! [Enter]
```

SDM Router Basic IOS Configuration

If the startup-config is erased in an SDM router, SDM will no longer come up by default when the router is restarted. You must build a basic config as follows. Further details about the setup and use of SDM can be found in the SDM Quick Start Guide:

http://www.cisco.com/en/US/products/sw/secursw/ps5318/products_quick_start09186a0080511c89.html#wp44788

Step 1.   Configure the router and PC IP addresses.

A PC-based web browser uses the router interface to bring up SDM. The PC IP address should be set to 10.10.10.2 255.255.255.248.

Note:

An SDM router other than the 1841 may require connection to a different port to access SDM.

```
Router(config)#interface fastethernet 0/0
Router(config-if)#ip address 10.10.10.1 255.255.255.248
Router(config-if)#no shutdown
```

Step 2.   Enable the HTTP/HTTPS server on the router.

```
Router(config)#ip http server
Router(config)#ip http secure-server
Router(config)#ip http authentication local
```

Step 3.   Create a user account with privilege level 15 (enable privileges):

```
Router(config)#username username privilege 15 password 0 password
```

Replace *username* and *password* with the username and password you want to configure.

Step 4.   Configure SSH and Telnet for local login and privilege level 15:

```
Router(config)#line vty 0 4
Router(config-line)#privilege level 15
Router(config-line)#login local
Router(config-line)#transport input telnet
Router(config-line)#transport input telnet ssh
Router(config-line)#exit
```

Notes

Notes

Notes

Notes

Notes

Notes

Notes